Crazy for Democracy

Crazy for Democracy

Women in Grassroots Movements

Temma Kaplan

ROUTLEDGE
New York • London

Published in 1997 by

Routledge
29 West 35th Street
New York, NY 10001

Published in Great Britain by

Routledge
11 New Fetter Lane
London EC4P 4EE

Copyright © 1997 by Routledge, Inc.

Printed in the United States of America on acid-free paper.

Kaplan, Temma, 1942–
    Crazy for democracy : women in grassroots movements / Temma Kaplan.
        p.   cm.
    Includes bibliographical references.
    ISBN 0-415-91662-3 (cl : alk. paper). — ISBN 0-415-91663-1 (pb : alk. paper)
        1. Women social reformers—United States. 2. Women social reformers—South Africa. 3. Social movements—United States.
4. Social movements—South Africa. I. Title.
HN49.W6K36   1996
303.48′4—dc20   96-18574
                                                                    CIP

Contents

Acknowledgments

MODERN TIMES ARE ALL PERIODS of upheaval when you are living through them. But from the perspective of an historian, the decades from the sixties through the mid-nineties may have been the most profound period of transformation women have ever experienced. When I directed a women's research center in the eighties and early nineties, people from the media frequently called to confirm what they already believed: that the women's movement was white and middle-class. When I said the opposite, that I think feminism's greatest impact can be seen in the way poor and working-class women of all colors have been linking women's rights and human rights, the press quickly hung up. So I decided to write this book.

The women discussed here don't frequently appear on television or in the papers; they are not stars. But they are very well known to tens of thousands of people whose lives they've helped to transform. Because they've welcomed me into their homes and movements and given me formal interviews but have also taken me into backwoods cabins, neighborhoods scorched by toxic waste, and squatter communities where they've lived, sharing family anxieties and teaching me about what political life can be like when democracy concerns itself with human need, they have been my teachers and mentors. My special thanks go to Dollie and Kim Burwell, Josette Cole, Lois Gibbs, Luella Kenny, and Regina Ntongana.

My friends who are also my family have shaped me and this book. Bennett Sims, whose sense of humor eases any situation, shares my curiosity and keeps me from hiding in a scholarly shroud. The best of all companions, he can walk any walk and talk any talk. T. J. and Lois Anderson weave together communities of politically committed artists wherever they go and have included me in these groups. With the style and wit of which only they are capable, Mary Gordon and Victoria de Grazia have inspired me to reach beyond old limitations. From Amy Ansara, Dolores Hayden, Nancy Hewitt, Luella Kenny, Claudia Koonz, Addie and Murray Levine, and Kathryn Kish Sklar, I have learned to think about politics over long distances.

Marianne Hirsch told me I was a storyteller and thereby gave me a voice. Ellen Ross and Dick Glendon, with Maud and Hope in tow, have always come through for me, giving valuable advice that has ranged from historical and medical practice to the use of sequins or the care of guinea pigs. Sheila Rowbotham, Dorothy Thompson, Radha Kumar, Naomi Rosenthal, Deborah Rhode, Deborah Silverman, and Judy Walkowitz serve in different ways as examples of what political commitment can do for the creation of engaged historical writing. Leo Spitzer, who brings people and continents together, has taught me to reveal the autobiographical dimensions of my political passions. Christine Stansell is as thoughtful and subtle a gardener as she is an historian, and has nurtured me both horticulturally and historically.

Karin Shapiro, Jacklyn Cock, Josette Cole, Michael Godsby, Sandra Klopfer, Sheila Meintjes, Regina Ntongana, Deborah Posel, and Laurine Platzky introduced me to the history and politics of South Africa and have stood by me even when they have disagreed with me. Barbara Weinstein, Helen Cooper, Lou Charnon Deutsch, and Adrienne Munich, through their own courage and intelligence, have set a high standard that I hope I can meet. Mary Yeager's commitment, energy, and generosity have seen me through good times and bad.

Acknowledgments

I don't know where I'd be without the shrewd advice and unconditional support of Deborah Valenze and Robert Moeller, who give the word *scholarship* new cachet. Both share themselves as well as their intellects, always helping to shape what I want to say, frequently realizing what I'm getting at more quickly than I do. Of course, neither is responsible for my excesses.

The American Association of University Women, American Council of Learned Societies, National Endowment for the Humanities, National Humanities Center, and Research Foundation of the State University of New York at Stony Brook have generously provided me with the resources to carry out the research for this book and time to write it. There is no way to thank them enough. I am especially grateful to Robert Conner and Kent Mullikin, who make the National Humanities Center the humane and nurturing place it is. Many new insights emerged there in seminars and conversations with Kate Bartlett, Susan Porter Benson, Steve Caton, Marianne Hirsch, Gil Joseph, Michael Maas, Ed Muir, Leo Spitzer, and Alex Zwerdling.

The most remarkable journey I've made in the course of this study has been my foray into the world of the third wave. Plenty has been said about Generation X that totally overlooks the work of young African-American, Asian, Latina, Native American, and white women born to lead through participation. In both the United States and South Africa, their movements combine the entitlement of feminism with those of cultural politics, bringing together a no-nonsense view of the world and rap, hip-hop, and township jazz. Whereas we in the first generation of second-wave feminism need one another's almost daily reassurance that we can and must cross the boundaries, the third wave will crest into the promised land. Thank you Abby, Abra, Angie, Anna, Bodi, Emma, Julie, Kim, Marva, Meg, Mia, Polly, Rosa, Olie, Shannon, Tanya, and, most of all, Laurie Liss, who always believed in this book, and Cecelia Cancellaro, Christine Cipriani, and Jeanne Park, who made it happen.

The first debt of gratitude is also the last. When I was lucky enough to spend a year in North Carolina, I kept coming across references to Warren County, North Carolina, and to the role that struggles there played in alerting people to the relationship between toxic waste and race. The name that came up repeatedly in connection with the movement was Dollie Burwell, and I set out to find her. When I finally did, her commitment, faith, courage, intelligence, and strength made me understand the world in a whole new way. After she heard me speak in public about her, her daughters, and the other grassroots women leaders discussed here, I nervously awaited her verdict. She told me, because of her interest in the other women and their movements, "now you really must finish the book." So, for Dollie.

Introduction:
Women Prophets and the Struggle
for Human Rights

A NEW GENERATION of women leaders is carrying out an invisible revolution. All over the globe women have been asserting collective rights to protect their children against pollution, disease, and homelessness. Not content merely to fight for improvements in the lives of their families and communities, many of these women justify their action by making broad claims about human needs and rights according to an interpretation of justice that they themselves are developing through their actions.[1] The women featured in this book have linked social need to democracy by creating clinics, schools, and local governments in the squatter settlement of Crossroads, South Africa; by protesting against the dumping of soil laced with toxic waste in Warren County, North Carolina; and by forcing the government to buy their contaminated homes in Love Canal, New York. They have grown from individuals fighting to survive to members of communities with collective identities. Taking for granted that all human beings are entitled to safe housing and a clean environment and that sometimes only women can secure them, women in the United States and South Africa frequently have transformed grassroots struggles into full-blown social movements.[2]

Though widely used, the term *grassroots* does not have a commonly recognized meaning. Grassroots generally implies being widespread and common, in the sense of being universal. The term also suggests being outside the control of any state, church, union, or political party. To the women claiming its provenance, being from the grassroots generally means being free from any constraining political affiliations and being responsible to no authority except their own group. Though such women generally recognize their seeming powerlessness against corporate and governmental opponents, they also assert their moral superiority, their right to be responsible citizens, not according to official laws, but on their own terms.

Women such as Dollie Burwell, Lois Gibbs, Luella Kenny, Kim Burwell, Regina Ntongana, and Josette Cole are hardly household names. Neither was the Reverend Dr. Martin Luther King Jr. in 1956 when at the age of 26 he became the leader of the Montgomery bus boycott.[3] Even after he and Miss Ella Baker helped establish the Southern Christian Leadership Conference (SCLC), few in the North or West recognized her name. Neither she nor the countless local women in church and civic groups all over the South attracted much attention.[4]

Dollie Burwell, who in 1982 helped launch the movement for environmental justice, combining civil rights and environmentalism, continues to work in The Warren County Citizens against Toxic Waste. She also served as registrar of deeds for Warren County, North Carolina; sits on the boards of the United Church of Christ's Commission for Racial Justice and the Office for Church and Society; and acts as a local leader of SCLC. But few outside the movement or the region know anything about her or what she continues to accomplish.

Her daughter Kim Burwell, an activist in the Leadership Initiative Project and its umbrella organization, the Youth Taskforce, helps direct a southern grassroots youth crusade, engaging young people from fifth-graders to people in their twenties, as she herself is. By focusing on local schools, civil rights, and the environment, Kim Burwell helps empower a new generation of activists, many of whom will remain in their home towns in the South to create a permanent core of citizens with a vested interest in politics and the necessary skills to make their voices heard.

Lois Gibbs, Luella Kenny, and the women of the Love Canal Homeowners Association first alerted Americans to the dangers of toxic waste in their own backyards and basements. Worried about the growing number of miscarriages and the degeneration of the health of the children in their neighborhood, formerly docile homemakers became enraged citizens, determined to win recognition of their predicament and redress of their grievances. Today, Lois Gibbs's Citizens Clearinghouse for Hazardous Waste, on whose board Luella Kenny sits, coordinates the efforts of seven thousand grassroots environmental organizations all over the United States.

Regina Ntongana and Josette Cole fought to end influx control laws, one of the legal pillars of apartheid in South Africa. Ntongana lost two children in 1973 because she, like millions of other South African black women, was expelled from her home in the city and was forced to live in the barren wastelands called Bantustans, where there was little food, water, or access to medical care. Ntongana moved her three other children back to Cape Town, constructed various shacks made up of what white South Africans had tossed away, and prepared to fight to preserve her life and the lives of her remaining children. Once she had a home, she had to fight alongside others to keep it from being bulldozed by the South African government, which was determined to expel her and the other black women who had established themselves in the city where they weren't wanted. The women organized to defend themselves and fought for eight years before being driven out of their homes. But they refused to leave Cape Town. They moved to other squatter communities in the city and formed an organization to help women like themselves fight the injustices of apartheid.

A theory of leadership that explains the activities of these women and countless others depends on the idea of charisma.[5] They are charismatic in the sense that sociologist Max Weber meant, insofar as they appear to have inherent magical qualities of authority that justify their ethical mission.[6] Yet unlike leaders who stand aloof, acting as stars, participating only in the most publicized meetings, these women pay as much attention to the nitty-gritty of daily organizing as to making points that register at the national level. In doing so they create new political cultures.[7]

Though three of the six women focused on here are deeply religious, their charisma lies not in their religion but in their commitment to promoting new ethical principles as the basis for democracy. Their moral fervor challenges the meaning of human rights and justice as the woman have known them. In Weberian terms, these women are prophets:[8] lay people who evoke a higher moral order. They would not blaspheme their inherited religions by claiming to be prophets, but by promoting ethical agendas for transforming society, they fulfill Weber's definition. What they are doing is reclaiming human rights on their own terms, redefining humanity and making demands for the social and economic support necessary to sustain it. Such women, with their strong personalities, abilities to pitch in, and high morale, gather together people with different backgrounds, areas of expertise, and status, helping create egalitarian movements.[9] Where a grassroots leader seems to enhance the ability of the group to reach a higher moral plane, she doesn't stand out herself so much as she helps the community come together.

The grassroots leaders considered here, despite their similarities, differ in the kind of leadership they exercise. Dollie Burwell has the mind of a craftswoman. She can imagine an improvement and carry it out from start to finish. She can dig in at the person-to-person level, going door to door registering voters as happily as when participating on presidential committees on rural development. The goal for her is always social justice. Some think the concept is utopian; she knows it is attainable. Whether she is in the forefront, arguing before cameras, or in the background, acting as a voting monitor in the first democratic elections in South Africa in 1994, she is always at the service of the same cause: helping create a just life. For her, that includes a healthy dose of democracy.

Regina Ntongana resembles Dollie Burwell in her self-confidence and her commitment to others who are trying to better their lives. As Ntongana, known to her friends as "Ma," frequently says, "We, as women, were feeling the pain." The pain had first to do with the injustice of apartheid, and now with the removal of formal laws discriminating against blacks and other people, with the inequalities of life where whites secure most of the benefits from the land while others live in excruciating poverty, without housing, running water, electricity, health care, or education.

If Dollie Burwell and Regina Ntongana are like artisans, seeing individual projects through from start to finish and participating whether or not they lead, Lois Gibbs, Luella Kenny, and Kim Burwell are more like orchestra conductors; and Josette Cole moves from one position of leadership to another. All can play most of the instruments, but what they usually do is put the notes together to create an ensemble whose power surpasses those of the individual tones. A synergy of sound.

Gibbs's organization, The Citizens Clearinghouse For Hazardous Waste, grew from her realization that others wanted to fight back, as she and her neighbors at Love Canal had, against companies that damaged the environment and against government bureaucrats who underestimated their determination to save their families from destruction. Luella Kenny sits on the board of the clearinghouse and also directs the Love Canal Medical Trust fund, distributing the financial settlement a group of homeowners won for the ailments they developed from living over a toxic waste dump. Kim Burwell, having grown up as Dollie's daughter in the movement for social justice in the South, has an historical vision and a sense of group process. Cole, one of the founders of the Surplus People Project in Cape Town, South Africa, began by aiding women like Regina Ntongana, then joined her for ten years working to achieve land and housing rights all over the Western Cape. When that no longer seemed sufficient, Cole moved on to work in more informal settings, entering into alliances with people who wanted to push the new South African government to recognize people's social and economic needs as well as their civil rights in the revised constitution of 1996.

To a certain extent Gibbs, Kenny, Kim Burwell, and Cole, by accepting leadership of organizations, making sure that the whole job of planning, coordinating, and campaigning gets done, miss the day-to-day pleasures and mobility of simply acting as members of a group. Lois Gibbs talks about the loneliness of being the one responsible for cheering people on, keeping their spirits up, having no one in whom to confide her own doubts, no one on whose shoulders she can cry. Gibbs and others who head grassroots organizations must be ready to carry their institutions alone while encouraging others to assume more responsibilities. Dollie Burwell and Regina Ntongana lead in different ways, acting as facilitators, expressing the views of people they talk to, working with individuals, shaping them into self-administering communities. By acting as political intermediaries, they help rejuvenate the organizations in which they participate.

But how could all this be going on without the public noticing? In part, it is because grassroots movements are mainly concerned with local issues, with what affects ordinary people every day. The media and public opinion are preoccupied with the spectacular, with the activities of celebrities. What's more, the participants in grassroots movements are ordinary women attempting to accomplish necessary tasks, to provide services rather than to build power bases. Therefore, the work they do and the gains they make hardly seem politically significant.

Initially, the women leading such struggles merely act according to what I have called "female consciousness."[10] By female consciousness, I mean that certain women, emphasizing roles they accept as wives and mothers, also demand the freedom to act as they think their obligations entail. Women in many societies and historical periods learn from youth that they will be responsible as mothers for providing food, clothing, housing, and health care for their families. When toxic pollution or expulsion from their homes threatens their communities, certain women will take action according to female consciousness, confronting authorities to preserve life. Far from being a biological trait, female consciousness develops from cultural experiences of helping families and communities survive.

Placing human need above unjust laws, South African women, struggling to win housing and create community, launched one of the leading social movements of the seventies and eighties. They acted as prophets and contributed to the destruction of apartheid in South Africa. Homemakers in Love Canal began by protecting the safety of their homes, and wound up alerting the country to the poisons beneath the soil of homes throughout the nation. Local housewives and ministers realized that their neighborhood had been chosen for the landfill because their neighbors were largely poor, black, and thought to be politically powerless.

Presupposing that collective needs should be fulfilled by authorities, prophetic women called the entire system of politics into question at Crossroads, Love Canal, and Warren County. But unlike other leaders and movements that have undermined the political systems we know, discrediting democracy itself, these grassroots women's groups have attempted, through moral claims for justice and human rights, to transform politics in far more democratic directions than ever seemed possible.

Such activists draw on an implicit theory of human rights, seeking to make community health a corollary of justice, deriving its power from commonsense notions of human need rather than codified laws. These women move back and forth between specific requirements for survival and principled demands for general goals such as justice. When a crisis ensues and the patterns of everyday life come into question because of health threats, housing shortages, or because of disruptions in the social order, such women sometimes argue that justice requires that they intercede. By justice, they often mean more balanced behavior, an end to violence, and equal distribution of social necessities. Recently, certain women of the working classes and subordinated ethnic and racial groups made claims for justice, representing their demands as selfless and their provenance as universal. They challenged rights of private property and unfettered markets, substituting a demand for economic equality and social transformation.

The particular brand of justice women evoke in these kinds of movements rests with fundamental human rights that no existing government or legal system now promotes. But these rights—to eat, have shelter, remain well, and live in peace—are so much a part of what every human being in every culture knows is necessary to survival that only tyrants are willing to say that others should not strive for them. Women such as those in Love Canal, Warren County, and Crossroads increasingly have compared their own collective treatment at the hands of powerful companies and governments that endangered the health of their families to violations of justice and human rights. And these women have not been alone. In grassroots movements all over the world, women activists have integrated social and economic demands into their conceptualization of human rights. To win their demands, women have formed networks of grassroots and private organizations known outside the United States as Non-Governmental Organizations, or NGOs.

The term NGO became familiar to many Americans for the first time in 1995 when the Fourth World Conference on Women, sponsored by the United Nations, met in Beijing, China and Americans got their first look at the invisible revolution on the move. United Nations' conferences on women had been held in Mexico City in 1975, Copenhagen in 1980, and Nairobi in 1985, to report on economic, social, political, educational, and sexual conditions of women during the U.N. Decade of Women (1975–85) and to vote on proposals for improvements.[11] In the early fall of 1995, determined to see what progress had been made, the General

Assembly sponsored another conference. Each of the U.N. women's conferences really had two parts: an official assembly of representatives from different member states, and the NGO Women's Tribunal or Forum, made up of women's grassroots and private organizations from all over the world. The goal of the Forum in Beijing was to exert influence on the Platform for Action, the official document the governmental conference of the General Assembly would issue at the end of its deliberations.

The sight and sound of twenty-six thousand women (more than one-third of whom were from the United States) converging on the Chinese capital caught the imagination of the international press. Because the American media were conscious of human-rights abuses in China and because First Lady Hillary Rodham Clinton headed the American delegation, the Beijing conference received widespread coverage. During the conference, the media dwelled on government harassment, bad facilities, exotic costumes, and absurd fears that lesbians would demonstrate naked in the streets of China. What the press seemed to miss was that women from all over the world were meeting to express their hopes for a transformed future.

The Chinese had wanted the summer Olympics to be held there in the year 2000, but because of human-rights abuses and bad facilities, the Olympics went elsewhere. As a booby prize, the U.N. agreed to hold the Conference of Women in Beijing. No one thought to stipulate that the NGO Forum would also be held in Beijing. Fearing the combined forces of tens of thousands of activist women, and troubled by the specter of demonstrations in Tiananmen Square, the Chinese government insisted that the activists meet in Huairou, a village about fifty miles from the center of Beijing.

Despite the difficulties of meeting so far away from the governmental assembly, with no regular public transportation during the day for the ninety-minute ride between the two sites, the NGO Forum made an enormous impact on the official delegations and on the document it produced.[12] Activists met for ten days in six two-hour sessions per day and about twenty sessions per time period. Those engaged in the struggle against environmental racism in the United States, such as Connie Tucker, executive director of the Southern Organizing Committee for Economic and Social Justice and a friend of Dollie Burwell's, took part in a session at which people from all over the world gave testimony about grassroots environmental action in their countries. They shared strategies and formed networks to coordinate resistance across national boundaries. A group working through the U.N. Habitat program discussed housing reform in war-torn Afghanistan with land and housing expert activists from South Africa, among them Regina Ntongana's friend Laurine Platzky, as others from around the globe debated about how to create new democratic municipal organizations in which women could hold equal power with men.

In another session women street hawkers, who had built businesses in Bangladesh with the help of the Grameen Bank, which provided $400 million in 1994 in credit amounts ranging from one dollar to about one thousand dollars in the form of small amounts of credit to poor women, talked about how they had banded together in groups of five to improve their own economic and social conditions.[13] There were sessions of the International Reproductive Research Action Group that has carried out qualitative studies in seven countries, in which grassroots women reported on how they experience their bodies, regulate their pregnancies, and negotiate for their rights within sexual relations and outside them.

Sometimes activities converged in ways the organizers and individual group participants might never have imagined. Increasingly, women's grassroots movements have made claims about human rights that the human-rights community had been reluctant to recognize: South African women who fought removals from their homes claimed that housing is a human right. *Monitorias*, grassroots health providers in the squatter communities of Chile, argued that health care is a human right.

10

Women from island nations in the Pacific, who have suffered 310 nuclear bomb tests (largely by the United States and France) over the past fifty years, explained how they were fighting against French and Chinese nuclear testing and against U.S. nuclear waste incinerators on Johnson Island in the South Pacific. They joined women from the Southwestern United States in claiming that a clean environment is a human right. Activists from Zimbabwe and Egypt argued that battering and genital mutilation violate women's human rights. But until the June 1993 United Nations Conference on Human Rights held in Vienna, the official human-rights communities insisted that human rights referred only to political and civil rights of individuals to be free from state violence.

Grassroots organizations, including the Women's Rights Action Watch and the Center for Women and Global Leadership, pressured the official human-rights organizations to discount the separation between so-called public and private life and to characterize as human-rights abuses such acts of violence as genital mutilation, holding servants as slaves, dowry death, and domestic violence.[14] By creating a third space that is neither public nor private,[15] grassroots activists have opened up an arena in which human dignity, not national law or custom, prevails. They have led a struggle worldwide to force the United Nations and, through it, member governments, to stop abetting the abuse of women.

One group that brought the experiences of grassroots legal and medical movements together were women of Zimbabwe, Zambia, and South Africa. Discovering that 42 percent of women in Sub-Saharan Africa report that they are beaten regularly and that 54 million African girls are victims of genital mutilation, southern African activists have presented these practices not as individual and cultural problems but as violations of human rights for which the United Nations and participating states should have oversight. Women from southern Africa led the struggle to view mistreatment of women in universal terms that make such treatment unacceptable whatever the religious, cultural, and traditional justifications. Effectively, these women and the majority of other participants challenged the notions that cultural context determines women's needs for bodily integrity. Women grassroots leaders from all over the world acted as prophets, attempting collectively to supplant cultural differences with universal ethical human standards applicable to all women.

Following in this prophetic strain, Lydia Kompe—known as Mam Lydia—a former trade union organizer, land rights expert, and now an African National Congress parliamentary delegate, also took part in the deliberations at the NGO Women's Forum. An ally of Regina Ntongana in attempts to win housing rights for women under apartheid and now in the new South Africa and a friend of Dollie Burwell, Mam Lydia's appearance in Beijing brought home to assembled grassroots leaders the potential political impact that grassroots activists can have in creating new democracies. South African grassroots leaders, who boasted of an interim constitution that ensured rights of sexual preference and barred domestic rape, and a Bill of Rights that includes collective aspirations for decent housing, employment, and health care along with civil and political rights in the revised constitution, spoke with confidence in Beijing. Because the claims for expanding the notion of human rights now comes from South Africans and other women from the developing countries, these ideas can no longer be stigmatized as representing only the views of former imperialists dead set on imposing "Western" values on the rest of the world.

The Beijing Conference was prophetic of the campaigns that grassroots women's international organizations will pursue in the future. The Platform for Action, passed by over 120 of the 189 governments participating in Beijing, places increased emphasis on a broad interpretation of human rights that makes sure to include women among human beings. Building on the 1994 Cairo Conference on Population and Development, which endorsed the view that population-control measures, including abortions, are matters of public health, and that women need education, access to birth control, health care, and freedom of choice throughout their lives, not just during their reproductive years, the Beijing document secured the gains.

The Platform for Action endorsed the findings of the 1993 U.N. Conference on Human Rights held in Vienna, which for the first time acknowledged that women's rights are human rights. (As Hillary Clinton echoed: "once and for all.") Perhaps, most important, the majority of countries represented in Beijing endorsed the priority of international human rights for women over national and customary law.

The theoretical issues raised in Beijing go to the heart of what politics will be in the twenty-first century. First, the questions Denise Riley and, more recently, Iris Marion Young have considered about whether we can speak of "women" at all when class, race, ethnicity, disability, and sexual preference mark such differences among women gain new currency as grassroots leaders blur differences in favor of universal human rights.[16]

While feminist lawyers have written the language of rights for women in national as well as U.N. documents, grassroots women activists have been less constrained by the language of existing legal systems.[17] Women in NGOs want individual rights, but they also demand greater protection for the communities for which they speak. In other words, they want to transform international priorities to fulfill human needs despite what customary laws or legal systems may dictate.

Regina Ntongana, Josette Cole, Lois Gibbs, Luella Kenny, and Dollie and Kim Burwell as well as the tens of thousands of activists in Beijing have embarked on a prophetic mission to create a new global community, and the notion of women's rights as human rights is intrinsic to it. Women's human rights now promise the right to a good life, free from torture, intimidation, scarcity, and pollution, with access to good education, health care, choices about childbearing, and meaningful work.

The Beijing Platform for Action does not solve the problems of pollution, homelessness, or violence against women, and even the signatories do not have to stipulate how they think they can implement the document. But commitments to international platforms set moral standards, providing NGOs with leverage they can use on their own governments, and enabling grassroots activists to organize across borders to compel governments to comply.

The women at Beijing and the Burwells, Ntonganas, Coles, Kennys, and Gibbses are pathfinders, mapping out new routes to democracy, or what Ntongana and Cole and other activists in South Africa would call "social citizenship." In South Africa in the nineties, that term came to include the rights of everyone to schools, jobs, health care, and housing. The women concerned with human rights internationally commit themselves to practical transformations in everyday life through collective action to achieve justice. That form of justice has never been codified in national or international law, but the increasing frequency with which women's groups have called for it in the twentieth century indicates that justice as a social as well as an ethical goal may be closer at hand than any of us had previously imagined.

2

Suburban Blight and Situation Comedy

DRIVING AROUND LOVE CANAL, a lower-middle-class neighborhood in Niagara Falls, New York, sadness overcame me. When I was younger and going through a horrendous divorce, people kept telling me that I'd be better off without my husband. But I missed my old life and couldn't believe what was happening to me. The women who formed the Love Canal Homeowners Association weathered much greater losses, including frequent miscarriages, dead and disabled children, cancer, suicides in the family, battering, and ultimately the loss of their homes. Despite the pride the women feel about what they accomplished, most of them would be happy to find themselves back in a Love Canal that no longer exists, baking cookies and taking their kids to dance lessons. Instead, like refugees, they live scattered in different neighborhoods and different cities. Several are in new marriages. Most of them have had to take jobs to support themselves and their families. Out of their efforts, two groups have formed dedicated to empowering ordinary people like themselves: the Love Canal Medical Trust and the Citizens Clearinghouse for Hazardous Waste.

Home and homelessness are frequent topics when you talk to people from Love Canal. Luella Kenny, the mother of seven-year-old Jonathan Michael Kenny, who died as a result of kidney failure after years of playing in the creek at the bottom of their yard, recently met the new owner of her house.

Kenny, a modest, soft-spoken woman, was back in Love Canal, giving an interview, when her successor came out of the house to see what was going on. He wanted to challenge her view that those houses remain unsafe and present a threat to the health of anyone living in them. He believes authorities who say all the pollution has been cleaned up. Luella Kenny takes solace in the fact that he is an older man without children or grandchildren. Kenny, like other former owners who sit with her on the board of the Medical Trust and of the Citizens Clearinghouse, still brims over with anger about what she believes are the continued dangers of Love Canal.

In fact, she seethes first about the contradictory position of the government, which argues that there never was any significant danger at Love Canal and then, that the government has cleaned everything up. Instead of monitoring the neighborhood and the people who lived and died in it, using the suffering of the former homeowners to some purpose, the government has tried to divert the canal, its streams, and people's memories. Officials now claim that the area is safe for habitation. Tuscarora Indians live on condemned property. Cheap housing is once again available to lower-middle-class people who otherwise could not afford their own homes. Young children play, as the previous generation of kids did, on earth where submerged chemicals bubbled up into yards and basements, dissolving metal pumps.

Americans like to believe in the good intentions of their government, and they frequently consider the absence of politics to constitute an ideal state of being. Hardly a person from Love Canal doesn't wish she could turn back the clock and forget what she knows about the government. Barbara Quimby, whose adult retarded daughter now lives in a group home, says she envies those who still have faith in authorities.

It took the death of Luella Kenny's young son and officials' efforts to pretend that there were no toxic waste in the creek where he played to jar Kenny into action. Kenny, one of the few Love Canal activist women who worked outside her home at the time disaster struck in 1978, is a trained scientist. When she recently spoke to ghetto kids in an enrichment program about what had happened at Love Canal, she realized that unlike most audiences, they immediately understood how devastating it is to be homeless and not have any rights. And when Luella Kenny and Barbara Quimby reminisce about living in motels for nine weeks and being treated as though they had committed a crime, it registers as one of the worst times of their lives.[1]

All Americans except the very poor think of themselves as middle-class. That means they live in single-family houses in which they raise their families, or so the homeowners of Love Canal believed. Barbara Quimby, who grew up in Love Canal, and Jim Quimby, whom she married right out of high school, believed in the American dream, and for the first part of their lives, they lived it. By the time Barbara was in her late twenties, they had nearly paid off their mortgage.

Barbara Quimby could have been a cheerleader. Compact and energetic, she is a quintessential American strong blonde, spinning with ideas and confident that she can put them in place. Never what you'd call "shy," she is filled with ambition and pride though not in a classic sense. She had— and still has—a fierce desire for what she regards as a "normal" Christian family life centered on home and community. Fury permeates her conversation. She had all she wanted when things started going terribly wrong. First came the diagnosis of mental retardation of her oldest daughter at age two. Then, after six years of heavy rains, in 1976 the basement of her house began filling with a black, viscous material that was corrosive enough to dissolve four or five iron sump pumps. Quimby hoped that whatever was happening would stop; she simply kept buying new pumps.[2]

Looking away could not last forever. Quimby and her neighbors, who preferred being homemakers to being activists, joined together to save their homes and children. The more they learned, the less public officials wanted to deal with them. From being largely apolitical homemakers they became shrewd political operatives, adept at using the media to get their messages across. In the course of documenting what happened to them, they alerted the country to a national and international threat.

Love Canal, a housing development in the city of Niagara in northwestern New York state, provided suburban homes where in the early seventies, for a $200 down payment and $150 a month, young, blue-collar families could be homeowners. Love Canal took its name from an actual canal left unfinished by a builder called Joseph Love in the late nineteenth century. The Hooker Chemical Corporation, a subsidiary of the Occidental Petroleum Corporation, which produced pesticides, plastics, and caustics, dumped over 82 different compounds in the canal between 1947 and 1952, according to the *New York Times*.[3] The city and perhaps even the U.S. Army joined Hooker in using the canal as a landfill for fifty years. Together they discharged up to 20,000 metric tons of toxic waste, including pesticides and transformer oil tainted with PCB (polychlorinated biphenyl), containing dioxin, a deadly chemical found in DDT and Agent Orange.[4]

Like asbestos, dioxin is believed to be dangerous to human health in quantities of a billionth and in some cases a trillionth or quadrillionth proportion. The pollutant attaches itself to chemicals such as benzene and toluene and travels with them through water, leaching into ground water if the water table is too high. Known to cause central nervous system disorders, severe rashes, liver and bladder ailments, stillbirths, and miscarriages, dioxin has been considered one of the greatest of all environmental hazards. According to *Niagara Gazette* reporter Mike Brown, "The mere tracking of minuscule amounts of dioxin on a pedestrian's shoes in Seveso, Italy [where a chemical plant blew up] was of major concern, and according to [another commentator], a plant in Amsterdam found to be contaminated with dioxin had been 'dismantled, brick by brick, and the material embedded in concrete, loaded, at a specially constructed dock, on ships, and dumped at sea, in deep water near the Azores.' "[5]

In 1956, a few years after Love's canal was filled, the chemical company handed over the land to the city of Niagara for a nominal $1 price with the proviso that the company not be held responsible for any health damage that might arise. The city permitted a school and a housing development to be built over the landfill, providing modest homes for young families, none of whom realized what lay beneath them.

Like many working people, Lois Gibbs, another young Love Canal homemaker, knew only too well how important the chemical industry was to the local economy. Her husband, Harry, was a chemical worker who earned $150 a week in the late seventies. They paid $125 a month on the mortgage, another $90 a week for necessities, and looked forward to the following year when they would have paid off their mortgage.[6]

As early as the late fifties, certain homes in Love Canal began resembling the set for *The Exorcist*. Take, for example, the home of Aileen and Edwin Voorhees. In 1959 the Voorhees found black sludge seeping into their basement walls. By the late sixties, similar disasters beset their daughter Karen Schroeder, who lived down the street. The Shroeder's third child, Sheri, was born on November 21, 1968, deaf, retarded, and with a cleft palate, a hole in her heart, and misshapen ears.[7] The Schroeder's house and garden underwent frightening changes. First their trees and plants began to shrivel and die. In 1974, after four years of heavy rains, chemical action beneath the surface of their swimming pool lifted it several feet into the air. When they took out the pool, the yard filled with a sludgy, watery mess.[8]

Debbie Cerrillo, another Love Canal homemaker, tried to grow tomatoes, beets, or even grass in the back end of her garden, but everything was stunted or gigantic. Of two packages of beet seeds she planted one year, only four beets formed, one as big as a basketball. Neighbors warned her not to eat anything she had grown. The Cerrillo's swimming pool also began to rise, showing rims of barrels around the edges.[9]

Not knowing that the local elementary school sat on a chemical dump, Lois Gibbs began to worry about her son. Within two months of starting school, Michael, an otherwise healthy child, began having convulsions, and the doctors thought he might have epilepsy. Then he developed asthma, followed by bladder irritations and rashes. After that, his white blood count declined.[10] Hoping simply to get her son out of the school, Gibbs went to the principal. He asked for a note from the boy's doctor. Even though Gibbs came back with two notes saying that her son's illnesses since starting school indicated some irritant, the school board adamantly refused to transfer the Gibbs boy. Unable to get her child out of the school, she began contacting her neighbors to see how their children were doing.

Gibbs, at first shy and inexperienced, forced herself to go door to door to discover what people in the larger community knew about what was going on at Love Canal. Her spirits improved once she rediscovered Debbie Cerrillo, someone she'd known when both were Brownies but hadn't seen since high school. Cerrillo's house, right next to the hidden canal, had huge puddles filled with chemicals seeping up from the ground.[11] Cerrillo, who had been the class clown, referred to the holes as elephant footprints. She speaks about her multiple "female problems," including her difficulty conceiving her children, as the result of growing up near Love Canal.

Embarking like Chicken Little, Gibbs and Cerrillo hadn't yet realized that the sky was falling. But they gathered other mothers who shared their concerns. As the two women and their allies moved down the streets closest to the school, neighbors recounted a litany of odd illnesses: childhood arthritis, hyperactivity, and, most frequently, miscarriages. Of the fourteen pregnancies that occurred in the neighborhood during one year (1979–80), only two had resulted in able-bodied infants. Officials later regarded such evidence as anecdotal and referred to the women as "hysterical housewives."[12]

While canvassing the neighborhood, Lois Gibbs and Debbie Cerrillo met Barbara Quimby; Pat Brown, whose

one surviving child had multiple handicaps; and Marie Pozniak, whose daughter Kimberly suffered severe asthma and
who herself contracted cancer and died. Pozniak's daughter's
asthma was so severe she had to be sent away to relatives
when her breathing difficulties increased.[13] Together the
mothers formed the Love Canal Homeowners Committee
(later Association), which ultimately gathered 500 families as
members. Between June 1978, when it began, and September 1981, when it succeeded in having the government agree
to buy all the houses of those who wanted to move away, the
Love Canal Home Owners Association was able to "work"
the media in a way that transformed isolated homemakers
into sophisticated political organizers and citizens.

Although articles had appeared in the local press during
the spring and summer of 1978, many of the people who
lived around the canal were unaware of what was going on.
New York state, following up on the alarm the newspapers
sounded, carried out some blood tests in June 1978, but did
not release the results until August. Learning that Dr. Robert
P. Wahlen, commissioner of health for the state of New York,
was going to issue a public statement on August 3, 1978, in
Albany about the test results, Debbie Cerrillo, Lois Gibbs,
and her husband, Harry Gibbs, drove 300 miles to hear the
prepared statement in person—wondering why no one had
made the announcement in Love Canal itself.

Calling the situation "a great and imminent peril,"
Whalen exhorted pregnant women and children under age
two to leave the area on the south end of the canal—without
explaining how they might do so.[14] Debbie Cerrillo, whose
family was one of the twenty who lived within the first ring,
in what turned out to be the rim of the canal, qualified. But
what about her husband or her older child or the people
across the street or down the block? What should parents of
three-year-olds do? The announcement could lead only to
panic, and it did. Having issued his statement, the commissioner refused to take questions, and fled the hearing room
in Albany. Gibbs and Cerrillo kept lower officials talking for
over an hour before beginning their journey home.[15]

Once back at Love Canal, they had little time to absorb what they had heard. Gibbs's mother, who had been caring for Michael and two-year-old Melissa in Gibbs's absence, told them the neighbors had gone over to the 99th Street school. Harry, Lois, and Debbie went immediately to an impromptu meeting of about 150 families in the street near the school. As homeowner Lois Eisner, who had had one miscarriage and a child who was born with a defective ureter that would result in surgery, explained, "Right now we don't know what we're going to do. My husband's parents live down the street, so we can't go there. My mom's only got a one-bedroom apartment. A decent apartment in this area costs $180 to $200 a month—we can't afford that with our mortgage payments."[16] Some people decided to organize a strike against paying taxes or mortgages until the government gave them further information.

Without any prior experience in public speaking or political action, Gibbs, just back from Albany, addressed the crowd, urging them to fill out health department questionnaires, detailing what was happening to them and their families. The next day, 500 people attended a meeting at the 99th Street school with a representative of the governor sent to help make plans to move out of the neighborhood a small number of pregnant women and children under two years old. But no one said clearly how long the exodus would last and where people would end up if they could move.[17]

One local woman, Bonnie Snyder, told a reporter that she had always been especially careful about the food her twenty-two-months-old adopted daughter ate. "I don't let her eat sugar. I open up my bread drawer, and I see 'no preservatives,' and I laugh. She's been breathing chemicals all this time. My dog is five years old. It has had fourteen operations for cysts. If we can get some money, we'll move out."[18] Standing in her muddy front yard, the foul smells of chemicals wafting up, Snyder presented a strong image of a mother looking for an escape route.

In fact, what differentiated the women of the Love Canal Homeowners Association from other protesters was their self-presentation as traditional mothers trying to do their job. "Radicals and students carry signs, but not average housewives. Housewives have to care for their children and their homes," Lois Gibbs recalled later.[19] The homeowners learned to use the news media to project that image of themselves as they pursued a strategy for saving their families. Familiarity with television, especially with situation comedies like *I Love Lucy* and *The Carol Burnett Show*, provided models of strong women who retained typical feminine qualities. Portraying themselves as housewives helped otherwise ethnically and religiously disparate neighbors forge themselves into a community. In fact, a by-product of the homeowners' movement was the blending of two immediately recognized images of women. One melodramatically presented women, especially mothers, as innocent victims. From this vantage point, the homemakers were caught in a plot over which they had no control. But by virtuously resisting, standing up for their families, they gained license to act against the forces of evil. The other image developed in situation comedies. There, strong women such as Lucy, played by Lucille Ball, attempted to win their goals but always in a way that did not enhance their own power.

The successful use of the news media came partly because local people were themselves schooled in television and partly because of the advice of academic supporters. From the first days when Lois Gibbs began to recognize that her son was suffering and that local officials worried more about their own images than about what was happening to her family, she had the advice of her sister, Kathy Hadley, and Wayne Hadley, her brother-in-law, then a biology professor at the State University of New York at Buffalo.

The Hadleys frequently left their young son with Lois Gibbs for child care, and the two families were close. Although the Hadleys moved away in the fall of 1978, Wayne Hadley, who had worked on government commissions and was astute about the news media, was around long enough to teach his sister-in-law a few tricks about getting her message across. Hadley taught Gibbs certain fundamentals:

namely, that reporters stay only for the first fifteen minutes of public events and that "talking heads" don't make good television. To get your message across, you have to speak quickly, in sound bites, and preferably wave or bang something.

The homeowners learned that they had to be seen in order to be heard. They acted in dramatic ways, making themselves colorful for print and television. At the meeting in August 1978, for example, where pregnant women and children under two were told to leave, Gibbs cast their predicament in epic terms: "You're treating us like the Titanic! Women and children first!"[20] Sociologist Adeline Gordon Levine writes of the response: "The news reporters, photographers, and television cameramen, trailing their gear and bathing the group in hot lights, recorded what was happening and inevitably became part of the scene themselves, while helping to turn the event into a nationally known and shared experience."[21]

The ability of the homeowners to shape their own images and broadcast their messages through the news media is something that brings a grin and a blush to the faces of even those women who would rather forget. Debbie Cerrillo will punctuate a story with an aside, saying "now we went out to manipulate the media" or "we had to regain the headlines." Even now they remember what events of national or international importance—such as the eruption of the volcano at Mt. St. Helens or riots in Miami—pushed them off the front pages and off the nightly news. Generally, however, reporters appear as conduits to a public arena that would otherwise have been unavailable to the homeowners. Unlike politicians and disgruntled neighbors worried about their property values, the media generally portrayed the homeowners in a favorable light. The homeowners did not have to feign their fears; all they had to do was show them—preferably on camera.

When a representative of the Federal Disaster Assistance Administration came to Love Canal on August 5, 1978, he spontaneously grimaced and held his nose when taken through one of the houses; a photojournalist was there to record his disgust.[22] Throughout the neighborhood, when frightened and angry people proclaimed, "Give me liberty, I've got death" and "Love Canal kills," they appeared on the news.[23]

The homeowners had a special opportunity during the late summer and fall of 1978, when New York Governor Hugh Carey faced a tough re-election campaign.[24] In September 1978, when the state came up with a hastily constructed plan for draining the canal, with few safeguards against releasing deadly chemicals into the air and onto the ground, Lois Gibbs threw a copy of the plan down on a table at a public meeting, and a local television news camera recorded her act.[25]

The medical investigator for the state, Dr. Nicholas Vianna, admitted in the fall of 1978 that residents from 93rd Street to 103rd Street, the area immediately over the canal, all might be susceptible to liver damage because of the degree to which the chemicals had spread underground.[26] In the midst of growing terror among the homeowners, seven-year-old Jon Kenny, Luella Kenny's youngest son, died of kidney failure on October 4, 1978. Relatively healthy children up until June, the three Kenny boys had suffered periodic rashes that doctors said were poison ivy. But Jon's real troubles had begun with swellings below his eyes and in his stomach. Once doctors detected proteins in his urine, possibly caused by chemicals, he spent three weeks in the hospital. After a brief period during which he was normal, he suffered convulsions and was rushed back for treatment in late September. After doing some checks, a doctor asked Jon how he was. The agreeable child answered, "Fine," whereupon the doctor commiserated with him, claiming that Jon's mommy was causing them both problems by imagining things. Luella and Norman Kenny took their boy home. Within two days, he had to return; he died a few days later.[27]

Better educated and more prosperous than many of their neighbors, the Kennys had bought a house in Love Canal because there they could afford a house on an acre of land running down to a creek. Luella Kenny had trained as a chemist and worked in cancer research, but even she did not suspect environmental pollution as the cause of her sons' minor ailments. When Jon began to suffer from kidney disease, she read up on environmental hazards. After Jon died—a death that officials still refused to admit had anything to do with the canal—she became active with the homeowners.[28] The autopsy showed at least one strange glandular change. Kenny said, "Children have a gland called the thymus. It is what determines the immune response. It usually disappears when children are fourteen years old. The autopsy report indicated that Jon's thymus was already shrunk. In the medical journals, all of the animal studies showed that a shrunken thymus is an indicator of exposure to dioxin. That's what was in our back yard: dioxin."[29]

What guided the homeowners was anxiety about their children. Having grown up in a community with fathers who had served in the Army—and Debbie Cerrillo's father had been a prisoner of war—the homeowners had trusted public officials. The decades of the civil rights movement and the Vietnam War, which discredited public officials in the eyes of hundreds of thousands of American citizens, had scarcely registered on the consciousnesses of the women of Love Canal, many of whom, like Lois Gibbs, had brothers who served in Vietnam. They had kept their faith in authorities. The story of Jon Kenny's death and their own experiences with doctors who wouldn't credit what the women said undermined the homeowners' confidence in doctors, challenged their trust in authority, and enhanced their sense of urgency about getting their families out of the contaminated area. Even today, when Barbara Quimby or Pat Brown speaks about their retarded or disabled daughters, who are now nearly the ages their mothers were when Love Canal struck, the mothers sigh and thank God that their beloved daughters are still alive.

As the government began excavations in the fall of 1978 to create a clay channel at the southern end of the canal to prevent seepage of chemicals into neighboring areas, the homeowners still wondered with fear and rage what would happen to them. In October 1978, people in the surrounding blocks begged to be moved out. With the help of a geneticist and biologist, Dr. Beverly Paigen, from the nearby State University of New York at Buffalo, Gibbs and her group gathered information about the diseases and ailments for which local residents had been hospitalized. They correlated those diseases with evidence about the apparent cracks in the clay lying between five and twelve feet below the soil. There appeared to be small creeks and a veritable system of drainage ditches called swales carrying the toxic wastes far from the canal, seeping into outlying neighborhoods.[30] Having submitted their medical records to the Department of Health, they all received the same telegrams stating that there was no danger and therefore no reason to remove them from the site.[31]

The group presented additional findings about miscarriages, kidney and liver ailments, and skin diseases to a hearing in Albany in November 1978. But state officials discounted their arguments. According to Gibbs, "They said there was no data to back up the claim. All we had was what people told us. It didn't mean anything because it was put together by a bunch of housewives with an interest in the outcome of the study."[32] Without consulting the material, a Department of Health official dismissed the report as "information collected by housewives that is useless."[33]

Despite the fact that by the end of 1978 and early 1979, the New York State Health Department had told residents not to eat or sell anything grown in their own backyards and had even begun running blood tests on local residents, officials would not admit that the neighborhood might be unsafe. The news in mid-December that dioxin had been found in the trench near 97th Street led the homeowners' group to demand that the state stop digging up the canal until they could prove that they could protect residents. Fearing that dioxin on the construction truck tires would spread, Marie Pozniak stood in the middle of the road in subzero weather in order to keep the trucks from moving. Others joined her, and they were all arrested. Pozniak complained in front of reporters, "My child's crying all the time. She wants to go out."[34] Pushing a baby carriage, Lois Gibbs and seven others demonstrated and were arrested. Eight more were jailed before the week was out.[35] Though Pozniak, Gibbs, and the others had never participated in demonstrations before the previous summer of 1978, they quickly learned that presenting themselves as outraged mothers—identities they really assumed—made them interesting to the news media and hard for government officials to attack.

The homeowners' group challenged the government over what gave mothers special rights. Even in February 1979, when the new commissioner of health for the State of New York, David Axelrod, agreed to pay to move and house pregnant women and children under two living between 97th and 103rd streets until the area was safe or the children reached the age of two, the state would still not admit a clear and present danger from chemicals in the neighborhood.[36] Taking the government's message to the airwaves, Dr. Nicholas J. Vianna of the Department of Health told the audience of CBS morning news on February 8, 1979, that the only verifiable odd health conditions at Love Canal were "fetal wastage," by which he meant miscarriages, birth defects, and low birth weights. Adeline Gordon Levine, the sociology professor who became an adviser to and friend of the women at Love Canal, observes that terms such as "fetal wastage" and "adverse pregnancy outcomes," though common in the scientific community, have an impersonal sound that belies the reality. The terms were associated with babies to whom the residents of Love Canal had given names and for whom they were grieving.[37] The numbers revealed that 36 percent to 46 percent of all pregnancies in Love Canal resulted in low birth weight, miscarriage, or deformity, and that one woman in four could expect a miscarriage.[38]

At the February 1979 meeting, when the pregnant women and very young children from the outer rings around the canal were ordered removed, the mothers of Love Canal ridiculed the secrecy and incompetence of those assigned to decide the fate of the residents. A secret blue ribbon committee, possibly made up of the same public officials who had ruled on gambling in the city of Niagara Falls, was chosen to determine the degree of danger. Attending the meeting, the women of Love Canal showed their scorn by wearing blue ribbons prepared for them by Debbie Cerrillo. Beverly Paigens, the scientist helping the homeowners, had a ribbon that said she was "an expert on housewives' data." Another wore a ribbon saying she was "an expert on blue ribbon panels." Another claimed she had become "an expert on listening to New York State bullshit." [39]

The homeowners group, realizing that only by maintaining media interest could they win any concessions from the government, decided that they needed visual representation of their plight. To raise money, the homeowners printed up T-shirts, which they wore around town along with red carnations to mark themselves and to voice their distress about the health of their families and the conditions of their homes. [40]

The homeowners decided to demonstate in Albany. The homeowners held a press conference, and, with an unwanted police escort, Lois Gibbs, Marie Pozniac, and several other homeowners set out for Albany carrying coffins as props. When they reached the capital, armed guards examined the coffins for bombs. Marie Pozniak, who had a cold, appeared to reporters to be crying. The other women, quickly covering for her, comforted her in order to shape the right dramatic message before handing the coffins over to one of the governor's aides. [41] Playing to stereotypes resembling Lucy and Ethel Mertz, the women frequently allowed themselves to be portrayed as silly the better to confront the government. Comedy and appearing in the role of victim allowed the homeowners to challenge authority and gain media support. Even as they were growing stronger and more self-confident, the homeowners presented themselves as helpless.

Had the women been feminists, they could have undercut their demands to be treated as full citizens by such actions. But the homeowners were desperate to save their community from disaster; they were willing to compromise their own dignity to survive.

When the state revealed in April 1979 that PCB was concentrated in the site at 176 per billion, the Love Canal Homeowners Association held a rally complete with dummies of the governor and the head of the New York State Health Department. Chanting: "Thanks to New York state, death is our fate. We don't want to die—Listen to our cry. We want out," they demonstrated at the parking lot of the school and burned the figures in effigy. Their public spectacle once again won them good news coverage.[42]

When I first spoke by phone to Debbie Cerrillo, I sheepishly asked her about these demonstrations, hoping she wouldn't think I was drawing attention away from the seriousness of the homeowners' efforts. She responded by saying, "I was the art director of Love Canal," in what I later came to recognize was her typical directness and zaniness.[43] Choosing the images was a collective effort, although both Cerrillo and Quimby credit Lois Gibbs with coming up with most of the ideas; Gibbs points to Cerrillo's genius at imagining political props.

In another incident, the less extroverted Luella Kenny witnessed the humiliation of officials outside the range of the media. When Kenny followed some inspectors down to the creek where her sons had played, she simply wanted to see what the officials were doing. No one was more surprised than she when a bird swooped down, scooped up a fish, began its ascent, and then plummeted to its death.[44] Kenny realized that birds, like the fabled canaries mine workers sent ahead, were sensitive to the same poisons that harmed humans. When birds and small animals die, it is time for humans to evacuate. The officials with typical distrust of and paranoia about the homeowners, turned around, accusing Kenny of having orchestrated the scene worthy of a sight gag in a movie.

Cerrillo, Quimby, and Kenny recount the war stories of triumph over adversity, but as Quimby frequently points out, she would have preferred skipping the whole thing and would still give anything to be back in Love Canal before she knew anything about toxic waste. By the second year of the struggle, beginning in the summer of 1979, the seriousness of what was going on made the pain almost unbearable. Marie Pozniak, who at first seemed more stern than the rest of the troops—as they called themselves—staffed the office and frequently was the rock others leaned on. When a man who had just learned that his wife had three months to live because her liver cancer was not responding to treatment came in, he was close to tears. In a macho community, where men were suffering not only from the pollution but from their sense that they were failing to take care of their families properly, crying in public was the ultimate indignity. Marie shunted him over to a side office, where she joined him while he cried in private, knowing that she wouldn't spread the story all over the neighborhood.[45]

In August 1979, when the city was attempting to create channels for the underground pool of toxic waste, more fumes were released, making countless people so ill they had to be hospitalized as a result of the noxious gases. Those neighbors outside an arbitrary line the state drew continued to live in the stench, a mixture of rotten eggs, vinegar, and ammonia, which they knew demonstrated the high levels of toxic chemicals in the air and water around them. One resident described the area at its worst: "I can't tell you what it was like on some days. It was hot, and the air would just hang there. The fumes were thick. They made your eyes water, or you coughed. Someone described it as similar to trying to breathe underwater. In the winter the cold wind would come off the river and blow the fumes away. That was bad enough, but in the summer you knew you were living on a chemical dump."[46]

To get them away from the neighborhood, from late August to the beginning of November, the city temporarily housed 125 families in motels at a cost of $7,500 a day. Officials told people that each member of the family needed certification from a physician in order to remain in the motels. People who had never before had a family doctor and were squeamish about medical authorities turned to Luella Kenny to help them decide how to get the certification they needed.[47] Lois Gibbs recognized that "the state couldn't continue to pay several thousand dollars a day for motels, although there was a court order that said they had to. It would be very embarrassing if women and children were thrown into jail. We relied on their unwillingness to jail us. It had worked in the past."[48]

Luella Kenny and Barbara Quimby recall how unbearable it was to live in the motels for six weeks. Motel managers treated the homeowners as homeless people whose presence detracted from the quality of the clientele. Kenny, unable to live with the dirt, cleaned all the windows in the room her family occupied. When the weekend came, the manager wanted her family to leave their room, desirable because it had a view over the Niagara River. She refused, saying she was not responsible for cleaning the entire establishment. Since the motel owners regarded people from Love Canal as a burden—despite the fact that the state paid handsomely for them—the homeowners received no special accommodations. The motel refused to provide lunches for the children and the men before they left early in the morning, so the homeowners were left to their own devices. Norman Kenny stopped at a 7-Eleven every morning and bought bread and fixings to make his two remaining sons their lunches.

Whole families and their pets shared one or two rooms. Luella Kenny said that because the family was living in such close quarters, she tried especially hard to keep things neat. She made the beds each morning before she left for work. Her tidiness resulted in a motel manager's wrath. He reported her to authorities, saying that her family's beds were not slept in and therefore that they were living elsewhere.[49]

Like other homeless children, the Love Canal kids living in the motels attracted the ridicule of schoolmates. One cruel trick was to turn out the lights and joke that people from Love Canal glowed in the dark. Frightened and irritable, the kids living in motel rooms had problems doing homework or concentrating on their studies.

Even the leaders of the homeowners' group were growing restless. The Environmental Protection Agency had carried out a pilot project examining the blood of thirty-six residents of Love Canal. On May 15, 1980, the report reached the EPA offices, and late the next day, on a Friday, Lois Gibbs was asked to alert the people tested that they would learn the results on Saturday morning. But before the team of experts arrived, the news appeared on the local radio station and on the front pages of the *New York Times* and the *Niagara Gazette* on May 17: one-third of those studied had damaged chromosomes.[50]

Those tested lived at a further distance from the canal than the 200 families who had already been evacuated after the government bought their contaminated houses. Of thirty-six so-called safe families, eleven couples, among them Barbara and Jim Quimby and Patricia and Jim Brown, were found to have broken chromosomes, believed to be responsible for miscarriages, birth defects, and cancer. Patricia Brown, who like Debbie Cerrillo had suffered frequent miscarriages, had finally given birth to a daughter who is disabled. The daughter has had cerebral palsy and severe nerve disorders for which she has undergone almost a dozen operations.[51]

Against this background of news about chromosomal damage, two other messengers of bad tidings came from the EPA. A physician and the public relations official from the Washington office of the EPA had remained in Niagara Falls, ostensibly to help people process the reports after the people tested had met in half-hour sessions with other EPA officials all Saturday morning. But the two troubleshooters were not available any time on Sunday or even on Monday morning to explain to the victims or their neighbors the significance of broken chromosomes, what might happen to them and their children, and what the government planned to do next. Outraged people congregated around the Love Canal Homeowners Association office on Monday morning and grew more and more violent as the day proceeded. When the officials appeared in the office on Monday afternoon at about 3:30 p.m., they were told it was not safe for them to leave.[52]

Dramatizing their cause had been a commonplace strategy among the homeowners, but holding the officials hostage escalated resistance. The women leading the homeowners had pursued peaceful demonstrations, pitting their own bodies against those of state officials. They had competed for—and generally won—the media's award for the chief victims. But many of the people for whom the homeowners had done unofficial counseling had grown increasingly angry—people suffering from depression; men furious that their own sense of masculinity was wounded by official callousness; men and women whose spouses wanted to leave or wanted to stay, contrary to their partner's wishes. Since local citizens had been dealing for months with seemingly insensitive and unresponsive officials, the two captives became surrogates for all the officials who for two years had failed to assuage the terrors of people whose lives had been overtaken by strange forces.[53] The modest homes of the people of Love Canal represented everything they owned. They could not afford to pack up and leave, yet they seemed to be endangering their lives and those of their children if they remained. The crisis in which they had found themselves for several years could have led the community to sit back and wait for the government to come to their aid. Instead, a group of homemakers had taken action.

On May 19, 1980, when Barbara Quimby came to work at the Homeowners Association, she found the raucous crowd ready to turn over cars and attack the EPA officials who had already gone into the office. Quimby sought shelter from the angry crowd, and Gibbs warned her that she might want to leave because the officials would be forced to stay. Quimby remembers how frightened she was by the mob, who were egged on by a man from outside Love Canal who had hung around for months, always urging more militant action and promoting violence.

Whatever else might happen, Quimby knew that she was scared to death to be outside.[54] She stood by Lois Gibbs, who decided to call President Carter. Forced to remain on hold for a long time while the White House switchboard tried to figure out what to do, the homeowners waited. Quimby shudders when she recalls how one of the EPA officials, pointing across the street, told her that an FBI sharpshooter could strike her dead from there without touching him. The tension built as Quimby, Gibbs, and some of the local teenagers who had joined them inside waited for the White House switchboard to call back.

Finally word came that state and national officials would decide by Wednesday, May 21, whether or not to buy the homes of the remaining families so that they could afford to move away. In fact, the FBI moved in on Monday night at 9:30 and rescued the two men, who kindly claimed they had no memory of any of the people with whom they had stayed all day. Had the captors been men instead of women and children, the hostages might have felt more threatened. As it stood, by keeping the men out, the homemakers and teenagers portrayed themselves as confused victims, and they got off with a reprimand from the U.S. attorney.[55] Actually, the media-wise Barbara Quimby recalls that riots in Miami, which flared up the same day, drove Love Canal out of the news and diminished the significance of the hostage taking. The Federal Disaster Assistance Administration agreed by Wednesday that 700 families would be temporarily housed at a nearby Air Force base at government expense, still leaving unsettled the question of whether the government would buy their homes.[56]

How little the women realized the significance of the hostage taking became evident when Barbara Quimby talked to her father a few days after May 19. He asked her "What about the children?" Confident that she was a good mother, that in fact everything she did was for her children, she explained, "The kids were all right. They were with my neighbor." "No," her father responded, "not during the hostage incident. What did you think would happen to the kids while you were in prison during the next twenty years?" "I *never* thought of that," she explained incredulously.[57]

In one of the final stages of the struggle, on May 20, 1980, the day after the hostages were taken and released, many people from the Homeowners Association had attended a meeting of the Niagara County Council, which had to vote on whether money would be given to buy them out so they could afford to relocate. A woman named Liz gave testimony. Lois Gibbs describes it: "Liz began to tremble. Her eyes filled with tears. She had moved out temporarily to protect her unborn child and her two-year-old daughter. She carried her baby Julie [the full] nine months. Everything seemed to be fine. But now, tears were running down her cheeks. She didn't bother to wipe them. She was in a trancelike state, reliving the birth of her child. Speaking very softly, she said her baby was stillborn, that it was dead. 'My little Julie is dead because of Love Canal. Please, I beg you to support the bill tonight before this happens again!' Liz could barely walk away from the podium when she was through, she was crying so hard."[58]

When the council members still voted against the homeowners, the latter staged a demonstration. Afraid of the hostile crowd, the council adjourned for forty-five minutes. When they returned, so did Gibbs. Under the television camera lights, Gibbs stood on a chair challenging the lawmakers to explain their negative vote. As two officers came over to tell her to get down or face arrest, one of them whispered to Gibbs and she recalled "that he had just called home to tell his wife he would be late. She asked him to deliver a message [to the demonstrators], thanking [them] for the overtime, [urging them] to keep up the good work and [telling them] that she was behind [them]."[59] The police, though not always sympathetic, were, like the homeowners, from blue-collar families and well understood how precarious their situation was.

After Gibbs was removed twice, she sighted an open door, but another police officer caught her eye and moved to stop her. In order to distract him, her friend Marie Pozniak pinched him on his backside and everyone, including the policeman, laughed as Gibbs slipped back into the hearing room.[60] This little act of bawdiness established a comical relationship between the police and the women just as the first policeman's wife earlier had emphasized their shared roles as lower-middle-class homemakers. A woman's sexual harassment of a man in authority also underscored the resolve of the mothers of Love Canal. By acting as sexual aggressors, they contradicted the image of asexuality and docility generally associated with motherhood in our society. By playing an uppity Carol Burnett instead of a victim in a soap opera, Pozniak and her supporters reversed stereotypes and took the upper hand.

Rebellious acts overcame for a little while the sense of despair that women such as Marie Pozniak felt when they reflected upon what had turned them into activists. "You go out and see someone carrying groceries into their home in another part of town," Pozniak said, "and they're smiling and happy and you resent them for it, because they have a safe home. Yours is dangerous. You're afraid of your own home. My family is going to pieces, and there are divorces all over this place. My husband is so desperate: There is no way he can get us out, no way for him to protect his family, and that gets to him. That gets to everyone."[61] The image of the lost home, the assault on the world that housewife-mothers had constructed, appears repeatedly in the nostalgia for what most of the former homeowners feel they've lost. But they refused to submit to self-pity, fighting on to save their families and their neighbors.

Local reporters, David Pollack and Mike Brown, both from the *Niagara Gazette*, had pursued the early stories about health problems, sludge, and strange transformations of the landscape at Love Canal. Local news reporters Miranda Dunne (ABC-TV) and Marie Rice (CBS-TV) remained devoted to the story. Sociologist Adeline Levine reports that in May, in addition to the regular news coverage they received, the Homeowners Association members were featured on the *Today* show (5/22/80), *The MacNeil-Lehrer News Hour* (5/22/80), *Sixty Minutes* (5/25/80), and the *CBS Sunday News* (5/25/80). Phil Donahue brought in forty homeowners for a show on June 19, 1980. Early June saw a few pieces on Love Canal on *Good Morning America*, as well as a PBS show, a segment of *Nova* titled "A Plague on Our Children," and a sequel to ABC's *The Killing Grounds*.[62]

The homeowners needed all the support they could get, since each time they won a victory, they were further from their exodus than before. To publicize their continued plight, the homeowners, who could not afford simply to abandon their homes, rented buses and went to the Democratic National Convention in New York in August 1980. With rubber rafts Debbie Cerrillo made as props, they called themselves the "Love Canal Boat People," comparing themselves to the Vietnamese refugees who were being hailed as heroes in the press. In front of Madison Square Garden, they chanted "President Carter, hear our plea. Set the Love Canal people free!" and "2-4-6-8! Help us now before it's too late!" Once again, the media found them interesting and gave their story big play.[63] Their willingness to make spectacles of themselves made them acceptable as comedy figures.

About two weeks after an appearance on ABC's *Good Morning America*, which played on September 19, 1980, Lois Gibbs was notified that President Carter was coming to Niagara to sign an agreement with New York state allocating $15 million for the purchase of the Love Canal homes.[64] The media coverage clearly had been key to the homeowners' victory. As Lois Gibbs explained, "We always saw to it that our protests had coverage, because that was really the only thing we had going for us."[65]

The buyout of the homes went slowly. The first house wasn't sold until November 15, 1980, just after Ronald Reagan was elected president. By mid-July 1981, nine months after Carter had signed the authorization for the buyout at fair market value, only 376 of the 550 families who wanted to leave had succeeded in selling their homes to the New York state agency established to buy them. Barbara Quimby recalls that Gibbs kept promising that things would be settled for good at the end of two weeks. As a result of the efforts of the Love Canal homeowners and other activists, the lame-duck Congress passed the Superfund legislation on December 11, 1980, and allocated $1.6 billion to clean up dumps throughout the country. But the law made no provisions for relocating people who lived on or near the dumps, or for providing them with health care for injuries they may have suffered from their exposure to toxic waste.

Lacking institutions through which they could exercise their will, and without common religious or political customs upon which they could build, the women of Love Canal created their own practices, drawing from disparate sources including situation comedies. A lot of what they did was staged for the television cameras because being photographed meant they would be heard. Indirectly, the Love Canal homeowners became astute television critics. They constantly analyzed their progress by their success as television characters. When Barbara Quimby imagines renewing her wedding vows on her twenty-fifth anniversary, she dreams of walking with Jim down the steps in Addie and Murray Levine's beautiful Victorian house in Buffalo. Even in fantasy, she compares herself to Carol Burnett playing Scarlett O'Hara, wearing the green velvet gown made from the drapes at Tara—but with the curtain rods still in.[66] Lacking other models for the behavior they knew survival required, the Love Canal women chose from among images presented by feisty women in situation comedies.

The way the Homeowners Association members tell their story, everything they did grew out of what they knew as homemakers and mothers. But their organizational abilities and the confidence they came to exude also deserves mention. The homeowners at first reached out to one another simply to compare notes, to discover whether what was happening to them was singular or typical of the neighborhood. Canvassing, which has always been an essential part of grassroots mobilization, became their main organizational tool.[67] But going door to door built up a sense of common interest. Activists also made use of the public hearing. Facing humiliation from public officials who challenged their knowledge and claimed they were overreacting, the women of Love Canal learned to turn ridicule back on their opponents.

The transformation of what it meant to be a homemaker in Love Canal over the three years of the community's struggles shows the way citizenship can sometimes grow out of conscious motherhood. Gibbs explained her sense of disquiet: "[H]ere I was giving press interviews, doing radio programs, and chasing a congressman, a governor, and the president with signs saying I supported him or that he was doing something wrong. Here I was literally screaming at the New York health department or the department of transportation. I never even knew these commissioners existed before all this. Now all of a sudden, I was in the middle of it—and I wasn't really used to it yet. It all seemed strange."[68]

Debbie Cerrillo attributes some of her own development to Adeline Levine, who was then a professor of sociology at the State University of New York at Buffalo. Levine contacted the Homeowners Association to see whether she could bring the students in her class on social movements to observe what was going on in the office. According to Cerrillo, who hadn't had much contact with academics before this time, Levine at first seemed remote. But staying around the office as she did, she gradually began helping out. She was especially helpful in teaching public speaking to the activists who were increasingly invited to address church meetings and gatherings of other people who found themselves in trouble all over the country. Needing support from outside the cities of Niagara Falls and Buffalo in order to win their fight to get evacuated, the homeowners had to take to the podium, and Addie Levine tutored them.

Cerrillo was not used to public speaking. She recalls how Addie Levine took her home and got her to express her thoughts and then Addie typed up the notes. Then they transferred Debbie's words to note cards she could hold. Still suffering from fear of public speaking, Cerrillo learned a valuable lesson: Levine taught her to pick out a sympathetic face in the audience and speak to that person as if they were alone. She also taught Cerrillo to picture those who might be scowling as sitting on the toilet, and imagine how embarrassed they would be to know Cerrillo was watching.[69]

Far from maintaining a distance, Addie Levine and her husband, Murray, a professor of psychology at the State University of New York at Buffalo, increasingly became the unofficial parents of the homeowners.[70] Moving out from relatively sheltered lives as homemakers, most of the Homeowners Association leaders lacked even the most basic survival skills as political activists. The Levines, who were about twenty years older than most of the homeowners, had been involved in liberal causes and recognized some of the ways activists suffered.

Many of the women who have participated in these movements have individually and collectively paid a price for doing things "good mothers don't do," such as forgetting their own child's birthday or missing recitals. Even today, when Barbara Quimby's retarded daughter calls from her group home and Barbara isn't there, she asks if her mom is at a meeting. Though Quimby's family seems to have withstood all the tragedies that have come its way, other families came apart or underwent painful transformations. Of the six central figures among the Homeowners Association members, one couple was divorced by the spring of 1981 and another within a few years. Not only do ordinary women, accustomed to polite dealings with those in authority, learn to confront those who call them "hysterical housewives," but they must also face their husbands and children, who accuse them of withdrawing affection and attention while pursuing political goals. Guilt about not being home, stress over taking on extensive community work in addition to their many tasks as homemakers, and worry over the harm pollution has already done to their families cause personal pain.

Addie Levine recognized that the low self-esteem of some of the women kept them from advancing. She helped some to deal with their own depression and others to come to terms with the increasing jealousy and resentment of their husbands. Two women in the neighborhood had committed suicide, unable to cope with the threat to their families and with their own entrapment as working-class people unable to abandon their homes and start over.[71] In cases where Homeowners Association members were actually in abusive relationships, Addie helped bolster their egos and encouraged them to recognize that they had brains and were creative, forceful human beings. And it was Addie who took them seriously when their own natal families urged the women to suffer through their husbands' abuse.

What remains is a lot of anger and some sense of victory. According to Debbie Cerrillo, the government paid off only the remaining mortgages, giving even "privileged" homeowners nothing for the money they had already invested and leaving them with little money for a down payment on a future house. Barbara Quimby grows irate when she recalls the way outsiders viewed the Homeowners Association. "As young as we were when we moved, we had only nine years to go on our mortgage—and it was at 6 percent. When they bought us out, mortgage rates were at 13 percent. We never would have put our houses on the market at that time. We never would have moved."[72]

The people I've talked to at Love Canal are furious about new people moving back into their places. Luella Kenny wishes that the government had set up a long-term research project to monitor the houses and the people. Since the contamination has been so widespread that no one would ever attempt to recreate it, why not study it? Having lost a child, she would like her family's suffering to serve some purpose.[73]

Barbara Quimby keeps trying to go somewhere where people won't identify her as coming from Love Canal. In addition to feeling as if the Homeowners Association lost— since the government is once again claiming the women overreacted and everything is fine—Quimby wants recognition that they did the right thing and saved their kids. As she explains it: "Say you're at the shopping mall with your kids. There are clowns over here and bargains over there, and you're having a great time. And then a fire comes. Even though you'd rather stay at the mall, you've got to get your kids out, because otherwise they'll die." Having grown up at Love Canal, Quimby has the hardest time adapting to other places. "I had a happy childhood, a Norman Rockwell life. I wanted the same people who'd known me all my life, who'd seen me going up and down in my baby carriage, to see me with my own kids. I wanted to show my kids the school I went to, my old house. But they're torn down. I can't share my childhood with my kids."[74]

Quimby feels pride tempered by regret about how things turned out at Love Canal. A devout Christian, she has been working on establishing Christian group homes for the severely disabled, in one of which her retarded daughter will live. But when the people with whom she worked on the project wanted her to do publicity, she refused. They knew she had contacts coming out of Love Canal. She knew that she didn't want to relive that experience, although she still serves on the Medical Trust that takes care of the medical needs of homeowners who won a settlement from Occidental Petroleum. Aware of her accomplishments but eager to choose when and where she gets involved in public again, Quimby jokes that she stays as far away from Luella Kenny as possible since she doesn't want to be close to the center of the action, doesn't want any publicity.

Over the eighties, many activists concerned with ending wars and violence increasingly turned their attention to the environment. A vast number of activists fighting to liberate their families from the dangers of pollution have been homemakers acting in their capacity as mothers protecting their communities. As writer Harriet Rosenberg notes, "The rapid growth of the Environmental Justice Movement in the last few years has thrust housewives into the role of community organizers."[75]

The way members of the Love Canal Homeowners Association learned to express themselves through the media would do a spin-doctor proud and doesn't necessarily fit into our images of how distraught mothers act. But women claiming to be defending their children increasingly are willing to demonstrate to oppose environmental hazards affecting their families. In publicizing environmental issues, playing crazy seems to have become an important part of politics. Taking their cue from situation comedies, housewives frequently try to mug for the cameras.

Women engaged in struggles for environmental justice are often viewed as oddities. They are told that they are hysterical housewives or crazy feminists. Or that they just aren't ladies. "Ladies don't take on an issue," Cora Tucker, a community activist from Virginia, explains. "I don't know if 'lady' is a compliment or not. I really don't like to be called a lady because my momma used to tell me that a lady was a woman who didn't know which way was up. And I really think we know which way is up. What we are is people. As long as we allow other people to make decisions, they're never going to make them in our best interest. Nobody makes a decision in our best interest unless we do it ourselves."[76]

Quimby takes refuge in her religious faith. She says that as much as she loves and respects Lois Gibbs, her faith in God, not Lois Gibbs, got her through the struggle. And Quimby's continued activism in religious social services, especially around health care and education for the mentally disabled, shows her inability to let go.

Debbie Cerrillo could have left the struggle at Love Canal when she and her family were moved out with the first group in August 1978. Instead she commuted in to work with the Homeowners Association. Once the others moved out in 1980, she lost her marriage, remarried, and moved away.

Luella Kenny continues to work in scientific research, but she's also the guiding force on the Love Canal Medical Trust. With money secured from Occidental Chemical

Company in an out-of-court settlement in which the company admitted no guilt, the trust provides medical care for those homeowners who sued. By continuing to set policy, Kenny has remained at the forefront of discussions about the personal costs of toxic-waste pollution.

Lois Gibbs, whose marriage also disintegrated, moved to Virginia, where she and her current husband, Stephen Lester, an environmental activist, founded the Citizens Clearinghouse for Hazardous Waste. Moving on, Gibbs has become an national arbiter on grassroots resistance to unimpeded toxic waste dumping and "management." Luella Kenny and Murray Levine serve on her board.

3

"When it rains, I get mad and scared": Women and Environmental Racism

WHEN I FINALLY REACHED Dollie Bullock Burwell at about 10:30 at night, we'd already been playing telephone tag for weeks. She'd just returned home after campaigning with Eva Clayton, who, one month later, in November 1992, became one of the first two African-Americans elected to the United States Congress from North Carolina since Reconstruction.

Exhausted, Dollie spoke relatively slowly over the phone, with a refinement and ease common to people from the northern borders of North Carolina. Despite the time and the fact that Dollie had been campaigning for months, her voice was energetic and enraged remembering how 40,000 cubic yards of PCB-laced soil had been dumped three miles from her backyard ten years earlier. "I was ticked off. I couldn't believe they'd dump that dirt on us—the landfill's a mile away from the school my daughter Kim went to and down the road from the Baptist Church," she said. "Everybody around here knows everyone's business. How did they get the land?" Like a person slowly waking from a nightmare, she stopped for a moment and recalled, "I became registrar of deeds in 1988; I never wanted to be surprised like that again."[1]

We arranged to meet in person in her office in Warrenton in late January 1993. Having driven up from Durham on a blustery day and arriving way too early, I wandered around town before going to see Dollie. I'd done a stint in

Mississippi in the mid-sixties, teaching at Tougaloo College outside Jackson. Despite the terror of those times, walking around small southern towns always conjures in me a sense of possibility from a time and place when interracial victory over white supremacy seemed possible—even inevitable.

With a population of scarcely more than five thousand, Warrenton is the county seat of one of the poorest, blackest regions in the state. Downtown consists of two city blocks along a main street. In front of the post office, there is the usual monument to white Civil War dead vying for attention with historic markers, pointing to the houses of Revolutionary War heroes and senators from the slave South.

The local stationery store, which sells the *Warren Record*, a weekly newspaper, also stocks books on local history, self-help studies, and the latest offerings of conservative Republicans. Postcards in black and white fill the racks with three scenes of downtown Warrenton at the turn of the century. But around the corner from the shop, opposite the library and the single-story county office building, is the Taste Paradise health-food store on whose front door is the motto "Cleanse your body with herbs." A few doors down is the Hercules Fitness Center. The sign out front has a black muscle man and a white couple dancing, seemingly indicating that, despite racial stereotypes, the center is integrated. If the war monument and historic homes look back to a sectional past, certainly health food and a sexually and racially integrated fitness center indicate that never before has American culture been so unified. For better and worse, there's a national culture, and the media have a lot to do with it.

Television aerials and even a satellite dish or two stood out along the country roads I'd taken between Durham and Warrenton. Thirty years ago, more naive and purist, I'd been shocked by the presence of television sets in the shacks of even the most abject sharecroppers in Mississippi. When I returned to Tougaloo after one weekend in the Delta and expressed my indignation to the campus minister, he countered by saying, "Hey, you've seen the schools. And Negro kids here can't even get into this new Head Start. What's better than TV to show your kid a world outside of Mississippi?" Talking about television recently to a friend who has lived in another small southern town for twenty years made me take stock again. He said, "It's not just television but cable that's changed the outlook of the South. When you can get thirty channels, local people no longer control what you know. You begin to make your own connections."

I was thinking about this when I first walked into Dollie Burwell's office. She told her male assistant she'd be talking to me, and we went to her ground-floor office, which opens onto a lawn and the street. Dieting after months of living on doughnuts and fried chicken on the campaign trail, she suggested we skip lunch and talk. A soft-spoken woman in her mid-forties, dressed in a long blue skirt, high black boots, and a heavy, cable-knit white sweater, Dollie seemed younger and more vulnerable than I had imagined. I wouldn't have picked her out as a prophet whose views about the connection between civil rights and the degradation of the environment is changing the way people around the country are thinking. Vernice Miller, co-founder of the West Harlem Environmental Action, and herself a force to reckon with, says when Dollie speaks even male civil rights leaders stop to listen.[2] Among women, that is high praise.

Dollie Burwell is a shrewd political leader, filled with confidence but also a little shy. It's hard to envision her giving way to anyone, but it's easy to imagine her cultivating the political opinions of people who usually don't know what views they have until they speak. When an opponent in North Carolina, exasperated with Dollie said, "She's a professional agitator—that's her profession. She just goes around making trouble," Dollie responded, explaining patiently, "Yes, I'm an agitator. Soap and water just don't do the job. Without the agitator, the clothes in the washing machine remain soiled."[3]

Like many American radicals, Dollie believes in the American system. So in 1978 she discounted rumors about secret, state plans to build a large toxic-waste dump near her house in rural Afton, a town outside of Warrenton. Where

Dollie lives could pass as an exurb to the uninitiated. Small houses on about one-quarter acre are interspersed with small fields producing tobacco or cabbages, now grown as an alternative crop. Dollie's three-bedroom house owes a great deal to her husband, Willie. Willie directs a local Job Corp facility, travels all over the country monitoring Job Corp programs, and has a small construction business on the side. If something can be fixed, Willie can fix it.

If Willie can repair the physical environment, Dollie can fix things in society—though she was not as conscious of her powers in 1978 as she is now. In 1978 Dollie fervently believed that the courts would protect her and her neighbors against pollution. She couldn't imagine why the governor would allow a landfill to be built in Afton. The sandy soil and poor drainage made that land a particularly dangerous place for a dump. Nevertheless, she became fascinated with what was going on in Love Canal in New York, and avidly followed stories on television and in the local press. She especially remembers seeing *ABC's News Close-up: The Killing Ground* in 1979, where local homemakers were shown fighting to get away from their contaminated homes. Although those women were white, Burwell immediately recognized the similarity of their struggle to the civil rights movement she'd lived through.

Growing up as one of the youngest of ten children of sharecroppers, Burwell says she didn't know they were poor until someone at school told her. Her mother made biscuits every day, and a pig or chicken on the farm assured that the family ate meat regularly. When the family were tenant farmers, as part of the contract, Dollie's mother had to do domestic work for the landowner's wife, but she bucked the system. Required to enter the house by the rear door, Dollie's mother went into the back with her coat on, took the broom from the closet, backed out the door, walked around to the front, swept, and entered through the main door every day before taking off her coat and starting to work in earnest.[4] With that pedigree in resistance, Dollie comes by dignity and a sense of purpose somewhat naturally.

Even as a teenager in the early seventies, Dollie led local struggles to improve the segregated black schools. North Carolina was one of the last states to integrate, and Dollie, who liked her community and didn't want to face the humiliation of being a supplicant, fought against joining the white schools. "We had what they called 'choice.' I wanted to stay with our black teachers and principals," Burwell said. "I liked it that way. In fact, I told my friends not to go over. But when they shipped us the broken equipment, the jammed typewriters, and soiled chairs, it made me mad. I wanted us to enjoy the best without giving up what we had together."[5]

Confident that the law would protect her and her neighbors, Dollie was nonetheless outraged in 1978 when she first learned that nearly 31,000 gallons of transformer oil filled with PCB had been dumped along two hundred miles of road in fourteen counties in central North Carolina some time around July 28, 1978.[6] Robert J. Burns and his sons, Randall James Burns and Timothy P. Burns, owners of a trucking company in Jamestown, New York, had been hired by the Ward Transformer Company in Raleigh, North Carolina, to dispose of the oil. The New Yorkers "obtained a 750-gallon tank and installed it in back of a truck . . . [V]alves were run from the tank through the wall of the truck so that fluid could be drained at will." Then the truck simply drove along at about 20 miles per hour, dribbling the contaminated oil along the highway.[7] In a similar case, the driver of a tanker revealed how, by leaving his valve open, he could go along a road in the rain, dropping a slick of oil filled with toxic wastes. According to that driver, "The only way I can get caught is if the windshield wipers or the tires of the car behind me start melting."[8]

The Burns family pleaded guilty in federal court to technical violations of the Toxic Substances Control Act and the Clean Water Act. The father got three to five years, and his sons received suspended sentences in return for testifying against Robert E. "Buck" Ward Jr. and Robert E. "Bob" Ward III of Raleigh. The judgment against the Burns family, rare as it was, did not make the problem go away. Despite a civil suit for $12.5 million filed by the federal government and the state of North Carolina against both companies, the state showed its own shortsightedness. Instead of incinerating and thus neutralizing the 40,000 cubic yards of contaminated soil resulting from the oil dumping, the state decided on the cheaper method of simply disposing of it in a landfill, disregarding the health of the largely black population destined to receive the contaminated soil.[9]

Little was done with the dirt for four years while the courts tried to decide how to dispose of it. A sixty-eight-year-old woman, Mame Stansbury, who lived with her sister near the small town of Arlie along Rural Road 1308, described what life was like after the dumping: "There was a brown streak along the highway" and the smell was "so strong that we had to roll our glasses up, and even with the glasses up it would get in your eyes and burn." They "rode by this stuff for months and months with [their] glasses rolled up, and it was awfully strong," she said.[10] The area around NC 43, NC 561, NC 5, and Rural Road 1308 in Halifax County remained polluted for four years.

Miscarriages increased and children were born with defects all along the roads where the toxic liquids had been dumped. In 1980, a local physician, Dr. Brenda Armstrong, claimed to see an increased incidence of congenital illnesses among her patients. Three weeks after the spill, Vicky Jordan, who lived about thirty feet away from one of the rights of way where soil was contaminated, had a stillbirth. A year later, she had a child with heart defects who lived only eight months.[11]

Then in the fall of 1982, twelve women who came in contact with the spill were found to have suffered contamination of their breast milk with Aroclor 1260, the exact form of PCB that was in the transformer oil. Most of the women lived along the road; one, Diane Griffen, 34, of Raleigh, had been looking at some land to buy and had noticed a "black, oily substance" on the road in October 1978, when she was two weeks pregnant.[12] All of this was what experts considered anecdotal evidence, but local people, calculating the increased threat, got worried.

The question was how to dispose of the tainted soil. Dollie, a legal secretary, had confidence that the state would find a safe way to dispose of it. Little could she imagine that the EPA would approve a 142-acre site near her home. The county Board of Supervisors, with a single black official, at first opposed the site, and with good reason. Although the U.S. Environmental Protection Agency recommended that dumps be located at least fifty feet from the water table in dense clay soil, the site where 20 acres were targeted for the landfill at Afton was within fifteen feet of water, and the soil was sandy. But, to the horror of local residents, on June 4, 1979, when the state requested a waiver, the EPA waived requirements for clay soil in the case of Warren County. More than any case that had come to light earlier, the case of potential PCB pollution in Afton opened the eyes of the nation, if only for a quick blink, to the relationship between seemingly powerless, poor, and isolated people of color and the pollution of the soil and water supply.[13]

According to sociologist Robert Bullard, Afton was chosen for suspicious reasons, among which is the fact that "Warren County has the highest percentage of blacks in the state," and 84 percent of Afton was African-American. Although blacks constituted barely one-quarter of the state population, they were 63.7 percent of the county population. Local people lived at two-thirds the per capita income of the rest of the state.[14] Descended from slaves who became tenants and sharecroppers, even the 13 percent of the population who were unemployed and sought work outside the county had roots going back at least a century in this part of the world. Many people had grown up without running water so that, unlike city dwellers, they knew where their water came from and how fragile life was without it. All local drinking water comes from wells, into which the PCB linked to benzene would almost certainly leach.

The state's blueprint for the landfill included covering the hole with plastic, pouring in the contaminated soil, covering the soil with more plastic, and planting grass above it. As one manager of landfills explained, "A hazardous-waste landfill can be described as a bathtub within a bathtub with an umbrella over it."[15] What he failed to say was that the "bathtubs" were made of garbage bags.

When the Environmental Protection Agency refused to take action by testing those along the highway to see how the chemicals may have affected them, and when the state moved inexorably to deposit the contaminated soil in Afton, local residents organized. The state, required to hold public hearings, scheduled them at Christmastime for early January 1979. Dollie Burwell alerted all the women and local ministers she knew, including the Reverend Luther G. Brown, pastor of Coley Springs Baptist Church, down the road from the proposed dump. She also got word to Henry Pritford, head of the local NAACP chapter.

Before rumors of the dump, few blacks paid much attention to the oil spill, but seven hundred local people, mostly women, came to the hearings in Warren County. "Most of the folks had not even been involved in the integration," Dollie Burwell remembers. Like her, they were frightened for themselves and their families. No one automatically connected experiences in the civil rights movement with local determination to prevent Afton from becoming home to a toxic-waste dump. Though Dollie first remembers hearing about the federal government's dump in Emelle, Alabama, in a private conversation with a woman at a SCLC meeting, Dollie now says "We were just talking. We didn't really know any of the people from those parts. We hadn't yet heard about the rashes and nervous diseases, of the miscarriages and suffering. We never thought about the fact that most of those folks were black."[16]

She later learned more than she wanted when she helped spawn an investigation into the connection between toxic-waste dumping and race, which revealed that race was the most significant determinant of uncontrolled hazardous-waste sites. Forty-one states send waste to Emelle, Alabama, where 86 percent of the population is African-American. Of the five largest disposal areas in the country, the Emelle site in Sumpter County represents 25 percent of the U.S. capacity for toxic-waste landfills. According to a report issued by the Commission for Racial Justice of Dollie's church, the United Church of Christ, "Three out of five African Americans or Hispanics in the United States live in a community with one or more uncontrolled hazardous waste sites. This represents more than 15 million African Americans and eight million Hispanic Americans."[17]

Dollie and her neighbors, none of whom regarded themselves as community activists, did not even begin to suspect the magnitude of the problem when they prepared themselves to ask questions at the January 1979 hearings. A mixed-race group of homeowners led by Ken and Deborah Ferruccio joined Dollie in forming the Warren County Citizens Concerned About PCBs. Now convinced that Governor Jim Hunt didn't really intend to stop with the 40,000 cubic yards of contaminated soil, but planned to turn the 142 acres in Afton into an East Coast Emelle, Dollie credits the Ferruccios and local women with making that impossible.

Ken Ferruccio, who grew up on the outskirts of Boston and still retains a thick, Kennedyesque accent, and Deborah, who was raised in Ohio, were dissatisfied in their jobs as school teachers in the Midwest in the seventies.[18] By chance, they met a couple from northern North Carolina. Seemingly on impulse, they decided to move to the town of Afton.

Ken Ferruccio is a philosopher by training. He likes to take ideas apart and consider them piece by piece. Few grassroots activists speak about the epistemology of this or the phenomenology of that, but Ken does when discussing choices the state and federal governments have made about where to site landfills. He also speaks in catchy phrases such as "The landfill puts Rosa Parks right in the back of the bus again" or "Justice is a living organism." Although in the struggle to save Warren County, Ken Ferruccio emerged as one of the most visible leaders, he prefers to hover behind the scenes deliberating, working out his arguments, estab-

lishing his facts, writing position papers. Ken's wife and partner is as much an activist as he.

At the time of the public meeting in January 1979, neither Ken nor Deborah had ever engaged in any political activities, and Ken had largely missed the domestic political
turmoil of the early sixties while serving in Vietnam. They
were most definitely not political activists looking for a
cause. As white, seemingly middle-class outsiders among
largely poor black and white rural people, the Ferruccios
simply did what they thought was right, and their neighbors
welcomed them.

Dollie Burwell and Ken and Deborah Ferruccio joined
forces. Dollie, determined at all costs to keep her neighborhood from becoming a dump, never thought of herself as a
leader until this time. But she turned to her church and to
the civil rights groups of which she had been a part since her
childhood.[19] Sharing experiences of racial oppression and a
history of fighting against it, SCLC, the United Church of
Christ, and the local people of Warren County set out to
make their plight known. The United Church of Christ was
born when white northern Congregationalists merged with
black southern Evangelicals in the late fifties. Although
African-Americans make up only 4 percent of its membership, the leaders of the church uphold a commitment to
racial justice rare among religious denominations. Dollie's
pastor, the Reverend Leon White, is a leading force in the
United Church in North Carolina, and someone she treats
as a wise and beloved uncle.

At the time of the toxic-waste landfill, Dollie and White
called on other allies, the Reverend Dr. Joseph Lowery, president of SCLC, and Floyd McKissick, former president of
the Congress of Racial Equality. McKissick, a civil rights activist who had led the efforts to integrate the schools in
Durham, about one hour's drive from Warren County, also
had had a long history in the northern part of the state. A
member of the Republican Party—which he insisted was
still the party of Lincoln—McKissick was just recovering
from a business crisis when struggles over the dump ensued.

Having secured land and big federal loans from HUD for a commercial and residential development known as Soul City, he had just seen the venture disintegrate. Designed to provide decent housing and incentives for industry to establish itself in the poverty-stricken northern part of the state, Soul City had attracted only a few factories, employing a total of fewer than two hundred people, before the commercial venture collapsed. The housing development, complete with a clinic and a section for senior citizens, was a great success and continues to function today. But the failure of the federal government to shore up Soul City was widely associated by local people with what they began to believe was a plot to turn Warren County and the contiguous areas into a dumping ground for the waste produced throughout the Southeast. If this was the government's plan, officials hadn't contended with the strength of local black political organizations or the mobilizing capacity of Dollie Burwell and the Ferruccios.

Dollie, Deborah, and Ken roused their neighbors and fellow parishioners, most of whom were women concerned with their family's welfare. Before the first act of attempted waste deliveries and demonstrations against them began, however, on August 21, 1982, a vandal slashed the plastic liner of the dump every twenty-five feet in twenty-foot incisions.[20] Rather than replace it, officials just glued it together, Dollie remembers with a sigh. The local newspaper claimed that after the damage, estimated at about $8,000, was repaired, the contractors would re-stretch the plastic above a large portion of sand. Then they would layer in five feet of clay above which the contaminated soil would rest. The state presumed that the five feet of clay would act as a filter, leaching out and collecting the PCB in the soil above it, all of this only fifteen feet above the water table. An additional two feet of compacted clay was to go above the soil, then an artificial liner, then protective material, then several feet of topsoil, which would be seeded. Downhill from the pit, authorities dug a hole to catch drainage water and keep it from filling a nearby stream. Before all this could begin, Ken

Ferruccio and others from the Warren County Citizens Concerned About PCBs had unsuccessfully tried to convince EPA officers in Washington to try a new method being tested at that time in South Carolina. There, bacteria that consumed the PCB was released in a contaminated pond and then was eaten by microorganisms, thus restoring the balance of nature; the government claimed this technology was untried and that the material had to be buried.[21]

The government scheduled the first dumping in Afton for Wednesday, September 15, 1982. Ken Ferruccio knew the movement needed publicity, and he got press releases to a journalist he knew in New York who thought events in Warren County newsworthy. Since by the early eighties, demonstrations occurred infrequently, and the connection between civil rights and environmental issues was a novelty, some TV stations and news media turned their attention to how events were unfolding.

The Sunday before the trucks were scheduled to roll, the Citizens Concerned About PCBs rented a flatbed truck to serve as a stage for a rally at the Afton school. Marching under signs saying "EPA Landfills Leak" and "Stop Toxic Aggression," demonstrators moved from the school, a mile away from the proposed dump, to the top of the road leading to the landfill.[22] Choirs came from all of the surrounding churches and, as in the civil rights movement, music became a source of strength and solidarity, helping to prevent the violence that would certainly have occurred without the participation of the clergy and their commitment to nonviolence. Reverend White suggested that demonstrators practice civil disobedience by resisting arrest and preparing to go to jail. And though many people objected, the strategy of nonviolent resistance that had been so successful during the civil rights movement prevailed.

When the first of seven thousand truckloads of contaminated soil rolled down the road, four hundred to five hundred demonstrators, mostly women, tried to stop it in front of Coley Springs Baptist Church, a short distance from the proposed dump. Highway patrol officers dressed in riot gear descended on the demonstrators, many of whom were too young to have ever seen the police in full battle dress earlier in the civil rights movement. Chanting "Oh Lord, don't let 'em drop that PCB on me," fifty-five people moved onto the paddy wagons. The protesters, who were also singing "We Shall Overcome," recalled civil rights demonstrators of decades earlier. Yet, the arrests themselves were notable: never before had authorities treated protesters against a hazardous waste facility so forcefully—and never before had large numbers of environmental activists been black women.[23]

When I asked Dollie Burwell why there were so many women in the demonstrations, she replied, "More women participate. Even in the hearings, you have more women. . . . You have more women at church. . . . More women saw the need to do something. . . . For black folk, it was the first time they really got involved. They saw it as someone destroying what my community is, destroying black folk and poor people.

"Before, when people spoke about the environment, they were talking about animals and trees. When you come in and say, 'We gotta save our lives or we gotta save our children's lives or we've gotta save our homes from this poison,' black folks can relate." Dollie herself had always viewed the Sierra Club and other environmental organizations as far removed from "what would affect my everyday living. I should've been concerned with the whales and birds, but I wasn't." When the need to resist became clear, "people in Warren County didn't really consider it as an environmental movement. People talked about their land, their surroundings, their health, the fact that they are poor would mean they have no health [care]."[24]

One reason Dollie and her neighbors were able to resist is that their land belongs to them, even if that's all they own. According to sociologist Robert Bullard, "More than 78 percent of the whites and 64 percent of the blacks [in Warren County] own their homes (nationally only 45 percent of blacks are home owners)."[25] Like the homeowners in Love

Canal, the people of Warren County have mortgage investments that make it impossible to pick up and go elsewhere. All the families in Afton except Dollie's and one other family have lived there for generations since Emancipation, and Dollie grew up in the neighboring county.

With the median income for Afton residents under $10,000 a year in 1982, people couldn't afford simply to leave. "And that's why," says Dollie, "I get scared and mad every time it rains. . . . The government is haphazard. To put that plastic in is not safe. It won't even be safe if it meets EPA standards. It certainly won't be safe when it doesn't."[26]

During the first week of demonstrations, between September 15 and 22, 1982, the highway patrol arrested more than 268 people. According to one newspaper, they "included teenagers, housewives with their hair in curlers and middle-aged men." People knelt down in the road in front of the trucks and prayed. The fifty-five people arrested the first day included Dollie and the Ferruccios. Thirty or so arrests were made the next day.[27] Dollie was released on her own recognizance the first day, but she had to post $500 in bond the second day. Nevertheless, she and many others kept returning to the demonstrations.[28] It was clear, however, that such disruption only delayed the trucks a little while and did not make the point the protesters hoped for.

At the time the dump was scheduled to open in September 1982, Dollie's older daughter, Kim, was ten. She had been hearing lots of talk about how PCB causes cancer and liver damage. Because she knew that Dollie already had had Hepatitis A, which affects the liver, she was worried and clung closely to her mother.

When the first demonstration to stop the trucks carrying the PCB-laced soil was set for September 15, Dollie presumed that people who knelt to pray in front of the trucks would face arrest. Because she was prepared to go to jail at least the first day, she was reluctant to permit Kim to join the march, but Kim insisted. Finally making sure that Kim had her father's and aunt's phone numbers, Dollie warned her daughter that they would be separated. She worried about what Kim would do when the police began to carry her mother and other women off to the vans.

When, in fact, the highway patrolmen arrested Dollie, Kim began to scream and cry hysterically. She wanted to go with her mother. The CBS evening news as well as the local news media were on the scene that day, perhaps because of the press release to the Associated Press. The national news caught Kim crying for her mama and explaining that she was "not afraid to go to jail, but I'm afraid of what this PCB is going to do to my people in Warren County," beaming an image reminiscent of children in earlier civil rights struggles and of the children gunned down in 1976 in Soweto, South Africa.[29]

At the end of the second week of the demonstrations, a group of women, Dollie Burwell among them, decided that they had to remain in jail to dramatize their commitment. Joining Dollie in refusing to pay bail were Ann Shepherd Turner, a long-time civil rights activist; Martha Nathan, widow of a Communist Workers' Party member slain in 1979 in Greensboro, North Carolina, in a confrontation with the Ku Klux Klan and the Nazis; Joycelyn McKissick of CORE; and Evelyn Lowery of SCLC.[30] They spent several days in jail. Burwell recalls the women having plenty of time in jail to talk about their public struggles and their difficulties in the movement making their voices heard. They thought their concerns about their children's health were being submerged in more general political rhetoric. And as women, they sometimes seemed to be ornaments rather than leaders.

State officials, on the other hand, had their own grievances. They complained about the way they thought the protesters used the media. Heman Clark, then secretary of state for Criminal Control and Public Safety, said, "We who try to put the facts out don't seem to have the same sex appeal"; the demonstrators, he complained, stole the limelight.[31] Dollie Burwell, herself, was surprised by the national media attention and thinks what was news was the connection between environmental issues and civil rights.

What the media saw was in part the result of Dollie Burwell drawing on her affiliation with national black organizations. She had phoned James Orange of SCLC in Atlanta early on, and the organization sent trainers who "really taught people" how to go limp as in the sixties. During the first two days, people had simply walked to the vans as the highway patrol ordered; but the officers didn't know what to do with demonstrators when they became dead weight.

Although the Reverend Benjamin Chavis, a civil rights leader who had spent three years in North Carolina prisons on trumped-up charges, was wary of being arrested again, he marched with the demonstrators on the third day. Dollie made him walk beside her because she thought she could protect him. Some "senior citizen women" were arrested, according to Dollie, and Ben overcame his own fears, claiming that they should go to the jail in a motorcade to reassure the old women. With some other seniors who had protested that day following her, Dollie left the demonstration in a van behind Ben. She saw the troopers flag him over and charge him with driving too slowly on U.S. 401, as she heard other troopers say, "That's Ben Chavis; we're gonna get him." The troopers waved her on, but she wouldn't leave Ben alone with them. They put Ben in the patrol car, and she followed. Exasperated, Ben called the situation "environmental racism," and seemingly gave birth to the term.[32]

By the end of September, about three weeks into the campaign, press interest in the fight began to wane though arrests continued. Demonstrators, who depended upon the media for getting their message out, read the newspapers every day and looked for themselves on TV. Dollie knew that "without the press you were fighting a losing battle." She frequently recognized Rick Staley from the *Henderson Daily Press* and the reporters from local Channel 11. But among the crowds, she didn't notice the *Time* magazine reporter or the people from the foreign press, learning only later that they too considered the protests newsworthy.

Dollie openly admits to trying to recapture the media's flagging attention when she called on Walter Fauntroy, the nonvoting congressional delegate from Washington, DC, a member of the Congressional Black Caucus and SCLC, to join the march. He came on September 27, 1982, with SCLC members from Alabama and Georgia. He flew into the Henderson/Oxford airport, but Dollie recalls that "he practically left the motor running" because he had to return to Washington for an important vote. Usually the demonstrators marched, people got arrested, and then those outside rallied in the late afternoon. That day, they altered the routine and moved the march to 9 A.M. so that Fauntroy could join them. Since he had immunity from arrest, he seemed safe. She persuaded him "to march a little ways," predicting that they would tie up the trucks more than the usual thirty minutes because people had learned to use their body weight to impede arrest. Dollie Burwell knew "in her heart of hearts that the North Carolina troopers wouldn't know anything about diplomatic immunity," least of all for a black man, but she talked Fauntroy into joining the kneeling and praying. She says the troopers grabbed him and paid no attention when he protested that he was a United States congressman. The officers threw Fauntroy and those who went limp into the same bus and charged them with resisting arrest.[33]

Seemingly by accident, someone had thrown over a bottle of ammonia in the bus where they kept Fauntroy for ten excruciatingly hot hours. Enraged by treatment reminiscent of police brutality during the civil rights struggles, he went back to Washington and ordered a congressional investigation about where hazardous-waste facilities are located. The report, which took several years for the General Accounting Office to prepare, examined four landfills in the Southeast and discovered that three were in poor, African-American towns. Under the direction of Charles Lee and with the help of Ken Ferruccio, the United Church of Christ's Commission for Racial Justice carried out its own study, and found that the racial composition of a community is the single variable best able to explain the existence of commercial hazardous-waste facilities in an area.[34]

Their findings, published in 1987 as *Toxic Wastes and Race in the United States,* provided a picture of environmental racism that demonstrators in 1982 could not have begun to imagine. The problems of dumping in the United States prevail wherever large numbers of people of color live. Memphis, Tennessee, with a black population of 43 percent, harbors 173 hazardous waste sites; St. Louis, with 27.5 percent, has 160; Houston, with 23.6 percent, has 152; Cleveland, with 23.7 percent, has 106; and Chicago, with 37.2 percent has 103.[35] And, according to Vernice Miller, of West Harlem Environmental Action, West Harlem, a district one mile long and half a mile wide, had the following systems under construction or online in 1992: "A malfunctioning sewage treatment plant which treat[ed] one-hundred-and-eighty million gallons of raw sewage a day, two municipal bus depots, a marine transfer station where garbage [was] collected onto barges for dumping, a crematorium [which released mercury from fillings], a six lane highway, a commuter rail line [on] which a four year old boy [had recently been killed], and a major route for the transportation of hazardous wastes. The one positive construction project . . . in this community [in the early nineties was] the building of a multi-acre state park—on top of the sewage treatment plant."[36]

The protests in Warren County marked this condition for civil rights activists and then for the nation to see. Once the furor over Fauntroy boiled down, the Ferruccios and Burwell feared that their movement would just disappear. First they decided to move the action in Warren County thirty miles away from Afton, to block the trucks as they came from the interstate to the road leading to Warrenton and Afton. But away from their base, local protesters couldn't muster the numbers. Returning to the dump site, on October 1, four women, three from Durham and one from Chapel Hill, formed a human chain at the landfill's entrance. Officers arrested them and charged them with resisting arrest.[37] Students from the University of North Carolina–Chapel Hill, Duke University, and East Carolina University began to participate during the third week. But as the novelty of the demonstrations began to wear off, new methods were needed. Children as young as four began to lie down on NC 1604 to stop the trucks, and they were arrested. If caught demonstrating a second time, they faced trials in juvenile court.[38]

While deeply involved in organizing resistance, Dollie says now that she never thought the community could keep the tainted soil out of Afton. She wanted simply to make sure that the state did not use the entire 142 acres for a permanent hazardous-waste dump, and there the Concerned Citizens succeeded in their goal. Heman Clark, charged with keeping the demonstrators from interfering with the deliveries of toxic soil, wailed, "I don't think any company would now try to put a toxic dump in there. They'd be crazy to try."[39]

During the protests, which lasted until October 27, 1982, state officials tried to ridicule the concerns of local citizens, who, in turn, confronted authorities. One of the leaders of local resistance, an older white woman in her seventies, Joyce Lubbers, attended a press conference Clark held to criticize the protesters in Warren County. Lubbers made sure the reporters heard her side, namely that authorities were "not coming out with everything." Since few local people believed the sanguine reports of state officials, she was confident that people would keep up the protests. "There's no way to stop people who feel their lives are in danger. We are fighting for our grandchildren's lives," she told the reporter.[40]

Though other environmental activists had carried on demonstrations in various places in the United States, the largely poor African-American demonstrators in Afton became, according to anthropologist Harriet Rosenberg, the first people arrested "in relationship to grass-roots anti-toxic movements. Not since the civil rights movement had African-American people in the South mobilized in such large numbers to demonstrate that they had reached the end of their rope and wouldn't have their human dignity and their very lives discounted because they were black and poor."[41] Two hundred mothers marched three to four miles every day and stayed in jail to protest against what was happening to them, transforming their struggle into one for "environmental justice" and against "environmental racism."

Heavy rains filled the dump with upwards of a million-and-a-half gallons of water before it was sealed. Shortly afterward, Ken Ferruccio and the Reverend White, hoping to keep the landfill in the news, led local people in a seventy-mile protest march from Warren County to Raleigh. Without police protection, the marchers faced hecklers, including members of the Ku Klux Klan, along their route. Mrs. Mosely, the woman who took care of Dollie Burwell's two-year-old daughter Mia, drove ahead of the marchers to scout what lay ahead and warn the demonstrators of trouble. As the heat of early fall continued, Mrs. Mosely bought cold drinks, and little Mia handed the sodas out the window of the car in which she was riding. Following the march, when the plastic covering the landfill ballooned out because of all the water, Ken Ferruccio protested by going on a hunger strike for three weeks.

More than a decade later, the thirteen-foot hole dug to capture water flowing through the facility has high concentrations of PCBs and traces of dioxin, the most deadly chemical pollutant known. Although the state government alloted $1 million in 1995 to detoxify the landfill, Dollie and many of her neighbors refuse to drink milk, eat vegetables, or eat meat produced locally.

When I asked Dollie whether she had immediately drawn a connection between civil rights politics and the new environmental threat, she said she never thought of the dump as political—by which she meant holding office; she thought it was about people's lives.[42] That's why she devoted most of her attention to making sure the women of the neighborhood and fellow parishioners came out to the meetings.

A commitment to life and service has, however, led Dollie Burwell to consider the importance of electoral politics. She thinks that had there been more than one black person on the county Board of Supervisors, they might have kept up the pressure on the governor through legal means and would have prevented or at least delayed the landfill. Others seem to have agreed that black representation would make a difference because later in 1982, Eva Clayton, a fifty-eight-year-old business woman from Littleton, North Carolina, ran for and won a seat on the board. Several blacks joined the school board, and one became sheriff. Since that time, more than 50 percent of local black people have voted in the elections, and sometimes their numbers rise to 75 percent.

Dollie says she wanted to become registrar of deeds because even though the state promised that there would be no other landfill within a fifty-mile radius of the dump at Afton, she wanted to make sure herself that no land was deeded to people for suspicious reasons. Her move into politics has not come without its price. Her opponent in 1988, a white racist, repeatedly referred to Dollie as "that darkie."[43]

Because Jesse Jackson was running in the Democratic primary, held in April of 1988, agitated white voters were turning out in droves to defeat him—and possibly other black candidates. Dollie knew that if the white people in Warrenton voted in large numbers, she had to turn out the much less numerous rural vote, including the four hundred Native Americans who lived around Hollister.

Dollie calls that campaign a lesson in humility since, as an African-American person whose whole life had been defined in relationship to whites, she had scarcely known or dealt with issues of concern to Native Americans. What seems to have stuck in her mind is that in North Carolina historically, white undertakers embalmed Native Americans, although blacks had to have separate funeral parlors. Dollie's brother told her, "Whoever gets your body says who you are." But, as in everything, she made up her own mind and decided to find out about Native Americans. She regards her first campaign as a period of intensive self-education, one that helped her make friends and win the vote of Native Americans, who cast the 350 votes by which she won over her opponent.

In 1992, various blacks decided to run for two newly created congressional seats, one of which went from the northeast of the state to Wilmington in the south. Representing 552,386 people, of whom about 52 percent were black, the congressional seats ran over twenty-eight counties. Having succeeded in getting districts established where blacks could win for the first time since Reconstruction, the local black caucus of the Democratic Party chose its candidates from among five black men. Against them, Dollie supported Eva Clayton. Active in civic affairs, Clayton won the primary and the election with help from Dollie and other women whose political experience lay in the community.

Dollie attributes the victory to changes in the South few have recognized. "It took a lot of educating. . . . It took a lot of hard work. Folks looked at what [Clayton] had been involved in. She had run for Congress in 1968. . . . She got 30 percent of the vote. She was also assistant secretary to Howard Lee for Community Development in the Department of Human Resources [in North Carolina], bringing sewage and water to small communities. It took a lot of work making people realize.

"The biggest thing was what happened to Anita Hill. A lot of women got mad. A lot of women didn't believe Anita Hill, but they didn't like the way she was treated. Everyone was glued to the screen during the Clarence Thomas hearings. Eva Clayton, in smaller groups, talked about how women had to be in government. She talked about Queen Esther and how she saved her people. When Carol Moseley-Braun won the Democratic nomination, it cleared the way for Eva. The media's proclamation that this was the year of the woman helped her. She got more press than any of her male opponents. Press followed her extensively, but she did not get the support of the black caucus. They treated her as if she were the spoiler. [At first] even the women were for the men," Dollie sadly recalled.[44]

In one of her campaign speeches, Clayton assumed a deliberately feminized position, using her sex to emphasize her uniqueness among a field of men. She claimed to "care about people. . . . I care about the quality of their lives. I care about whether they have good jobs, education and health care, whether their families can be secure in their communities."[45] Dollie believes that Clayton showed women's commitment to improving everybody's life.

For Dollie, there is no contradiction between saying women are more capable of fulfilling human needs in the public sphere than men and saying women deserve equality. Dollie, who happily admits to being a feminist, sees continuity between feminism and other civil rights activities. Unwilling to argue for women's community activism as an extension of female self-sacrifice, Dollie and many other female African-American grassroots leaders have assumed special positions as spokeswomen for women's rights as human rights. They are linking feminism, civil rights, welfare reform, and environmentalism.

Cora Tucker, a speaker at the Women and Toxic Organizing conference of the Citizens Clearinghouse for Hazardous Waste in November 1987, explained: "People don't get all the connections. They say the environment is over here, the civil rights group is over there, the women's group is over there, and the other groups are here. Actually all of them are one group, and the issues we fight become null and void if we have no clean water to drink, no clean air to breathe and nothing to eat. They say, 'Now Miss Tucker, what you really need to do is go back to food stamps and welfare. Environmental issues are not your problem.' And I say to [them], 'Toxic wastes, they don't know that I'm black.' "[46] Dollie concurs, and both Tucker and Burwell have attempted to rectify the situation by working with a variety of community-based organizations and participating in Lois Gibbs's Citizens Clearinghouse.

Dollie, Ken, and Deborah cooperate so well despite racial differences because they recognize that racism makes everything people of color do more difficult, from merely surviving to catching the attention of authorities. Ken and Deborah Ferruccio know that the dump is in their backyard because most of their neighbors are black. In fact, it is Ken,

more than anyone else in Warren County—black or white—
who has stressed the civil rights aspect of the siting of the
dump in Afton. He sees the dump as a violation of the Four-
teenth Amendment; he views environmental threats as violations of every local person's civil rights.[47]

Whereas Dollie lives among people she grew up with,
many of whom are her relatives, the Ferruccios knew no one
in Afton when they moved there but thought it was a place
where they could raise their kids decently. Though Deborah's sister and her family followed, the Ferruccios are insider
outsiders. Dollie speaks of telling her friends in elected office
to go down fighting rather than submit to certain trends in
Washington and the state legislature; the Ferruccios call
some of the same people corrupt—or at least opportunistic.
Dollie presumes all black people keep the poor in mind in all
the decisions they make. Ken presumes that people vote
their economic interests, and that black business people are
no different; he believes that they are more interested in
profits than in the welfare of the black community. The Ferruccios, especially Ken, think about class a lot, though he
doesn't speak in class terms. So while Dollie regards the black
leadership in North Carolina as nearly kin, and certainly as
friends, Ken and Deborah make more distinctions. As
whites in a largely black community, the Ferruccios are the
rarest of all people—independent thinkers who trust their
black friends enough to criticize them.

Emphasizing the ethical aspects of living free from the
hazardous waste in the landfill, Deborah and Ken have recently succeeded in getting the Episcopal Church in North
Carolina, which is mostly white but has some black congre-
gations, to support the establishment of the Ecumenical Environmental Leadership Council, which Ken and Deborah
direct. The Ferruccios have grown closer to the church as they
have withstood Ken's being fired from a local community college where he taught; a retreat from 1987 to 1990 to Florida
to look for work and a safer place to raise their two children;
and their return to Afton, where they live in a constantly ren-
ovated log cabin up a dirt road that resembles a hiking trail.

Dollie herself readily acknowledges taking strength from her religious faith and finds her organizational base in her church. As in the civil rights movement, in the environmental justice movement, the churches have acted as nerve centers from which news radiates. Secular political supporters sometimes underestimate the truly religious elements in the demonstrations, such as the kneeling and praying in front of the trucks. For Dollie Burwell, as for so many other activists in the South, religious faith "was everything" in the development of her political consciousness. Now a member of the national board of the United Church of Christ, Dollie finds encouragement in social activism and contributes to keeping her church committed to political struggle.

In the dark hours of the soul, Dollie Burwell turns to God. "Even now when it rains and I get crazy, I have to fall back on my faith." Yet, for Dollie, faith is a two-way relationship. "We did our part," she explains. "The people in Warren County did our part. We went to jail. We did what we could do. A lot of the people have given up, but you have to reach back down into your spirit for the last bit of faith. Every now and then the Lord will show you." She proudly recalls that at the First National People of Color Environmental Summit, her old friend the Reverend Ben Chavis introduced her by saying, "God speaks to us through an African-American woman."[48]

4

Homemaker Citizens and
New Democratic Organizations

PREPARING TO REGISTER voters near her home in rural North Carolina on a warm, early October Saturday morning, Dollie Burwell carefully ironed a blue cotton dress so that she would look good when she knocked on people's doors. She drove to a nearby settlement she didn't know well and talked to a few people who were happy to fill out the registration form. One of the political innovations of the past thirty years is that anyone can register to vote by mail or in their own homes. The limitations even liberal states such as New York used to place on people's right to vote—one year in the state, four months in the county, and thirty days in the election district—were whittled away in the seventies and eighties by those who wanted to expand the franchise to include people who move frequently, students, and the homeless. In early 1995, largely through the efforts of organizers Frances Fox Piven and Richard Cloward in the citizens' group Human Serve, which lobbied for the National Voter Registration Act (the so-called Motor Voter Bill), people could even register to vote while they waited in the interminable lines at the Department of Motor Vehicles or at welfare offices.[1] But going door to door as Dollie was doing is still the principal means of registering people in the South.

Burwell knocked on the door of an eighty-year-old woman who had never cast a ballot and began chit-chatting like the neighbor she was, trying to persuade the old woman, who doubted that she could make it to the polls at her age, that she could have an absentee ballot mailed directly to her house. When the woman still hesitated, Dollie realized that something else was bothering her: she could hardly sign her name. Afraid of being humiliated because she couldn't read or write very well, she broke out in smiles when Dollie promised that she, her daughter Kim, or some other neighbor could come over and help the woman read the ballot when election time came around. The old woman told Dollie how pretty she was.

During four hours that Dollie wandered from house to house that morning, she registered only about ten people. But numbers were less important to her than talking to fellow citizens, hearing what they thought about their lives, and listening to how they voiced their concerns. For Dollie, as for many voting-rights activists in the United States over the past thirty years, registering people to vote is not simply about accumulating registration cards; it is about persuading ordinary people to take charge of politics; it is about creating a truly democratic society.

Though few of the women in Warren County or in Love Canal have given much thought to citizenship, they are concerned with democracy and regard simply talking to people as a precondition for it. At a time when media coverage frequently shapes what people know—and activists compete to present their own images to a larger public—face-to-face contact still provides a way to assure that everyone has a voice. Conversation creates and enhances citizenship as people learn to stand up for their rights by comparing notes about what is going on, confronting authorities, and working toward a solution, gaining confidence about perceptions they might otherwise think are awry. Dollie Burwell does not separate efforts to get people to vote from attempts to get them to stand up for their right to a clean and safe environment. For her, as for political scientist Mary Dietz, democracy is "the form of politics that brings people together as citizens."[2]

Burwell, Lois Gibbs, and Luella Kenny all share a notion of democracy that entails justice and the creation of a political community. As far as these particular activists are concerned, justice is not limited to rights under the law, but to what they think the law was designed to protect: the well-being of citizens and their access to the social resources necessary to sustain their lives. According to Lois Gibbs, "Justice is about choice; it is the goal and democracy is the process."[3] Gibbs recalls that before Love Canal she thought that "if something was wrong, the appropriate folks would make things right, or they would get the government to right the wrong": the government would simply find the resources to protect citizens. Part of what outraged Gibbs, the other homeowners in Love Canal, and the citizens of Warren County was the sense that although they had obeyed the law and paid their taxes, the government had broken its contract with them. Instead of protecting them, authorities put a price on the heads of their children.

Accustomed to trusting their government, the homeowners were outraged at officials who discounted the prevalence of miscarriages, birth defects, degenerative nervous conditions, and local people's sense that they were under attack from the chemicals seeping into their homes. By refusing to see that the homeowners were not exaggerating about what was happening to them and their children, authorities dismissed the seriousness of their suffering. Local homemakers, who became the leading spokespeople for conditions at Love Canal, might well have identified with Ingrid Bergman as Charles Boyer's wife in the forties film *Gaslight*. In order to take charge of her estate, Boyer tries to convince Bergman, his wealthy wife, that she is having a breakdown; he says that the footsteps she hears every night in the attic and the gaslights that flicker in her room are mere hallucinations. Learning that he has in fact betrayed her by secretly going up to the attic actually relieves her: her husband may be treacherous, but she is not crazy. Lois Gibbs compares her awakening to what happens "when you find out your government really does not work for you, and your heart's broken for a long time before you get angry."[4] That same sense of despair followed by relief mixed with anger overtook the homeowners as they gradually realized that if justice was to be achieved, they would have to achieve it themselves. For them, getting the government to take their health seriously was learning to assume their full responsibilities as citizens, learning to act democratically as a community.

If citizenship had once meant paying taxes and fighting for the nation—and therefore only men were full citizens—the activities of women like Dollie Burwell and Lois Gibbs have transformed its meaning. Dollie, when driven to explain what she does and why she works in so many areas with so many organizations, responds that she doesn't see any difference between fighting against the landfill, registering people to vote, or bringing combs and lipsticks to women prisoners. What she is interested in is service.[5] She's concerned with what she can give, with sharing, with equality.

The human relations she wants to create and the sense of what real democracy would mean don't rest with a single organization or a single doctrine—though you find out what balances her when you attend Oak Level Church with her on a Sunday. When Mam Lydia Kompe and other South African women officials came to Warren County in November 1994 to compare the conditions of rural women in the American South to their own country, Dollie took them to her church. A small building down a paved road off Interstate 85, the main north-south highway in North Carolina, Oak Level sits on land once owned by an African-American woman who was so fair-skinned she was presumed to be the daughter of the planter on whose land her mother had been a slave. With a small portion of the land he deeded to her, she founded the church and served as one of its deacons, a position unthinkable for most women at the time.

The church that now stands consists of a modern room with comfortable benches and cushions. On an average Sunday, after the service in which the Reverend Leon White's sermon deals with a social issue such as teen pregnancy, Dollie's daughter Kim will be found gathering the youth for some demonstration. Dollie exchanges news and pleasantries with her neighbors and discusses current events with her minister and friends. The tone is festive, as local people delight in each other's company. All are decked out in beautiful clothing. Although the Reverend Andrew Young, one of Dr. Martin Luther King Jr.'s chief aides during the civil rights struggles, used to say that one day black people would wear their good clothes to work and wear their overalls on weekends, "Sunday best" still has meaning in black churches.

Dollie's ideas about organizing and creating new democratic associations flow from her experiences in her socially active church. Her strategy for mobilizing people resembles what Cesar Chavez described. Having organized Mexican-American migrant farm workers into the United Farm Workers Union, he explained his method: "First you talk to one person; then you talk to another person; and another person." Gibbs recalls that when she began at Love Canal she "didn't know that what I was doing was called 'organizing.' We didn't use that term. We called it talking to people, getting them together, reaching a decision and taking action—for the survival of our children and ourselves."[6] Dialogue—talking things through and talking to everyone—is the basis for the new democracy that Chavez, Burwell, and Gibbs represent.

Burwell is a visionary, but she seldom takes charge, and she almost never takes credit, preferring to participate as one among equals. She carries her ability to make people like her and each other from one cause to another. Dollie's ideas about citizenship and democracy extend from her church sanctuary to her community to the international arena. In the summer of 1993, she traveled to South Africa with a group of black and white women from the United Church of Christ. When the delegation met with white women from the Dutch Reformed Church, a bastion of apartheid, the white South African women seemed to ignore Dollie and the other black women with whom she traveled. Dollie felt uncomfortably invisible and now, looking back, she laughs bitterly and says that they probably thought the African-American women were the maids. In fact, one white South African woman spoke scornfully about her own servants because they didn't speak Afrikaans, when, as Dollie later remarked, "she didn't speak Xhosa or any of the other African languages herself."

Then the white South African woman spoke about how chaos would ensue if Nelson Mandela's African National Congress succeeded to power. She thought it was obvious that black Africans would run the country into the ground. Dollie recalls that she kept praying, hoping to hold her temper. When she finally couldn't stand the conversation anymore, she told the women from the Dutch Reformed Church that white Southerners had spoken the same way about Jim Crow and that, although things were far from perfect in the American South now, greater justice had been good for everyone. "Democracy will come," she pronounced to the assembled group.[7] As Dollie said at the beginning of one of her many interviews, "talking is my thing."

In April 1994, when South Africa called for foreign monitors to supervise the first national elections in which black Africans could vote, Dollie joined the International Church Monitors for Peace and raised money so that she could return to South Africa. Fearful of the violence, she showed what a good organizer she is when she wrote letters to every minister, requesting them not only to pray for her, but asking them to tell her on what days and during what hours they would pray. She says, "I knew they were not going to pray for me all the time, so I wanted to be sure they'd really pray by making a specific commitment."

As she was going down in the hotel elevator in Johannesburg to see where she'd been assigned, she had another conversation with God: "Out of the thirty monitors from the United States, I'm the only one from Warren County, so small a place that no one's hardly heard of it. So if I'm here, you must want me to be here. Now, if you see fit to send me to the Natal [the most dangerous place in South Africa at the time], it must be part of your plan. And I'm not asking you, I'm telling you—I expect you to protect me."[8] She became a voting monitor in Natal, and she saw ten voting-rights workers carried away when they were wounded in a brutal attack by Inkatha forces hoping to disrupt, discredit, and delay the elections. But she also had the pleasure of being present when Nelson Mandela came to see how that polling station was doing after the violence. Without exaggerating her own significance, Dollie is aware of the historic importance of South Africa's first democratic elections on the lives of her children, her neighbors, and the African-American community that forms her base of support.

For Lois Gibbs, achieving justice lay with organization. During the crisis at Love Canal, letters poured in from other places, from people facing similar predicaments asking for help. One day, according to Addie Levine, she suggested counting the letters lying around. She claims there were three thousand; "3,126," corrects Gibbs, with a characteristic deep-throated, gurgling laugh. She says, "I remember that because it was a sort of stepping-stone to my life." But that wasn't what made her decide to launch her organization. What did "was the call from the woman in Texas whose son was dying of brain cancer."[9] The woman said that she believed her son's illness was caused by toxic waste, and after he died, she wanted to work in some organization to make sure no other kids suffered as he had. Realizing that no such organization existed, Gibbs decided to start one.

By the time the government bought Gibbs's house in Love Canal and she could leave with her children in March 1981, her marriage had disintegrated. At first, she wasn't sure where to go with her two children. She thought of moving elsewhere in Niagara Falls. But, having become wise to the ways of the media, she was afraid that once the homeowners had evacuated Love Canal, the area would lose its attractiveness. That left New York City and Washington, DC, Since she was born in Grand Island, New York, a stone's throw from Love Canal, she considered herself a small-town girl and did not think she could manage life in New York City. She moved to Arlington, Virginia, and started life as a single mother.

Stephen Lester, a toxicologist for the Environmental Protection Agency, who had been assigned to Love Canal, had, according to Debbie Cerrillo, "sat on the fence" for a long time.[10] Although he was at first skeptical about the homeowners' claims, he respected them and explained things to them. Increasingly, he became convinced that they were right about the relationship between their health problems and the spread of the waste out of the canal area into their basements. Resigning from EPA, he supported Gibbs's effort to form her group.

Ralph Nader also agreed to help Gibbs, and he suggested holding a reception at the Carnegie Foundation to launch her organization, the Citizens Clearinghouse for Hazardous Waste. A week prior to the opening, the *Washington Post* interviewed Gibbs and published a profile of her. That same week, Gibbs learned that the foundation prohibited fund raising, and since she had no money, running the organization as she was out of the basement of her house in Arlington, she decided that one of her new allies should serve as "father of the bride and collect envelopes." Because of the *Post*'s profile, her reception became the social event of the week in Washington. Instead of the fifty to one hundred well-wishers she expected, four hundred fifty people showed up, forcing Gibbs and her associates to open the envelopes and send someone out for more wine and cheese.

"The troops" [as the women who had staffed the homeowners' office in Love Canal called themselves] came down from New York at their own expense to join Lois at the party to announce the formation of the Citizens Clearinghouse for Hazardous Waste. In their last major appearance together, the group—consisting of Marie Pozniak, Barbara Quimby, Grace McCoulf, Luella Kenny, and Joann Hale—eased Lois's nervousness at the reception. Gibbs still mists over when she remembers that her team came to help her launch her new organization.[11]

Then the troubles began. Because so many people showed up at the reception, Gibbs thought people would back her financially. But that was not the case. Some potential funders thought she was arrogant, presuming that she had something unique to offer, something different from the official environmental organizations such as the Sierra Club or the Audubon Society. Then there was the matter of who she was. Several people she contacted called her to task for being a thirty-one-year-old woman without a college education, let alone a business degree in management; they saw her as a bad bet to head an organization. She was devastated: "I thought they were going to help me. I thought they were my friends. It was sort of like breaking my heart again."

Then a potential donor invited her to meet him in a downtown bar in a hotel to discuss funding. She was petrified. Seeing herself as unsophisticated and sexually vulnerable, and fearing the worst, she half-seriously told her friends and colleagues Steven Lester and Ron Simon that they should come get her if she hadn't returned by a certain time. Without any rescue, she met the backer and came away with the initial $25,000. The Citizens Clearinghouse was on its way. Gibbs appointed a board of directors, which initially included her, Steven Lester, and stalwarts from Love Canal: Murray Levine and Beverly Paigens, the scientist who had aided the homeowners. Luella Kenny joined the board shortly after.

The next step was to figure out what to do and what not to do in the attempt to "rebuild democracy from the local level." One of the first actions they took was to publish a newsletter, announcing the Citizens Clearinghouse for Hazardous Waste, Inc., which subtitled itself, "A Grassroots Environmental Crisis Center" designed "to assist other victims of toxic wastes."[12] Gibbs herself also did a lot of speaking, attending a big rally at Warren County at the end of the second week of demonstrations there in September 1982. A video made at the time reveals Gibbs as fiery but respectful of local conditions. She drew the media to her, but made them shine their lights on the Warren County struggle, not on the clearinghouse.

Gibbs and her associates tried through the clearinghouse to help others avoid the pitfalls that had first impeded the homeowners. For one thing, outsiders of every political stripe had converged at Love Canal, and some were more aggressive than others in the way they dealt with the inexperienced homeowners, whose leaders were mainly homemakers. The homeowners divided into factions, with the group Gibbs led remaining the largest. A segment that came to be known as the People for Permanent Relocation was also largely made up of homeowners, but it incorporated among its leadership people from outside the community, some of whom were impatient with the pace of the homeowners and frequently attacked Gibbs and "the troops" personally. They became known as the Action Group.[13]

Hoping not to repeat the mistakes of the Action Group in a different context, Gibbs was adamant that the clearinghouse people merely help others deal with their own fears, explaining to them how to hold democratic meetings and teaching them how to get their messages across to the media. To connect the clearinghouse to people who were trying to right a wrong in their own community, they developed a system of regional field representatives. About ten political activists became troubleshooters for the clearinghouse, available to travel to areas where hazardous waste had generated community opposition. In return for their expenses, the representatives helped people organize. The regional field representatives were not supposed to become leaders of local struggles. Thus the representatives wouldn't go into a community without an invitation, and they wouldn't vote on decisions affecting local strategies. "We have a principle that must never be violated by any staff member: the people who are directly affected by an issue or policy must make the decisions on what will be done about it," Gibbs says.[14] Field representatives couldn't speak for anyone else; no matter how much experience people in the clearinghouse had, local people were presumed to know their own situation better.

Even more important, the representatives had to let people make their own mistakes rather than intervene and take over. As Gibbs later explained, "A trained, professional organizer will let people fail, if by failing they learn. A professional organizer places a higher value on building long-term, deep-seated community power, and sometimes *losing* a fight (but learning from it) is a way to build this power. . . . The organizer would rather build the group than win the issue."[15]

Drawing on memories of Love Canal, where many of the older homeowners, fearing the loss of their homes more than the toxic waste, opposed attempts to have the government buy them out, Gibbs always emphasizes that democracy is about having the right to choose. That is why the Homeowners Association did not attempt to get the government to condemn all the houses in Love Canal. Choice—and the right of people to choose something different from the majority—was what set the Homeowners Association on the harder path of getting the government to evacuate those who wished to leave Love Canal, permitting others to stay. Whatever else Gibbs believed, she did not believe that one plan fits all community struggles. Although Gibbs doesn't say this, the principle was one of direct democracy: one person, one vote, and only those affected by local conditions have a right to make decisions about how to settle the grievances.

The field representatives taught people that writing, printing, and distributing fliers calling for a meeting was not enough; people had to go door to door in the community and speak directly to local citizens, finding out what their grievances were and convincing them that the best solution to their problems lay with each other. Divvying up tasks so that everyone did something not only helped people develop their skills, but also gave them a sense of participation. Since people got depressed when negotiations dragged on, the representatives advised holding periodic parties, celebrating their organization if nothing more. They advised people to learn as much as possible about their opponents.[16]

Never a membership organization, the Citizens Clearinghouse for Hazardous Waste was what its name said: a clearinghouse. Activist Will Collette, who had honed his skills in other community movements in the seventies, made Gibbs an offer: If she would pay him $25 a week for six months, he would put together funders from nonprofit organizations and others committed not to polluting the earth; then the money coming in would pay his salary and all the other expenses.[17] One of the group's first publications came in 1983 with the pamphlet called the *Leadership Handbook on Hazardous Waste.* If forming a network in which members felt a single identity was necessary to any movement, Gibbs and Will Collette, who had gained the title of program developer at the Citizens Clearinghouse, had to teach people how to do it. Putting together a handbook to teach would-be leaders how to create organizations may have seemed impertinent at first, but Lois Gibbs had had to learn from scratch how to organize; she was just passing on what she had learned. Despite help Gibbs got from her brother-in-law Wayne Hadley early in the struggle, and good advice from Beverly Paigens, Addie Levine, and Murray Levine, she always believed that the homeowners group would have had a six-week head start if they had known the "formula"; she hoped to provide that service for those who came after.[18]

Even though the homeowners' association later became outraged and outrageous about the government's unwillingness to buy their houses, at first they were quite shy. Gibbs was quick to realize that people starting out had to feel their way, and they often could not brook ridicule. So the handbook guides them in doing research—that is, finding out basic information. It tells them how to find out who is in charge, and how to build up the strength of the group before taking their arguments to city hall. It also cautions them about getting things right when talking to the media.

Belief in democracy entails some sense of history, or at least it has proven to be the case among the people of the clearinghouse. The handbook was followed by *Love Canal: A Chronology of Events that Shaped a Movement,* a desktop publication that the clearinghouse put out in 1984. Authorship is attributed to the "leaders of the Love Canal Homeowners Association," and the guide is filled with witticisms and acute observations about the political importance of seemingly trivial events. For instance, a citation for October 10, 1978, says: "Construction was to begin today. Turned into a media event with only one shovel full of dirt being removed."[19] Successive pamphlets, with their uniquely American sense of the immediate, are guidebooks for cooking up trouble for those authorities who do not take human need into account, and who do not equate democracy with social justice as the clearinghouse leaders did.

As with other community activists, Gibbs is well aware of how race divides most localities of the United States. When her young daughter came home from school in Virginia and said that *Roots*, then playing on television, was all wrong, that black people had never been beaten or lynched, Gibbs was appalled. Gibbs told her about the civil rights movement and firsthand experiences her friends had had. But Gibbs also blamed herself: "It's my responsibility for laying down what she learns in school and telling her the truth as I see it. . . . Part of rebuilding democracy is educating the adults so that they can educate the children." Because she is so interested in teaching the next generation, she is writing a children's book called *Democracyville*. She says that there is plenty in Dr. Seuss about democracy, but she wants to make her hopes for the future clear in her own book.

Gibbs seems assured that she knows what it will take to overcome racism and its legacy in this country. She says "diversity has to be approached differently in different regions." Each racial group must decide "who they are and where they fit in and who they delegate as their leaders." Conscious of the different claims of race, the board of the clearinghouse consists of "50 percent community of color." But not coming from a political background in which as a white person she would likely feel very guilty toward African-American people and other people of color, Gibbs bristles at the view that she and the Love Canal homeowners had an easy time because of their race. Gibbs knows that the clearinghouse is frequently portrayed as a white organization by foundations and government officials claiming to be helping people of color. Sometimes even people who are part of the clearing-house, such as members of a certain black community in Florida, say to her, "Do you think we are not being evacuated because we are black?" She retorts, "No, it's because you are not organized well enough." She thinks experience and organization is what enabled the Homeowners Association to get out of Love Canal and that the same will work for other communities regardless of race. But, unlike many white community leaders, she is very conscious that certain beliefs drive a "wedge between black and white people," and she is determined not to let them. One of the rare few who accepts differences in leadership style, local goals, and strategy, Gibbs simply encourages people to strengthen the informal social networks they have developed around a given issue and sustain those relations. Gibbs says—and it's hard to doubt her—that she is not trying to build up an organization, that her goal is to "rebuild democracy from community to community."[20]

While Gibbs is on the outlook for people such as Dollie Burwell who engage in permanent mobilization, Gibbs and the others at the clearinghouse also know that people who participate and then try to re-establish what they consider "normal life" are important. Gibbs argues over and over again that "everyone has something to contribute . . . [and that] networks are made up of people who've had experiences" of pitting their own judgments against those of authorities, even if they no longer participate in ongoing struggles.

Gibbs's program for organization prizes what people know rather than any specific skills. She is quick to say how significant she thinks homemakers are whether or not they engage in social movements. Many of the activist homeowners of Love Canal and the demonstrators in Warren County, North Carolina, did try to resume their earlier lives. Some withdrew, as Debbie Cerrillo did when she divorced her husband and moved away from Love Canal. The self-assurance that she had gained through her activities, freeing herself and her neighbors from the threat of dangerous toxins in their homes, remained hers whether or not she continued to work in an organization.[21]

As a result of living at the boundaries between private and public lives, Gibbs and her allies Luella Kenny, Barbara Quimby, Debbie Cerrillo, Pat Brown, and many of the other activists in Love Canal became different kinds of citizens. Debbie Cerrillo thinks she became a citizen for the first time: Before Love Canal, she hadn't even voted. Once she became part of a community in struggle, she began to view democracy as synonymous with helping her neighbors, being part of a community that was being held hostage by officials. Commitment to getting her neighbors out of houses they thought were killing their children without losing all that they owned made her believe in the rule of ordinary people rather than government officials. "I [had] never even voted. Now I was telling the president of the United States, Jimmy Carter, who offered to pray for us, that we didn't want his prayers, we wanted his help," Cerrillo recalled with a laugh.[22]

When Cerrillo was a central force in the Homeowners Association, she'd helped a community in New Jersey resist the siting of a toxic landfill near them. But once she moved away from Love Canal she wanted a new life or some approximation of the old life, free from thought about toxic waste. In her new home far away from Love Canal, her reputation as a dynamic organizer followed her. Local people discovered who she was and tried to engage her again, but she had had enough. She is now content as a school-bus driver. She believes that working with the Love Canal Homeowners Association even after her own family moved out was part of what she was morally obligated to do. As far as she is concerned, that fulfilled her responsibilities to her childhood friend Lois Gibbs and to her other neighbors. Cerrillo remains close to people in Niagara Falls, baking elaborate christening cakes and bringing them to her friends and daughters who, despite histories of illness, continue to live near where they grew up. Even with Cerrillo's wizardry as a craftswoman and artist, talents that she valued in herself before Love Canal, she had never thought much of her other abilities and felt no drive toward participation in public life. But, like the others who formed the Love Canal Homeowners Association, she developed confidence that she, not authorities, can judge what is right and wrong, and she maintains a strong belief in her own newly gained skills.

As a result of experiences outmaneuvering officials and creating linkages among disparate people and ideas, most of the leaders of Love Canal and Warren County changed their views about the world and their own place in it. In one way or another, they each have come to hold views about democracy and social justice that they never held before. Unlike poor people, the homeowners had had few contacts with government bureaucrats, seldom faced authorities who treated them rudely, seldom had what they said dismissed without consideration—until Love Canal. The conflict with the government changed their perspective on authority. Before the crisis, they generally did not feel class discrimination. When they began to recognize that what they had thought were individual health problems were epidemic in their neighborhood and that their distress seemingly did not matter to authorities, they were outraged. Experiences with government callousness once the threat from toxic waste became clear made local people challenge their previous beliefs that they would be treated equally regardless of wealth. This was an awakening that shattered childhood beliefs in the reliability and evenhandedness of the government.

Mutual caring became the driving force in the lives of all the leaders. A sense of connection that had previously extended to family in the case of Lois Gibbs and Debbie Cerrillo, to family and church groups in Barbara Quimby's and Pat Brown's lives, or to family and participation in a semi-professional Polish choir in the case of Luella Kenny, included a wider realm after Love Canal.

When in 1985 the Medical Trust Fund board was established with $1 million of the $20 million settlement Hooker Chemical, now Occidental Chemical, agreed to provide for the 1,328 people from Love Canal who agreed to an out-of-court settlement, Gibbs, Kenny, and Quimby agreed to serve on the board. Never before had a private endowment been established to deal collectively with past and future ailments of a group of people poisoned by their homes. The fund, which requires a minimum payment to avoid nuisance claims, provides money toward annual physicals, payment of prescriptions, and treatment of disabilities associated with having lived at Love Canal. Administered by an insurance adjuster who reviews the claims, only the official and Luella Kenny, the chairperson of the board who must sign off on the checks, know who is receiving benefits. Special cases, though anonymous, must be considered by the full board, which meets about twice a year. The issue the board must consider is how to judge ailments of those who left Love Canal more than fifteen years ago.[23] Being part of those self-defined communities, and believing as most of the former activists do that they have greater responsibilities knowing what they know, has given all the leading participants in Love Canal a sense of citizenship and democracy they never formerly held.

Similar changes overtook the activists in Warren County. Even with the right to vote or eat in any restaurant where they can afford to pay the check, blacks in North Carolina still suffer from poverty, and with the landfill, Warren County has sunk to having the lowest per-capita income in the state. More than 60 percent of its population receives some supplemental government aid. For Dollie Burwell, rectifying the economic condition through rural development constitutes the new struggle for democracy.

Dollie Burwell herself wages her campaign for democracy through electoral politics and community organizing. She worked actively for Eva Clayton in all her campaigns, registers voters, and takes a lively interest in the Democratic Party. Once Clayton joined the Congressional Black Caucus, Dollie and Kim Burwell frequently attended events the caucus organized in Washington. Dollie remained as registrar of deeds until 1996. Unlike most of the other activists in Warren County or Love Canal, Burwell maintains her optimism about working in organized politics. And she becomes angry when she recalls that some people say she can no longer speak as a grassroots activist because she once held political office and she confers with elected officials.

For her, grassroots is where you come from and what your commitments are. So even in relationship to elected officials, her intuitive response is to take to the streets. Speaking about one of her senators, Jesse Helms, who represents pretty much everything she opposes, she has zany proposals. In 1990, in a dead heat with Harvey Gantt, a liberal black candidate who had been the Mayor of Charlotte, Helms played the race card, promoting fears that blacks would take power in the state and that poor whites would suffer. Dollie wanted to organize a bogus "blacks for Helms," with banners and hats in hopes that Helms's racist constituency would be so afraid of black people that the mere suspicion that some liked Helms would discredit him. It is hard to say how seriously Dollie considered this strategy, but talking about it years later, she shows more and more excitement. "Since white people in Warren County hate Reverend White so much, they'd get very nervous about voting for Jesse if they thought Reverend White really supported him."[24] Dollie's outrage against Helms rests on the values she upholds in which she sees him deficient: commitment to justice and to social service. Sounding like the Democrat she is, she disparages Helms for not even delivering to his own constituency: "He doesn't even care that white folks are losing their farms just as black folks have."

While a lot of talk in American domestic politics today is about urban decay, Dollie Burwell thinks that the disintegration of rural America is partly to blame. She believes that rural development would keep people from migrating to the cities and would enable people to sustain community support networks that are largely missing in urban areas. Trying to understand what Burwell means by "rural areas" and "rural problems" is not always easy for city people. Because it is so difficult, we have a running joke about what is rural. In her hometown of Afton, where small fields and houses share a road, as in eastern Connecticut, she explains what she thinks defines rural areas: distance from medical care and grocery shopping and the absence of public transportation.

Well aware that the Research Triangle Park—between Raleigh, Durham, and Chapel Hill—is one of the most prosperous regions of the country, providing jobs that attract skilled workers from all over the United States, she points out how impossible it is to get there or to nearby Duke University without private transportation. "Here we are, next to Duke University, one of the major medical centers in the country, but can people get to those hospitals? Not even people in the outlying areas of Durham can get in unless they have a car," Dollie complains.

Her goals as a community organizer resemble those of her South African friends—to find ways not just to establish profit-making enterprises but to assure that the profits spread to masses of local people who find sustained employment in those projects. She mourns the failure of Soul City to attract industry to her region. Yet she proudly drives visitors around what remains of the development: the modern housing largely for retired people, the clinic that serves people from all over the county, and the child-care facility. While the public transportation grid that would have made Soul City a resource for all the northern counties of North Carolina never found support, the development continues to benefit and serve as a model for Dollie's own thinking about how to increase the access of her poorest neighbors to the resources they need to establish a good life for themselves and their children.

Dollie Burwell resembles Lois Gibbs in her vision of how democracy incorporates social justice and citizenship, but she has taken a different path from Gibbs. Instead of creating a single institution—even a clearinghouse—Dollie Burwell has participated in a multitude of organizations. Filtering all her activities through the lens of civil rights, Dollie can bring the force of the Southern Christian Leadership Conference and the 1.7 million-member United Church of

Christ to bear when there is racial discrimination in Warren County and its environs. Until she learned that Leon White, her pastor at Oak Level Church, once said in an offhand remark that she might have less impact because she lacks her own organization,[25] Dollie's participation as an environmental activist, a civil rights fighter, and a member of the board of governors of her church seemed to be an obvious and effective way to exercise her citizenship.

Yet, without a single institutional base, the politics in which African-American women such as Dollie Burwell participate remains largely invisible because it closely resembles housework: it includes a lot of different tasks, many of which are done daily without much drama. Except around the landfill, Dollie has received very little media attention and claims not to miss it. She wonders whether some people get "dependent on the media . . . and without the media they don't realize they exist." She is certain that the real work goes on locally, and sometimes she thinks that if it were up to her, she would dissolve some of the national organizations and just keep the locals.

People who lack experience in community struggles frequently imagine that all political ideas emanate from professional political leaders in government and policy centers. Dollie Burwell's political life testifies to another process whereby local concerns generate ideas about broader issues. And yet Dollie, who prides herself in being a rural person and derives her strength from that identity, doesn't fully realize that she and those like her are re-invigorating democracy by creating associations in which masses of people who have not previously participated in politics can engage.

One of those local democratic movements that often appears as an outside force but really has multiple local origins is feminism, which has developed since the seventies. While neither the Warren County group nor the Love Canal group thinks of itself as feminist (and many in both groups distinguish themselves and what they do from feminism), they all recognize that part of the discrimination they suffered had neither to do with class nor race but with their sex.

Dollie has confronted the well-developed sexism of certain civil rights leaders to whom she is close. When Floyd McKissick, former head of CORE, made fun of the local chapter of the National Organization for Women (NOW), which had invited him to speak in the early eighties, Dollie called him on that and carefully explained to him that stereotyping any group of people, whether by race or by sex, increased the power of their real opponents who didn't want to see any of them gain power over their own lives.

While Dollie Burwell thinks that feminism and justice are part of the same effort, the former leaders of the Love Canal Homeowners Association are more ambivalent. Because of fertility problems, probably due to toxic poisoning, Debbie Cerrillo had difficulty getting pregnant and had four miscarriages before she adopted one child and then went on to bear two, one of whom had birth defects corrected by surgery. She recalls "hating the women demonstrating for abortion rights when I was so desperate to have a child." Lois Gibbs remembers that she and her friends thought the women they identified as feminists from television seemed laughable, perhaps even a threat to the hopes they had for family, children, and a home. Though Lois Gibbs now says she is committed to the principles of equality, she still thinks "the word [feminism] has got to get bulldozed . . . [because] it has bad connotations that turn off blue-collar people."[26]

Gibbs says that she is not interested in feminism but in justice, yet she definitely recognizes sexism in the movement. In her speech to the Women and Toxic Organizing Conference that the clearinghouse held in November 1987, Gibbs said, "We all learned, as women in local fights, that we had to deal with the constant put-downs from men—whether they were friends or foes—who lacked respect for us in our fights just because we are women. Sometimes we had to deal with this by being even more assertive; sometimes we had to handle this problem by being less so, and getting others to do what men felt we were incapable of doing." In the same speech she voiced what is a common view of non-feminist women in social movements; Gibbs talked about why women are such good organizers: "I . . . decided that this training in running a home was one of the key reasons why so many of the best leaders in the Toxics Movement—in fact the overwhelming majority—are women, and specifically women who are 'housewives' and mothers."[27]

Gibbs, Burwell, Ntongana, and countless other women activists attribute their initial involvement in politics to the need to protect their children and their rights as housewives and mothers to intervene when the safety of their homes was at stake. When women who follow the social dictates of their societies about how to be a good wife and mother find themselves unable to fulfill their roles adequately, those who decide to take action frequently do so in the name of their families, not themselves. Because they speak as citizen mothers rather than individual citizens, neither they nor the various feminist movements with which they coexist view them as feminists, and they're not. But the fact that women agitating around health hazards in their neighborhoods often are called "hysterical housewives" brings feminists and nonfeminist women activists together.

During another speech at the Women and Toxic Organizing Conference, a longtime civil rights and environmental activist, Cora Tucker, recalled how she overcame the charge of being hysterical. She said, "I used to get upset and go home and cry, 'I'm a hysterical housewife.' I've learned that's a tactic men use to keep us in our place. So when I started the stuff on toxic waste and nuclear waste, I went back . . . and a guy gets up and says, 'We have a whole room full of hysterical housewives today, so men, we need to get prepared.' And I said, 'If men don't get hysterical, there's something wrong with them.' From then on, they stopped calling us hysterical housewives when we came to present an issue."[28]

Tucker highlights another hidden theme among women activists, feminist or not, and that is a sense of superiority to men who treat them badly combined with a certain scorn for men who act in ways women portray as juvenile. While women such as Tucker frequently claim that their interests lie with men in their group, they presume without discussion that those same organizations are divided by sex. If the men of their own communities fail to acknowledge what having women in them contributes to the struggle, men in authority are even more contemptuous of women. Barbara Quimby, who is the most unwilling to be viewed as a feminist of the former leaders of the Homeowners Association, said that officials' treatment of local women as hysterical belied the justice of their concerns over what was happening to the children. Like many women activists before her, commitment to being a "good girl"—obeying the rules her parents and ministers had laid down: marrying, having kids, trying to take good care of them—were all mocked when officials called her righteous concerns crazy. Adjusting her claims as a mother to the demands of gaining social justice made Quimby and her neighbors into activists, and even womanists if not feminists.

Gibbs herself recognizes the burden women leaders bear because they are women, one reason she arranged the Conference on Women and Toxic Organizing. As a leader and a woman at Love Canal, Gibbs found herself quite isolated: she remembers how hard it was to be the one who always had to be optimistic, who had to cheer up "the troops" when they were faltering. Lois Gibbs couldn't afford to let her guard down, admit her worries, or vent her anger, so she kept a diary. She now explains that she survived by "filling it with cuss words."[29] Both she and Luella Kenny, in different ways, became the ones whom others looked to for advice and support. While Luella and her husband had each other and the Polish choir in which they sing to help them escape the pressure, Gibbs suffered in a disintegrating marriage. Like many former homemakers who become activists, here and abroad, she couldn't depend on her husband psychologically since "he needed the same level of support and cheering and sense that we can do it as the troops."[30]

Gibbs did get a measure of support from Marie Pozniak, Debbie Cerrillo, Barbara Quimby, Grace McCoulf, Joann Hale, and Luella Kenny. Since Lois wasn't doing much cooking, the others brought food to her house to feed her family. They also gathered at Lois's on Friday nights to giggle like teenagers while their husbands were in the other room watching sports. That camaraderie—that sense that women could understand women and that ability to act silly, even bawdy, to let off steam—found its way into Gibbs's practice in the clearinghouse. At one conference only women attended, women spoke openly about ways they handled sexually aggressive men. Showing themselves to be "tough in that way," the women discussed how they hate when men look them up and down: "They agreed that the thing to do is to stare at a man's crotch. They think their fly is open, but they don't dare look down or touch, so they rush to finish their conversation and leave."[31] But individual men aren't the only problem. Gibbs rails about the organizers of a recent conference: "Out of ten grassroots leaders, there wasn't a single woman except one who was responsible for organizing the break-out sessions into workshops." Gibbs is well aware of what kind of discrimination women face and is proud that the tough community organizers she knows stand up to injustice at home as well as in their other struggles for social justice.

Dollie Burwell is more comfortably feminist than Lois Gibbs, but she is less willing to tie her political identity to a single cause—feminist, civil rights, environment, or the Democratic Party. Creating and working through an organization as Lois Gibbs has done gives the continuity that has enabled her to launch national campaigns, in her words, "to be a player," as the Audubon Society or the Sierra Club is. But it also requires a substantial amount of time spent doing bureaucratic work, raising money, publishing a newsletter, and reassessing organizational structures—tasks that activists like Dollie Burwell clearly don't enjoy.

Dollie is a perennial foot soldier, a leader who leads by participating. Unwilling to occupy an office other than the one she was elected to as registrar of deeds or to do the fund raising and office work necessary to maintain a national organization, Dollie likes to be out knocking on doors, speaking with the people, getting their ideas and translating them into actions she takes alongside them. What Dollie is able to do with her membership in the Southern Christian Leadership Conference and the United Church of Christ is to keep her options open and move with the issues rather than with the organization.

When a local teenager called Dollie in tears because she had just been fired from a supermarket that had never before hired a black person, Dollie took action. The teenager's cash register had come up short on her first day of work. Instead of presuming that the young woman had made the wrong change or that someone else had made a mistake at that register, the manager simply let the girl go. Dollie went to bat for her, arguing that if a white teenager had made the same mistake on her first day of work, the manager would have criticized the young person, but would not have fired him or her.[32] Dollie confronted the manager in her capacity as a member of the Southern Christian Leadership Conference and got the young woman's job back. For Dollie, this was as important a victory as any she ever won.

Dollie Burwell may not have an institution of her own, but she is a troubleshooter in her community, frequently identified with opposition to toxic-waste dumping and just as frequently seen as a representative of the Southern Christian Leadership Conference. Often, according to Dollie, the Reverend Joseph Lowery, who ostensibly directs the conference, responds to questions about activities by joking to reporters that local people never tell him anything. SCLC, the organization that Martin Luther King Jr. became identified with, always consisted of ministers and the work done in their parishes all over the South. Dollie considers it to be as much her organization as Lowery's, but when Dollie in concert with others wins some victory, news of it does not reverberate to the conference. Because national television and print journalists generally cover only campaigns designed to confront national laws, the constant work restructuring society, making changes in people's expectations, establishing new codes of human behavior that organizers like Dollie

Burwell carry on seldom get reported. This makes traditional black organizations such as the Southern Christian Leadership Conference, CORE, the National Association for the Advancement of Colored People, and the Commission on Racial Justice of the United Church of Christ seem less active than they are. The same is true for the more than seven thousand local organizations that fit under the umbrella of the Citizens Clearinghouse for Hazardous Waste.

While the demonstrations and arrests of over five hundred people in Warren County publicized the Commission on Racial Justice in 1982, the commission did not and does not direct activities in Warren County. The reverse is true: large demonstrations brought the issues of environmental racism to national attention and enhanced the commission's position. Then the commission launched the study *Toxic Wastes and Race*, showing that toxic-waste dumps and incinerators are overwhelmingly located in neighborhoods in which people of color predominate, and held the People of Color Environmental Leadership Summit in 1991, as a result of what Dollie, the Ferruccios, and their neighbors did.

Social movements certainly do not depend on who gets credit, but failure to recognize how widespread and long-lived activities around civil rights and toxic-waste disposal are makes people think that civil rights movements and popular democracy are dead in this country. The opposite is true. Seldom have so many individual citizens, especially women, taken action to improve their health and protect their homes as part of their political birthright. The clearinghouse has been well aware of how overlooking the accomplishment of these groups comes, in fact, because the movement against toxic waste is largely in the hands of women.

Ongoing organizations such as the clearinghouse increasingly awaken people to the need for social justice outside of the environmental field. Members frequently feel, as someone from the clearinghouse expressed it, that "our thinking about the world changes as a result of our negative experiences with the government and industry. We see how corporate influence is used by the government against the health of the people, and we see injustice being done in other parts of society. As a result, we may think about and take on other issues that we haven't been socialized to deal with—like racism and sexism."[33] Local people frequently raise these "new" issues as they realize that the conditions that forced them to take action are part of broader patterns requiring democratic solutions.

Activists who have had the experience of reaching out to one another through telephone trees and now by electronic mail to solve a single problem sometimes use those same networks for other issues as well. For example, though lacking a single organization, Dollie works on a variety of issues that concern her. Recognizing the importance of these networks to the work they do, after a year's study, in 1995, the clearinghouse decided to reorganize. Instead of having its own regional field representatives, the clearinghouse switched to a strategy it calls an Alliance of Citizen Organizers. The organization invests in local activists and sponsors them to organize in their own region.

Instead of sending people out from Falls Church, the clearinghouse has chosen individuals such as Dollie Burwell, who are clearly rooted in their own communities. The idea is to "give them money to work with local communities. Hook them up electronically. [They'll be] like chapters or field officers. The only requirement is to help other groups and build up other groups. [The idea is to] build on indigenous networks, [to] invest in building democracy at the local level," according to Gibbs.[34] The new representatives are insiders, who can speak with local people because they are part of neighboring communities in the same state or region. The clearinghouse is interested in finding those who are in community struggles over the long haul, and when Gibbs speaks of this new model she vibrates with excitement: "This is a new model that has never been done before. The model takes people and builds an alliance with them. People say the local community is concerned with a single issue and once that issue is over, they're going to go back home." According to Gibbs, that's not true for the Dollies of this world. At another time, deflecting a compliment, Dollie seemed to agree. She said, "There are thousands of Dollie Burwells all over this country."[35]

Whether conscious of it or not, what those thousands are doing here and abroad is transforming the concept of "human rights." While the official human rights organizations tend to focus on narrow views about what constitutes bodily integrity, trying to protect human beings against indignities such as torture, only in the nineties have feminists succeeded in getting rape considered as a violation of human rights. Recognizing that dioxin accumulates in fatty tissue and puts women, especially poorer black women who survive on carbohydrates, at greater risk than other adults, Dollie Burwell sees that as a violation of human rights. Commenting upon EPA chief Carol Browner's 1994 statement that PCB shouldn't put an "undue burden" on local women, Dollie responded that not only shouldn't it be allowed to put an "undue body burden—it shouldn't be allowed to put any burden at all."[36]

Disagreements about terminology, such as "undue body burden" or disputes about the obligations of authorities to maintain the health of local people and whether health is a human right, drive community-based movements of women. To extend consideration of human rights to insistence on homes free of death-inducing pollution or even, as in Crossroads, South Africa, the right to have a home in a city, defies traditional notions of the body, which has focused on the individual body rather than the body politic.

By reconceptualizing human rights, activists such as Dollie Burwell and Lois Gibbs have also redefined political communities. Until recently, citizenship rested on a narrow definition of who held rights in a city-state or a nation. In the hands of the Burwells and Gibbses of the world, the community has extended beyond the old boundaries to include the globe. That is not grandiose. In an age of multinational corporations and global markets, which determine financial and policy decisions everywhere, local communities are, if anything, more important. Paradoxically, as the power of all but five or six nations on earth declines relative to the corporations and the international banks, grassroots activists and their local struggles increase. Social movements refuse to engage the Goliaths on their own terms, but do them damage with their slingshots.

The kinds of organizations to which Dollie Burwell belongs, which coordinate efforts made locally and internationally, and the kind of activist consulting Lois Gibbs and the Citizens Clearinghouse for Hazardous Waste provide, entail respect for alliances and confederations that groups involved in environmental and civil rights struggles have increasingly activated. By maintaining their rights to define democracy, citizenship, and human rights, and by enabling others to highlight the issues as they see fit in their own communities and contexts, movements such as those in which Dollie Burwell and Lois Gibbs have engaged have expanded the possibilities for democratic process.

Gibbs is well aware from her own experiences at Love Canal that "if we could organize community by community and get people to participate, people will rise to the occasion." But as one man she frequently quotes said, "No one ever gave me permission to think about these things." Gibbs and Burwell think democracy entails permission for everyone.

5

Generation X, Southern Style

THOSE SKEPTICAL about Generation X ought to meet Kim Burwell, a twenty-something grassroots leader. Calm, soft-spoken, and self-confident, she participates in a vibrant new civil rights movement that has extended its concerns to environmental justice and feminism as well as to overcoming the racism that permeates the schools and the economy. Dedicated to empowering young people to strive for social justice as they see it, Kim views herself as a freedom fighter, devoted to enhancing democratic practices in the communities of the South.

Kim Burwell, according to her reckoning, has been a grassroots leader since she was ten, and perhaps that's what accounts for her belief in the political potential of youth. In the sixties, student activist Tom Hayden (now a California state senator over fifty) cautioned us not to trust anyone over thirty. Kim, who spends her time organizing young people in the South, believes that youth are politically dynamic, do not quibble about the larger picture, and do not insist that all possibilities be worked out in advance—which she thinks means that "they give themselves more wholeheartedly to new democratic movements than their elders."[1]

Kim's political views—and those of the civil rights and new left movements of the sixties to which she is an heir—rest on commitments to participatory democracy, to the potential for self-government inherent in all people. Her principles entail deep respect for the ability of poor people, particularly youth, to decide how to improve their own lives. By pursuing the belief that empowerment—that sheer self-confidence—can be applied to winning those rights and then preserving them, she also is helping to transform the words *justice* and *equality* to include commitments to a broad definition of human rights.

To secure these goals, Kim Burwell has joined a national organization, the Leadership Initiative Project (LIP), founded in 1989 by another North Carolinian, Angela Brown. The organization is part of the Youth Task Force, originally launched in 1992 as the youth division of the Southern Organizing Committee for Economic and Social Justice. Kim, who spent two years in college and now teaches pre-kindergarten to three- and four-year-olds from impover-ished families, went to work in her late teens at the head of-fice of the Commission for Racial Justice of the United Church of Christ in Cleveland, Ohio, though she still thought of herself as working for the South. While in Ohio, she got involved with the Transport and Communication Workers Union and with Louis Stokes's successful campaign to become the first black mayor of Cleveland. Following the election, she went to Alaska for a brief period. Homesick and dissatisfied, she returned to rural North Carolina as the first trainee of the Leadership Initiative Project.

LIP's inaugural event was to gather fifty young people (ages twelve to eighteen) and youth (ages eighteen to twenty-five) for a Young People's Congress in March 1990 to discuss black culture, black-on-black violence, and continued racism in the schools. Having grown to over 500 members, the project's goal has been to develop a cadre of local leaders, rooted in their own communities and dedicated to justice and social change.[2] To achieve those ends, Kim attempts to develop the potential of other young people: "Now I work . . . as a project consultant. And what I do is go throughout the state of North Carolina and organize other youth groups . . . or go into communities that have issues that need to be ad-dressed or that the young people want to address or want to organize around. And I make sure that they are self-sustaining so that when I pull out they'll still be functional."[3] Rooting itself in rural North Carolina, LIP coordinates its work with others through the Youth Task Force.

Under the stewardship of Angela Brown, who is barely in her thirties, the Youth Task Force (YTF) attempts to build alliances throughout the South and Southwest among black, Native American, and Latino young people.[4] Brown, a distant cousin of Dollie and Kim's pastor the Reverend Leon White, grew up in Wilmington, North Carolina, a center of civil rights activism in the seventies. Angela Brown went on to get a BA in philosophy and religion at the University of North Carolina at Wilmington. She worked toward a master's degree in religion at Southeastern Baptist Theological Seminary in Wake Forest, North Carolina, but she became distressed about the absence of young people in the current movement for social justice in the South. Destined to be a preacher, she speaks another gospel: the need to develop a new generation of leaders.

Brown remembers dropping to the floor at age seven when she heard a bomb go off in the grocery store near her house in Wilmington. A beautiful seaside city, Wilmington has a history of grace and refinement that derives from wealth that slaves created and from the city's commitment to the old racial relations. Having largely escaped civil rights activities in the fifties and sixties, Wilmington was a bastion of resistance to racial equality in the seventies.

When the bomb exploded, police accused ten civil rights activists, who became known as the Wilmington 10, of setting the explosion and of being responsible for a murder that took place at the door of one of the activists. Most of those charged with the bombing and murder were high school students. Only Ben Chavis, who was in his twenties, could by any standard be considered an adult. Emphasizing what you can see in news footage of the time, Brown notes that a preponderance of those sitting in, being fire hosed, and riding buses to win civil rights all over the South were young people.[5]

Like Kim Burwell and Angela Brown, 75 percent of the members of the LIP and the Youth Task Force are black women who began by focusing on community-based environmental projects but who have gone on to expand their activities to political odd jobs around racial tracking in the schools, economic inequities, police brutality, and sexism within and outside their movement. When a young person was killed in a churchyard in Enfield, North Carolina, in the mid-nineties, LIP organized a Unity in Community march of three hundred young people to protest. Unable to get a permit from police, who were implicated in the murder, local youth with Kim as backup won the support of the town council, telling them what the young people wanted, why they wanted it, and when they wanted it. Then, lacking a permit, they took over the streets. The self-organizing of youth was what, according to Kim, made the mobilization successful. "I don't see that you can have [an event] for young people [that] old people are planning, because they're not talking from experience. . . . They're not young anymore, so how do [they] know what young people want?"[6]

The bravado about youth comes from the concern Kim and Angela share with other black leaders that the black movement is in disarray and that young black people are drowning in drugs and despair. Alienation from schools that don't teach, growing crime and homicide rates in rural as well as urban America, and a lack of jobs pervade communities throughout the United States. For rural areas, there is the added worry of environmental pollution as farms, which can no longer be a family's sole support, are turned into huge dumps for the waste produced by industries in the cities. As Kim and Angela write, "Our generation faces a myriad of problems! We lose seven (7) young sisters and brothers to violence each day; the U.S. imprisons more of its people (particularly youth between the ages of 16 and 30) than any other industrialized nation; one out of every eight (8) young women will be diagnosed with breast cancer, and for black women, the death rate is twice as high; communities of color continue to be targeted for the siting of hazardous-waste facilities; and poverty rates for both urban and rural families are increasing. Unfortunately, social ills such as violence, increased crime rates, poor health conditions, and environmental degradation are not just examples of community deterioration, they are also perpetuating factors, and young people are the primary beneficiaries."[7]

Rather than give in to frustration, Kim may perhaps exaggerate the special skills young people possess. Promoting her generation's leadership of democratic struggles to emancipate themselves, Kim and her roommate, Minnie White, exhort their minions, saying, "Our generation is punking out! The majority of us are confronting drugs, sexism, violence, racism, miseducation, classism, etc. Yet, we aid the continuation of these cycles by sitting back watching these elements strangle the life out of our communities or at best sitting around intellectualizing and debating the struggles and tactics of the past. We have not engaged actively in creating new tactics to confront the problems of our day."[8] But Kim and her mother, who founded the Free African Youth group at the Oak Level church they attend, have committed themselves to empowering young people.

In Warren County, people travel twenty miles to a supermarket or a doctor; the houses are far apart; and farming still sets the standard for work, although few people derive a living from agriculture. The county suffers from many of the same social problems that afflict the cities, among them unemployment, drug addiction, and a high incidence of teen pregnancy. The Free African Youth tries to provide a social life, sports, trips, and solidarity to keep teenagers from feeling isolated.

If Kim goes to the extreme of idealizing black youth, it is only because American society as a whole has disparaged them. By reaching out to young people through dances, games, high school assemblies, and by aiding in local struggles, Kim, Angela, LIP, and the Youth Task Force have built up networks in Alabama, Georgia, Mississippi, and Louisiana, as well as in North Carolina. Their constituents are mainly fifteen- to twenty-five-year-olds, though they also work with younger kids. Kim thinks that it is easier to organize young people because they are modest: "They don't think they know everything . . . , don't insist on knowing all the pros and cons. . . . I usually start with fourth-, and fifth- and sixth-graders." She likes the fact that they have simple questions and "their goals are not so broad . . . and we're able to achieve them quicker." Kim has the grassroots organizer's commitment to trying to win intermediate victories rather than ultimate goals. She thinks victories whet appetites for more activity and increase people's confidence about the possibilities for change. One reason Kim worries about adults setting their goals too high is that she is afraid of having people be disappointed, which makes it harder to win their support for the long haul. With the young and very young, though they ask a million questions, any improvement can be viewed as a victory, according to Kim.

Like many American activists, Kim roots contemporary struggles in history. But like many people in their twenties, Kim has a partial knowledge of history—a mixture of heroic myths and family stories, of legends and secrets that do not appear in clear images or sequences. For example, she knows that her grandparents, Dollie's parents, who died when she was quite young, grew tobacco, but she doesn't know what their position had to do with slavery. Few people do know. The northern part of North Carolina, a tobacco-producing region, was never, like Mississippi and Alabama, a land of large cotton plantations. Small farms using slave labor had produced tobacco. After slavery, many black families remained, intermarried, and took the names of the plantation owners: Bullocks (Dollie's maiden name) married Burwells; everyone in the county or nearly everyone is kin. Since people move out of but not into Warren, Vance, Franklin, Granville, and Henderson counties, where Dollie and Kim work and where unemployment is high, people in the county tend to come essentially from the same families as they did one hundred years ago.

Kim wonders what might have happened if black people had received the forty acres and a mule the radical Republicans wanted to provide for former slaves after the United States won the Civil War. Had the program succeeded, Kim's grandparents would have been small landowners. Instead, they grew a crop and shared its proceeds with the landlord. Dollie's mother, who bore fourteen children, of whom ten lived to adulthood, also had to work as a domestic servant for the privilege of farming someone else's land. Although Kim does not know the history in detail, she feels outraged that her grandparents, whom she scarcely remembers, worked so hard for so little.

A sense of injustice, tempered by belonging to a church and community that reveres her and her family, propels Kim to believe in democracy rooted in community. But whereas Dollie held public office and travels widely as a member of the board of the Southern Christian Leadership Conference and the United Church of Christ, despite trips to Selma and Birmingham, a conference in New Orleans, and periodic conferences in the West and the Deep South, Kim tends to stay home and work locally as much as she can. Dollie inhabits a racially integrated political world structured largely—as the civil rights movement was—around church networks and affiliations; while Kim, Angela Brown, and their generation, despite their religious commitments, work through more secular, black institutions. Though grassroots youth organizations are increasingly visible in the black community, most of adult white America knows very little about them.

Kim does, however, participate in integrated youth activities. When Kim returned from a weekend conference in Durham, about one hour's drive from Warren County, she said very little about what had gone on. When her father, Willie Burwell, who doesn't speak much or go on demonstrations, but takes in everything from his seat at the family computer he built, asked what she learned, she said, "a lot." Like most young people and prisoners of war, Kim gives elders her name, rank, and serial number and keeps most of her thoughts to herself. What Willie finally got out of her was that the conference—which had dealt with networking in new democratic movements—was largely white, mostly young and male, and almost exclusively gay. Kim found the white part more difficult than the male or gay.

No woman is a hero to her daughter, and therefore Kim, who actually works closely with her mother in community-based environmental projects, subtly rebels against Dollie, too. One of their main arguments occurs over how to organize democratically. In a mixture of teasing and genuine pique, Dollie and Kim joke about their disagreements, neither ceding to the other in her expectations that her own way is the best one for achieving democracy and social justice. One place where their sparring gets funny is in their disputes about what constitutes a "real" grassroots leader and to what degree Kim should put up with male leadership.[9]

Kim, impatient with someone she worked with, wanted her mother to agree that the person we'll call Wilson Jones was a bad grassroots leader. Kim argued urgently, "He's not working for the movement. He comes in with his plans and doesn't consult with local poor people. They don't get to develop themselves. You do not go back into your community once you have been absent and take over. You do not do that because you separate people. You alienate people when you're trying to pull your community together."

Dollie, concerned that grassroots leaders not be asked to be perfect, ruminates: "Wilson probably never had a steady job. And I've always said there ought to be some kind of fund for grassroots organizers because they don't have health benefits, they don't have vacations, they don't have nothing. They may have a decent suit, but they may not even have that." Kim claimed that those criteria did not matter. What made her angry was that Wilson did not consult with people, did not listen to suggestions, but simply told people what to do, thus keeping them from developing. For Kim, efficiency was no excuse for acting in what she considers undemocratic ways. For her, as for Dollie, democracy and the practice of enabling the vast majority of people to exercise power is the highest goal. Neither woman, mother or daughter, wants to be considered undemocratic. And if there's rivalry, the competition is over who is more in touch with the community.

Since they have to fight, at another time Dollie and Kim argued about whether it would be better to order two buses or one for a demonstration in Selma, Alabama, to commemorate the thirtieth anniversary of Bloody Sunday. On Bloody Sunday a civil rights demonstrator was murdered after crossing the bridge at Selma on the eighty-mile march to Alabama's capital in Montgomery. Dollie claimed that people would want buses at the last minute. But Kim, who was largely responsible for raising money to hire the buses and provide food for the sixty kids she was committed to bringing, did not want the additional burden—and cost—of another bus.[10] When I saw Kim and Dollie about eight months later, Kim remembered that I had overheard the argument and she proudly told me that Dollie had been right, that in fact, people crammed into cars and vans. In all, the anniversary march had attracted three thousand participants, about twenty-eight hundred of whom were young people.

In local civil rights organizations Dollie Burwell has generally been the adult voice who calls for more attention to youth and for the creation of more projects giving young people real power. Now, Dollie increasingly says, "Kim will organize that." But Kim insists that most older people are not really giving youth their due. One story that Kim likes to tell deals with the initial conference of the Youth Task force, scheduled to take place at Xavier College in New Orleans in 1992 at a conference on environmental justice the Southern Organizing Committee for Social and Economic Justice had organized. Olie Taal (the daughter of the committee's director Connie Tucker), Kim, and many of the other young people from North Carolina chartered what they called a freedom bus and were on their way to the meeting. Hearing that there was a struggle about a Super Fund site in Columbia, Mississippi, the young people stopped off, joined the demonstration, and got back on their buses. Arriving in New Orleans too late to make their presentation on environmental justice at the time on Friday evening's program they had been assigned, they were outraged when Connie Tucker and the other adult leaders rescheduled the young people's presentation for 8 A.M., on Saturday before the programmed events were to take place at 9 A.M.

At 8 A.M., there wasn't a young person in sight. But at 9 A.M., as the five hundred adults settled down for the scheduled program, more than five hundred young people from the newly formed Youth Task Force, made up of thirty different grassroots organizations, came marching in chanting, "Fed up, fired up, won't take it anymore" and "No justice, no peace!" Dollie, representing the "elders," remembers at first being angry and then, laughing: "We taught them too well," she recalls. Forcing the program to be reorganized, the young, mostly female, largely African-American crowd explained their need for equal recognition, and their objections to paternalism—and maternalism—on the part of those older than they.

Both Kim and Dollie remember how hard a young Native American woman cried, upset because she objected to the other youth showing lack of respect to their elders. Dollie and Kim both tried to convince her that by demonstrating for justice, the young people actually honored those who had taught them never to accept a subordinate place in life.

Kim's political career began early in life. Her first march was for her godfather, the Reverend Ben Chavis, one of the Wilmington 10 and later chair of the Committee on Racial Justice of the United Church of Christ and head of the NAACP from 1993 to 1994. "I was about two," Kim recalls. "My ma had me in the stroller marching for him and the Wilmington 10. So it's been in me ever since the beginning. She actually marched with him when she was pregnant with me, and they became good friends, and I became like a baby of the movement, I guess. . . . When it was time for marching, my mother never left me home. She'd always take me with her."[11]

Kim's own campaigns have permitted her both connection to and liberation from her past. She remembers demonstrating with her mother to release political prisoners and to oppose capital punishment. She recalls being frightened when she and her mother had to stay at the homes of strangers. "Now it doesn't frighten me because I'm older, but when I was younger it used to terrify me because I didn't know whether I would be separated from my ma or not."[12] Kim has seldom been far from Dollie since.

Kim's formative political experience, the one that shaped her views about participatory democracy, was, of course, the initial movement against environmental racism. She considered herself at ten not as a child but as a shrewd organizer who knew how to resist the toxic onslaught on her community. "September 14th [the day before the trucks were scheduled to roll in], Channel 5 came to one elementary school and wanted to know what the kids thought." That night, the community met and decided on a march the next day from Afton Elementary Old School to the community church. That leaked to the press. The Reverend White and others came down. Kim asked her mom if she could join the demonstration. Dollie said "Ask your daddy." Willie said "Ask your mamma." Kim, wily child that she was, didn't ask anyone.

The next day, while Dollie was ironing Kim's clothing for school, Kim said she was going on the march. "My father's not very politically inclined, but he's gotten used to my mom." Nevertheless, he was afraid that Kim would get lost or panic if Dollie got arrested, as he knew she might. "I know how to make a phone call to my aunt," Kim countered, and the deal was struck.[13] Sister Mia, only two at the time the landfill was established, found care in the hands of an older white woman whose son was an active participant in the marches.

For Kim, memories of organizing form the matrix of coming of age and inextricably tie her to her childhood. "I had been used to marching so they asked me to be a marshal. They tied a little orange, orange or yellow, red some kind of thing on my arm. . . . But when I got to the first road block, it scared me to death. So I went in the front with my momma and we start sitting on the side of the road and stuff, and they started jerking folks. . . . I started boo-hooing and crying, and for some reason it seemed as if all the cameras in the world . . . everyone just focused on me and wanted to know why I was crying . . . and when they pulled her, I went frantic, I went chaotic . . . and I was like, 'I wanna go with my mamma,' and they said 'You can't go with your mamma,' and I said 'I wanna go with my momma.' "14

When Dollie was arrested the third time and decided to remain in jail for a few days rather than post bond, Kim immediately adjusted her routine. "Where the old jail was they had a fenced-in yard, and they used to let them out . . . There would be a whole lot of people all the time around the fenced-in yard, and they would always let them out into the yard. So I got to see my mom every day." The community pitched in and met together every night at the Coley Springs Baptist Church, down the road from the dump. Kim recalls that she "actually got off the bus there, ate there, and halfway slept there, and did homework there."15

Kim likes the baby she was, and the mother with whom she has always shared political commitments. She recalls being at the center of resistance from the beginning of her community's struggle: "At the age of [ten], when I figured out what was going on with the landfill, . . . I headed up my fourth- and fifth-grade class members, and we wrote letters to the governor. Then I started participating with older kids at the high school, and they wrote letters to the governor. . . . We had a black Monday, where none of the kids went to school. So it's been constant."

Although Kim had been on marches before, she'd never worn a gas mask or encountered the police. Despite the increased fear, Kim says now that she "believed that [she and her neighbors] were actually literally going to stop the trucks, that they were going to turn around and go back to where they came from."[16] Following the period of mass demonstrations against the dump in Warren County, when the water and gases in the dump caused it to rise up, local people, with the Reverend White and Ken Ferruccio in the lead, marched. When that failed to get the governor to agree to detoxify, Ken went on a hunger strike. Kim marched, but she'd leave for school reluctantly and found excuses not to go out to recess at school or to play out of doors at home. Kim remembers "getting all psychological," afraid to eat local food or drink the water. Like many of the other children in her school, she experienced stomachaches.

Kim was perpetually worried about the dump down the road from their home and less than one mile from the school. Thinking that contamination was like a bomb that would explode, killing everyone, Kim believed that Dollie would immediately contract cancer and die.[17] "I just knew it was PCB, and it caused cancer. And I had heard all these terrifying stories about Love Canal and Cancer Alley [the polluted stretch between New Orleans and Baton Rouge, Louisiana] and I just didn't want my community to get like that, and I said, 'I don't want my mom or my dad to die of cancer, and this is racism.' "[18] It was Dollie who, realizing that the children think differently from adults, demanded that a scientist go to the schools to explain to the children that whatever poison there was from the PCBs in the contaminated soil would develop slowly.

The dump and the invasion of her childhood were enough to set Kim off on a life dedicated to redeeming the land. She says now that, "I know with myself even with the landfill, my goal was to . . . one day have the state come to the position that they will detoxify, and now we have succeeded, so that is a goal that I've accomplished, and it's making me continue to go on."[19]

For Kim Burwell, the civil rights movement lives on because she has helped to sustain it in her own area. Many people forget that the movement of the fifties and sixties concerned a variety of issues including access to public services, such as buses, public swimming pools, lunch counters, and voting as well as gaining the right to go to good schools. Kim, herself, is well aware of how diverse the movement for social justice must be and how localized, if ordinary people are to gain power over their own lives. In the early nineties, Kim organized three busloads of youth from neighboring Vance County to go to Selma, Alabama, for a campaign against a racial tracking system that had resegregated the schools. Few outside the South realize that by placing all white children in more advanced classes and all African-American children in the lower groups, despite test scores, many of the public schools in the South have effectively re-segregated. When the kids from Vance returned from Selma, they organized against their own tracking system and suc-ceeded in ending it.

Direct action has been particularly evident in the move-ment for racial justice and against environmental racism that Kim helped launch with her neighbors in Warren County. Other young people are also beginning to realize that their homes in the rural South and Southwest are being targeted as dumping grounds for waste from industrialized areas. Kim, Angela Brown, and others in LIP and the Youth Task Force devote a lot of their attention to helping kids resist the onslaught of waste-disposal industries in their regions. So Kim was particularly delighted with POP TARTS—People Organizing People to Acquire Recognition through Speak-ing—when it held a teach-in to expose the ways local offi-cials were colluding to permit a hazardous-waste recycling company to establish itself in their community. And in 1994 Kim took a busload of young people from Vance, Franklin, and Warren counties to Birmingham to join local groups fighting against the siting of a transfer station in that city.

The "Peace in the Streets" campaign opposing the trans-fer station decided to celebrate Martin Luther King's birth-day there on January 15, 1994, with a rap concert sponsored by the city council, which donated money for use of an au-ditorium. A high school group was marching into the hous-ing projects to announce the show and get kids to come when a white police officer ordered the kids associated with the Youth Task Force to get out of the street. Then he drove a car into the crowd and tried to capture the young people's red, green, and black flag, the symbol of black unity modeled on the African National Congress's banner. When the kids wouldn't scatter, he called in a 1040 alert, signaling that an officer was down, and other police came from all over Birmingham in full force. Two police officers broke their wrists beating teenage demonstrators. The police brought in dogs, hosed the young people with water, Maced the junior high and high school age demonstrators, and arrested fourteen young people, including an eight-year-old boy.[20] Olie Taal, Connie Tucker's sixteen-year-old daughter, was maced and her fifteen-year-old cousin had a dreadlock ripped from his head. For trying to intervene, Olie and three others were arrested, although the city dropped charges when the mayor supported the students.[21]

Kim calls it an old-style civil rights struggle, especially because the Youth Task Force went around to traditional black colleges from Texas to Washington, recruited six hundred to seven hundred young people, and returned to Birmingham to demonstrate their right to march. Although the opponent was a company that specializes in waste management and not voting monitors or the Ku Klux Klan, Kim believes the parallels to the earlier campaigns are only too obvious.

As a new civil rights activist, Kim also devotes herself to cultural change. Kids from neighboring Franklin County asked Kim to help them to organize Black Leaders About Social Change, which fought for the introduction of African-American history and literature courses and demanded that the schools hire more black teachers. And in the late spring of 1995, Kim escorted 125 youths to Window Rock, Arizona, for a meeting with young people from the Navaho Nation, attempting to build coalitions between Native Americans and blacks. Kim also sees her job as engaging a process of educating the parents who were afraid of having their children go so far away and afraid of what might happen to them outside a majority-black community.

She inspired the parents' trust just as she wins the hearts of their children.

Like her mother, Kim is patient and confident. Like her father, Kim gains her power from holding steady. Using the family computer to set up databases and taking advice more easily—but not very easily—from her father than from her mother, Kim is part of a generation that is revolutionizing grassroots organizing through high-tech solutions. But not all her abilities come from her use of technology. Kim was the first LIP intern, going through its program for a year, attending conferences and classes. Part of what she learned and has always practiced is how to teach people to participate in changing their own lives through direct democracy. In fact, Kim regards her work as successful when local organizations take over the campaigns that most concern them and don't have to call her. "LIP won't always be here. We're an umbrella, but we won't always be there. . . . The key ingredient is if it is a young people's movement, it should continue as a young people's movement." Like Lois Gibbs and Dollie, Kim is afraid of a tendency for organizers to overcontrol the movements of which they are a part. Kim says, "The young people should do what they want to do even if it is wrong because you have to learn from your mistakes."

One project Kim has undertaken with LIP and the Youth Task Force is the National Black Youth Agenda for the Year 2000, launched at the thirtieth anniversary commemoration of Bloody Sunday in Selma, Alabama, held between March 3 and 11, 1995. Attempting to attract young black people from all over the country, the call attempted to root the new movement in the history of black struggle. As the flier proclaimed "Whether you walk to the beat of the drums of Malcolm, Martin, Douglas, or Fannie; carry on the work of the Nation of Islam, the Black Panther Party, SNCC, or SCLC; it really doesn't matter at this point. What matters is whether or not we are going to pick up the baton from the brothers and sisters who have lived and died on the black battlefield or will we allow their living and their dying to be in vain?"[22]

Like many of the movements of the sixties, the Youth Task Force is attempting to create a new generation of black leaders, capable of governing their own affairs. Committed to feminism as part of that program, the schedule of events for the Selma commemoration included a two-day women's conference on "Invisible Giants" of the Voting Rights Movement, organized by the Southern Christian Leadership Conference, W.O.M.E.N., and the Voting Rights Museum at Concordia College in Selma. Kim and Angela Brown recognize that sexism in the black community weakens the possibilities for creating democratic institutions, and Kim views recognizing unsung women heroes as part of her mission. "At the commemoration of Bloody Sunday we actually honored women who participated in the voter rights movement and in the civil rights movement that had never been honored before because . . . unless you had a husband [who] has a big name, you never get commemorated or honored. So . . . we . . . went to communities and found women [who] had demonstrated their abilities and their greatness, and we honored them. One of the women [who] came . . . [was] Miss Rosanel Eaton . . . from Louisburg. She was the invisible giant. . . . She rode down on the bus with the young people. . . . All the young people know her because she was their teacher or their teacher's aid. . . . So she knows all of us."[23]

Both Kim and Dollie recognize that southern organizing frequently depends on a local woman. Kim says when you go into a new town, you must always find the Aunt Janey or the Miz Ella. The woman frequently does not see herself as a political leader, but she knows everything that goes on and, without her, nothing will happen in that town. Dollie notes that her own mother, who probably never went to a meeting in her life, would take care of local kids when their mothers went knocking on doors, raising some local issue or registering people to vote. Kim says that there is almost always an older woman in town to whom all the local kids turn for advice, solace, and even a chewing out when they deserve it.[24]

While Kim shares her mother's respect for the place black women have historically played in grassroots organizing in the South, Kim is less moderate about her feminism than her mother. Kim Burwell is certain that women of her generation won't stand behind their man—they'll be out in front of him. She is fond of saying that "behind every great man is a great woman," but she means that more sarcastically than it first appears. Despite the fact that in the era after the Million Man March in Washington in October 1995, official black leaders speak with increasing urgency about the need to enhance male egos as well as their sense of responsibility, Kim is having none of it. She says to the men in her organizations, "If I have to stuff envelopes, you have to stuff envelopes. If I need to write a flier, you need to write a flier."[25]

She is well aware of the connection between the civil rights movement and the development of feminism. "Civil rights did as much for white females as for blacks. [But] we still don't have the same agenda, even though the agenda should be the same," she says. Yet Kim's experience lies almost exclusively in political groups that women organize. Clearly, as a strong leader, Kim herself has had some trouble with men her own age.

Despite hopes that the men of Generation X would be more comfortable with strong women, Kim has not found that to be the case. Kim says, "They fear me. I've heard guys say, 'You talk too much . . .' or that type of thing. . . . You just have to speak up, and I think once women speak up more, they'll get more attention." In Kim's experience, women get the ideas and then find a man to present them, not because they lack confidence, but because, according to Kim, men have such a "superiority complex" that the women are happy to have men take the credit so long as the job gets done. "It's usually the woman's intuition or idea [that promotes a project]." But, she claims, "because of a superiority complex, the [men] want to take over all the time." Recently, Kim notes, "it's become more prevalent that a woman will say, 'Forget it,' because they ain't doing it right. So we just gonna do it ourselves."[26]

Kim is certainly not as willing as her mother to defer to black ministers. Dollie, raised in more conformist ways, feels that she should not antagonize the ministers, but should get their attention when necessary; Kim says she simply can't deal with them except, maybe, the most elderly of them. When asked whether from her perspective elderly means sixty, she says, "more like seventy or eighty." Here again, Dollie, who seldom criticizes her daughters in front of them or behind their backs, steps in and tries simultaneously to reason with Kim and to highlight her own objections to writing off whole groups of people.

Dollie to Kim: "It's true, there's a lot of sexism among the ministers, but you gotta know where they're coming from. Sometimes I just say to them, 'Now, be quiet. I have something to say, and you have to listen.' There's a lot of subconscious sexism, and they're not used to listening to women. But sometimes they have to."[27] Kim, because of her belief in a division of labor in organizing, thinks that if someone young has to work with the black ministers, it should be her old roommate, Minnie White, who can be charming. Or, looking to specialization by generation, Kim thinks Dollie or Connie Tucker, Dollie's contemporary, should try to cajole the ministers into listening to women's points of view.

Other problems rest not with gender but with class. A lot of what has been written by and about Generation X presumes everyone in it is white or middle class and lives in New York or California. And then, of course, there are the gang members and the gangsta rap singers, who are overwhelmingly male—and misogynist. Kim Burwell and the people with whom she works don't fit any of those categories. Viewing themselves as pioneers, the people around Kim are not willing to conform to any stereotypes about race or sex just because someone tells them they must. But Kim recognizes that she has some special skills to work with the roughest, most impoverished, least privileged young people. Unlike Dollie or even Angela, Kim seems to prefer to work with young people others dismiss as rough or out of control.

And, like her contemporaries, she is schooled in hip-hop and rap music, which Kim tries to adapt for the little children she teaches in nursery school.

Kim is justly proud of what she and her partners have accomplished, proud of what young people have done, and eager to reclaim her community in the South as a vibrant place. "I tell my momma, if y'all were going to let young people handle this, the landfill would already be detoxified." When Kim testified before one of the governor's commissions investigating the effect of the dump thirteen years after it had been established, Kim said: "I'm tired of people in my county hurting. There's no industry here. I can't get my classmates to come back into the county for even a class reunion. . . . It all boiled down to . . . the dump. [When it] was placed here, all property values went down, no industries wanted to come, and I [am] just tired of it."

Since Kim has been in campaigns for social justice so long, she has an historical perspective on what has been going on. "The movement . . . not just civil rights, but . . . environmental racism, . . . educational racism, . . . social justice—everything is going through this recycling process: I can tell from reading the history of what happened in the sixties. . . . It's re-evolving. It's so hard to wake our elders and say . . . with police forces putting the dogs out . . . these things are re-evolving. And now [young people] are more conscious of what their elders had to go through."[28] But Kim says, "I'm not afraid anymore . . . because I feel I owe my community something . . . and I also owe my elders something because they are the ones that taught me."

Some people have worried that overexposure to political activism in their childhood would turn some young people against the causes in which their parents engaged. The six-year-old daughter of politically active friends of mine, when learning that her parents were taking her to another party, asked astutely, "Is this a real party, where people sing 'Happy Birthday,' or is this a blah, blah, blah party?" Of course, it was the latter. Dollie's daughters had similar experiences, but they don't seem to have suffered from them.

The Reverend Leon White says one of Dollie's greatest accomplishments is that wherever she's gone politically, she's managed to take her children along with her. Kim Burwell and her sister, Mia, though very different in their styles and experiences, are their own women as well as being Dollie and Willie's daughters.

Kim and Mia have each had two activists to contend with: their mother and one another. Each daughter seems to keep the family stride while creating her own steps. In the early nineties when Dollie urged her church, the United Church of Christ, to recruit young people, they called on Mia. Mia was to give an introductory speech at the church's annual meeting before a speech by Andrew Young, former aide to Martin Luther King Jr. and ambassador to the United Nations under President Carter. Mia, who was scarcely nine at the time, lambasted the church and the civil rights movement as a whole for failing to address what was happening to young people. Her jeremiad was so compelling that Mia got a standing ovation, leading Young to claim she was a hard act to follow. Although the church did not immediately start a youth program, they did send Mia, with Dollie and Kim as her companions, to Angola for a month when the church received an invitation to participate in a youth conference.[29]

Like many older children, Kim seems proud that she has the primary bond with her mother, but recognizes her sister's talents: "I more so grew up with it 'hands on' than my sister did. She knows when there are injustices being done, and she addresses them differently than what we probably would. We're quicker to take an action than she would. . . . When she feels that there's an injustice, that there's no other way out, she doesn't have a fear of taking action. But if she feels that there is another way out, she's gonna figure that way out." Mia's willingness to march becomes a standard by which Kim judges Mia's continued attachment to the family. Kim seems reassured when she says of Mia: "She marches with us. [At] the last commemoration march on Washington, she was a marshal."[30]

Demonstrating and "taking action" is the lifeblood of politics for Kim Burwell as it was for the Student Nonviolent Coordinating Committee, formed primarily among young people in the South in the sixties. Those afraid of the always present potential for leaders to become bureaucrats want all leaders to be in direct contact with the large numbers of people—in Kim's case, youthful people. Kim therefore favors mobilizations and enjoys the talents of the young people with whom she works for creating and sustaining such activities. Having done so much of the hard work of organizing—writing the fliers, hashing out the differences, hiring the buses—Kim also enjoys the theater of politics. For her, marching with the young people in whom she so much believes is a way of enacting democracy and living her hopes for social justice.

6

"We sleep on our own graves": Women at Crossroads

REGINA NTONGANA, a field representative for the Surplus People Project (SPP), sits behind her small desk with its red plastic cylindrical pencil holder and compartments for clips and notes. Wearing red socks, brown moccasins, a brown cotton skirt, a pale green sweater, and a woolen cap against the indoor chill of the rainy July winter in Cape Town, South Africa, she wouldn't be taken for a victim or a political philosopher. Nor would she ever think in those terms. But as a squatter, she became a grassroots activist working for the rights of other homeless women.

Regina Ntongana, known as "Ma," learned about activism from her mother, a domestic worker who belonged to the African National Congress. Ma was born in 1939 on the outskirts of Cape Town, near Elsie's River, a mixed community of blacks and the people the government called "Coloureds." She lived with her grandmother in Beaufort West, a railroad junction in the hot, dry, or tundra-like northern Cape, and had a conflicted relationship with her mother. Ma recalls misunderstanding why her mother was always engaged in struggle, constantly demanding her rights. Ntongana's mother told Regina that if she didn't understand, didn't feel the need for dignity, nothing would explain it. Ma, however, does not attribute her own fierce commitment to justice to her mother, but to her pain. "I gave me over to my people—how we are suffering."[1]

Her anguish came from apartheid, a political system upholding the fiction that white settlers had created South Africa from a wilderness, and that people of color, particularly black Africans, had no rights to interfere with the way whites ran their country.[2] By dividing people along arbitrary color lines and by keeping groups separate spatially as well as legally until customs of racism prevailed, the government established its authority over every aspect of life. "Influx-control" laws, imposing passes that governed employment and residence rights in the cities, formed one of the foundations for apartheid. In effect in different and increasingly vicious forms between the 1890s and 1986, these laws shaped South African society by establishing a nefarious urban housing policy that also discriminated against women.[3]

Apartheid, the systematic legal separation of the races in South Africa, effectively began with the Black Urban Areas Act of 1945. This law prohibited the mobility of all people of color and precluded them from moving where they wished, making women particularly vulnerable. In order to qualify for the privilege of living in the cities, people of color had "to produce proof that they were born [in the city] and [had] lived [in the city] all their lives." The second category of people who qualified were "contract workers who [had] worked continuously for one employer in the area for at least 10 years or for more than one employer for at least 15 years." The third grouping consisted of "wives and unmarried sons and daughters, under the age of 18, of those who qualified for the first two categories." The final section included "certain contract workers who obtained permission from the manager of a labour bureau to reside in an area for a set period."[4]

With the help of computers, "influx-control" regulations, replaced by so-called orderly urbanization rules in July 1986, permitted the South African government to monitor the movement of people of color. The emblem of influx control was the passbook, an internal passport listing employment and residential history. Representing the 15 percent of the population that was white, authorities imposed pass laws not only to regulate labor but to assure that there was no urban unemployment and no public services expended on anyone, least of all mothers or children, who were not directly creating wealth for employers. Pass laws meant that people of color, especially women, negotiated almost every move they made with some official of the state: as if they were on parole, they had to check in every few months and plead with some bureaucrat that special conditions, such as a child's illness or their own pregnancy, required them to remain in the city. Women's constant negotiations to preserve their families made motherhood a public activity among women of color. The government's lack of concern with the basic survival of African people marked apartheid as a genocidal policy—and one of the most sexist systems of government ever known.

The law restricted older Africans, those without steady employment, and married black women with children to poor rural areas called Bantustans, with no schools, no hospitals, no job opportunities in industry or agriculture. Able-bodied African men gained passes for jobs in the mines or cities only when work was plentiful. Even when mothers received passes to the city to earn money, it was generally to serve as live-in housekeepers and nannies for other women's children. Staying with the white family, working six-and-a-half days a week, not only precluded raising one's own children, but it exposed women to sexual attacks from the master of the house and his sons.

When Jezile, the protagonist of the novel *and they didn't die*, is forced to go to work for the Potgieters to support her children, she is wary of the father's growing wish for her attention. One night after the husband had bloodied his wife in an act of domestic violence and disappeared from the main house, Jezile returned to her room in the backyard and found him stretched across her bed. Claiming to love her, he began to hold her down and raped her. "Afterwards she curled up like a ball at the opposite end of the bed and winced and whimpered like a wounded animal."[5]

Apartheid's policy of reducing Africans to foreign "aliens," undocumented workers in their own country, deprived women like Jezile of any fundamental prerogatives against exploitative employers. Apartheid also exacerbated the housing shortages that have plagued advanced industrial society in the past two decades. By withholding from mothers of color rights to settle in the cities, South Africa doomed them and their children to starvation and ignorance. As the government attempted to consolidate its power in the seventies, it imposed yet another layer of restrictions. According to the Admission of Persons to the Republic Regulation Act of 1972, which granted citizenship to black South Africans in the Bantustans, "foreigners," a category that now included most blacks, could be deported even if they had a legal job under the old law.[6]

Despite being a native, Mrs. Ntongana, having married a worker who came from the rural areas, was no longer entitled to live in Cape Town. Once the "homelands" were created, women, children, and the aged were assigned to these deserts and wastelands, where it was impossible to eke out a living. As Mrs. Ntongana explained to Josette Cole, a field worker for the Western Province Council of Churches, "We as women, we had a feeling because we were the people who really felt the pain. We were the ones who were staying in the Transkei and Ciskei. We were the ones with nowhere to go." Ma did not want to leave her children and work full-time for a white family, as her own mother had done. She complained that "as women we were worried about a better future for our children. Never mind you are married or not, we wanted to stay together as family life. . . . Our aim was to see our children growing up in front of us. We wanted to blow the government down to allow us to stay with our children. That's what made us come together as women." Her militancy, derives in part from her sense of righteous indignation about the treatment of women as mothers. Women like Regina Ntongana, by their struggle to establish homes in the cities, helped undermine apartheid and contributed to the view that housing has some relationship to social justice.

Like other countries in which the government idealizes motherhood and denigrates single mothers, the South African government disparaged all women of color and effectively shattered stable families, making married women into single mothers even when they and their husbands preferred to stay together. Ma claims, "A white man can carry his wife like a briefcase but for blacks it's just like divorce. Other women did know that their husbands qualified to be here— it was just the women who did not have rights."[7] But, in fact, able-bodied men in their prime could secure work permits only for the length of their jobs; if they were laid off for whatever reason, they could lose their passes and have to leave the city. In addition, men were expected to live in single-sex barracks known as hostels and, if they were contract laborers, they could return to their families for only one month a year.

The men, prevented by the system from living with their families, sent money back for child support when they could, frequently finding new relationships in the cities, abandoning their wives and children to slow death in the infertile countryside to which they were assigned. As the fictional political leader in the novel *and they didn't die* explained to the other women, "We are the dumping ground. We live all our lives without the help of our men and when they are useless we must receive them back and care for them." Recognizing that men were victims of structural problems, earning little, being forced to live apart from their families to earn anything at all, the fictional leader in the novel realizes: "Even the most loyal of our men can only send back a pittance to support their families. And many fail even to do that—we blame them, but really it is the government that is to blame. When our men get lonely out there they meet other women and new families grow and we are forgotten. When our men have failed to provide for us, they have taken their frustration out on us; when they have been put into prisons for a thousand possible infringements of the law, we have suffered."[8]

When the men disappeared, the women faced even greater hardships. Without wage-paying jobs, women couldn't even gain residency in a city unless they had been born there and had never left. If domestic workers, women generally lived with their employers, leaving their children in the countryside to be raised by relatives to whom they sent their wages. Single women working in factories frequently had to live in hostels of their own. But women trying to keep their children with them could earn a living in the cities only by illegally doing day work or hawking provisions for a small profit. Those women who had domestic jobs cleaning houses by day worked long hours for very low wages since their employers knew that most of them lacked passes and thus were subject to expulsion if they came to the attention of authorities. Willing to do almost anything to remain, approximately 90 percent of women who lived in the townships or squatter communities, fully twenty-five or thirty miles from the white residential areas of the cities, did some form of domestic labor.[9]

As if surviving economically in the urban areas was not hard enough, the women faced harassment and arrest for merely being there, leading to about two million arrests for pass-law violations between the sixties and the eighties. Moving around to escape the police, begging with officials for yet another extension of passes they had to bring a sick child for treatment, many women finally succumbed and agreed to leave the city and settle in rural areas. A woman of color described how the passes determined her life in the sixties: "Once every six months I had to go to Observatory [an office in a section of Cape Town near the city center] where they would give me a closed envelope with a paper inside to take to Langa. And at the Langa office they took my pass book and read the letter, which told them how many months they had to stamp in my book. Every six months it was the same again—go to Observatory, go to Langa, and they stamped my pass book. . . . That is the way we know life. We don't mind about justice, about whether a thing is right or not. We know of people who came to Cape Town after 1960 who were given permits and houses, and we who have been here much longer must leave. We don't mind anymore. Our lives are upside down anyway. We're used to it. One person gets the pass, the next one doesn't. It's come to be so that we don't care if we have a pass or if we don't. If we feel we want to visit relatives we go. We don't worry about a pass. If they catch you, well, they catch you. That's the way we know life."[10] By subjecting everyone who was not classified as white to frequent contact with bureaucrats, the government carried out constant surveillance. Short of keeping a gun to each person's head, influx controls probably provided the most effective form of state terrorism the government could devise.

Nowhere has the effect of influx controls been more poignant than in Cape Town, one of the most beautiful cities in the world—and the one from which the government tried to exclude black Africans entirely by declaring it a "Coloured Preference Area." The blue waters of the South Atlantic and the Indian Ocean join at Cape Town to wash the beaches that lie below Table Mountain, Devil's Peak, and Lion's Head. But the majesty of the landscape is a Potemkin village. The view from the other side of the mountains, from the vast sand dunes called the Cape Flats, where by the mid-nineties nearly two million people lived, is entirely different from that of the white population stretched along the foothills.

Housing in the squatter settlements ranges from plastic tents to corrugated metal shacks. Frequently a few water spigots serve thousands. Latrines and the bucket system of waste disposal usually provide what sewage system there is. One step up are the vast sandy human parking lots, cement slabs with water attachments and toilets to which former squatters were allowed to move when the government conceded their need to stay in the city. Only the scale of the squatter communities—which like Khayelitsha have come to house close to a million people—and the way the natural beauty of the sand dunes mocks the misery of the people trying to survive on them distinguish the settlements from shanty towns all over the world.

Never have poverty and the inequities of housing been more clearly the result of government policy than in South

Africa. Apartheid used housing as a means to stem the tide of migration by people of color. Whatever their income, blacks simply were not permitted to buy or rent houses in Cape Town.

Among the townships of South Africa, Sharpville and Soweto have become the best known abroad because of the massacres that took place in them. Yet Crossroads, outside Cape Town on the treeless, wind-swept sand dunes south of the airport, served as home to about one hundred thousand black people before most of them were driven out in May and June 1986.[11] South African authorities envisioned Crossroads and its collateral settlements, known as KCT, Nyanga Bush, and Nyanga, as a transit camp whose inhabitants were en route to the misnamed, rural homelands created in the seventies. But the violence of the outcry about Crossroads contributed to ending influx controls.[12]

Crossroads itself emerged in 1975. Because of the economic expansion of Cape Town between 1968 and 1974, the number of migrant workers increased by over 56 percent, leading African contract laborers and their wives to establish informal, illegal housing. But as the recession began in 1974 and intensified over the following years, the government increased its efforts to restrict migration. The population of Crossroads principally came from people who had just migrated to Cape Town that year or who came from other squatter settlements in Cape Town. Mrs. Ntongana, who was one of the founders of Crossroads, recalls about her neighbors that "some people came from the townships, some were women who were staying with their men in the 'single' quarters. They come with their husbands here and built their homes. There were some people whose houses were demolished by the Board of Inspectors."[13]

Blacks suffered special repression in Cape Town. They were harassed for pass violations and forced to pay higher fines there than in any other place in South Africa. And the majority of those without passes were women.[14] Because authorities, hoping to consolidate blacks in one place the more easily to ship them out, told them to go to Crossroads in

1975 and 1976, women assumed that they had a legitimate right to settle there. Mrs. Ntongana, speaking at the time, said: "We are resisting because the inspectors said, 'This is your area. . . .' The council took the people who were staying among Coloured people and brought them here. It is because we have no place. We want to stay with our husbands. Women have lost their husbands before—we don't want to lose our men. There was even a white inspector who told us to go to Crossroads. We were not aware that they were going to kill us here. We were in other areas and they said, 'Come to Crossroads.' "[15] The women who settled there had not wandered into an area where they could put up makeshift dwellings; they believed they had been sent to that precise spot. Having obeyed officials, they felt entitled to conserve the homes they had built.

Beginning with no more than twenty shacks in February 1975, about four thousand people, living in approximately one thousand shanties, filled Crossroads by April. In 1978, twenty thousand inhabitants in three thousand handmade dwellings consumed an area of approximately two square miles in which only one street, the Street of Mice (Mpuku), had a name.[16] Out of this wilderness, people constructed a community.

According to Mrs. Ntongana, they "worked very hard to build this home. We cleared the bush, then we laid down mats. We initially built up a shelter to prevent the wind from blowing at the primus stoves. On the first night we were not able to put on the roof (the zincs), and we were told to build some toilets ourselves. Then we were only able to get water pipes installed after three months, as a result of some nurses, I would think. We had to fetch water from the Coloured families on the other side of the road."[17]

By marrying someone from the Transkei, Regina Ntongana lost her citizenship in South Africa and became a citizen of an artificially created state in a barren, rural area. Between 1976 and 1981, she and more than eight million other blacks were deprived of their claims to the rich lands and cities of South Africa.[18] Even earlier, Mrs. Ntongana and her children were forced to leave the Cape and move to the Transkei wasteland. In the Transkei, where the population density was 84 people per square kilometer as compared with the 19 people per square kilometer in the white-dominated areas of the country, food, work, and medicine were in short supply.[19] When Ma was incapable of saving two of her toddlers, who died in 1973 without proper medical care, she returned to Cape Town to protect her remaining children. Thwarting the government's prohibition against blacks living in Cape Town, that year Ma settled her children in Brown's Farm on the outskirts of the city, on the bleak road to the airport. Other black women joined her. But their presence threatened the government, which attempted to control urbanization as a way of maintaining white power.

For African people such as Regina Ntongana, constructing a dwelling in a squatter settlement provided the only chance for survival. Literally creating homes from scraps of wood and metal found in dumps, tens of thousands of black people had begun to put down roots in Cape Town by the seventies when the government intensified its enforcement of influx control legislation, driving out people they claimed were illegally in the Cape.

Headlines from that period increasingly featured bull-dozers, which along with armored personnel carriers, nick-named "mellow yellow" or "green machines," depending on their color, began to make visible the triumph of force over justice. Accounts about who populated the squatter settlements such as Crossroads broke on the conscience of people in northern and western countries, though the gendered nature of the repression was at first hardly recognized. Within two years of the founding of Crossroads in 1975, shanty towns surrounding it fell to the bulldozers. In August 1977, Modderdam had been destroyed, and 10,000 people made homeless. Three months later in November 1977, Unibel's shanties, on the grounds of the university campus near Bellville (now the University of the Western Cape), had been plowed under. Once these camps disappeared in the late seventies, Crossroads became the only sizable black squatter camp in Cape Town.

Not content with Crossroads' remaining, the police raided it on September 14, 1978, which resulted in three deaths, including that of a baby. Mrs. Ntongana described the scene: "The people were frightened and were backing away from the dogs. A young woman who was holding her two-month-old baby to her breast was pushed over in the crush. People fell on top of her and the baby. When the panic was over, we heard the woman screaming. Her baby had stopped breathing and was dead." Later on September 14, a group of twenty women, led by the Women's Committee, marched on the courts in Langa, demanding that they too be arrested, arguing that "the men did nothing to deserve being arrested. Neither did we, so we wanted the police to arrest us too." Despite efforts to force the Crossroads women to go to the Transkei, the Women's Committee of Crossroads stood firm.[20] They claimed that whether single or attached to men, they deserved passes of their own. In fact, the women increasingly forged ties to one another. According to Josette Cole, who was arrested along with Crossroads residents in the September 14, 1978, raid on the community, the extremity of the women's situation enabled them to "keep the authority which their mothers had to give up. It is out of this group that the concept of a more self-sufficient female world is emerging."[21] Collective self-reliance under a crisis situation forged the women into a group that trusted its own judgment.

The women of Crossroads, by claiming certain prerogatives based not on law but on their standing as human beings, transformed housing into a human rights issue. Crossroads brought the message home. Resembling a refugee camp and lacking toilets, sewage-disposal systems, or schools until local women led campaigns for government aid or created these social services themselves, Crossroads became an emblem of the personal costs of influx control. Its story also demonstrated the organizational abilities of ordinary, uneducated women as they attempted to craft a more just social system out of the extreme poverty in which they lived. Paradoxically, despite the law forbidding them to settle, those who lived in squatter communities, though there illegally, also had to pay rent and the costs of removing human wastes. As unemployment rose in the seventies, compounding the hardships of inflation and general recession, rents and service charges also went up.

Whatever competitors housing had for the title of the leading irritant, the unbearable condition of life in the squatter communities ranked high. Not all the displaced people had escaped from the Bantustans. Take, for example, Dora Jassen, who was known as the "Mayoress Vrygrond." From a land-owning family in Rondevlei, in the hinterland of the Northern Cape, her property, which she had inherited from her father, was condemned by the local council in 1975. Paid a mere 1,500 rands (the equivalent in dollars at that time), she was told to go to Vrygrond, a black settlement, while the government looked for other accommodations for her. Nine years later, she and her three married children lived together in a shack in the Vrygrond Township along with nearly two hundred other families. Such townships, which had become the principal settlements urban blacks occupied, lacked basic services. In Vrygrond, for example, all the families depended on only five water spigots from which all water for drinking, cooking, and washing had to be drawn.[22]

Though Vrygrond and other settlements subjected people to the same inhuman conditions, it was the efforts of the government to forcibly dislodge people from the shacks they had built to shelter their families at Crossroads that caused it to gain prominence as a human rights violation. For the workers whose labor they needed, the government provided barracks. Those whose husbands lived in dormitories were forced to sneak around, further humiliating women like Mrs. Ntongana who recalled, "When you come down to Cape Town you must go share your sleep with your husband in bachelor quarters, run up and down early in the morning because of raids, and come back late in the day again. It was these things that made us decide as women we had enough."[23] Many others, including people who were starving in the outlying areas, came to Cape Town seeking work.

When official census figures put the black population of Cape Town at 114,164 in 1978, the real population was closer to 200,000, according to anthropologist Pamela Reynolds.[24] She estimates that over 40 percent of those living around Cape Town lacked permits. A large proportion of undocumented people were women, and Reynolds claims that Cape Town was the only place where arrests of women for pass violations exceeded those of men.[25]

Mrs. B., an early settler of Crossroads, had had a temporary one-year permit to be in the Cape Town area in 1970 because she had a nine-month-old child who contracted polio. In 1975, a white inspector "indicated to us that here at Crossroads there was an area that is being allocated for Africans. They told us that only those women whose husbands were qualified to be in Cape Town should go to that area. And we asked for direction to that area."[26] When they arrived, there were a "lot of trees and just a few houses."[27] Hoping that if their husbands received steady work the women would get residence permits, the women stayed put and began building dwellings.

Housing at Crossroads varied. Despite the frequent floods on the sandy soil of the Cape Flats and the city's windy and rainy winters with temperatures in the forties, some lived in plastic tents lined with cardboard and paper. Others had grander dwellings, consisting of corrugated iron or sheets of zinc for walls and rooves. Wood and cardboard formed the floors, providing a dangerous setting for the paraffin stoves and candles that provided all heat, cooking facilities, and light. One woman said, "We sleep on our own graves."[28]

A month after the founding of the settlement in February 1975, the first eviction notices came, and the men and women formed separate committees to deal with the threat. Jane Yanta and Elizabeth Lutango led the ad hoc Women's Committee, which acted as a mutual aid society. They contacted the Black Sash.[29] Originating as the Women's Defence of the Constitution League in 1955, the Black Sash opposed the Nationalist government's attempts to change the country's constitution in order to disenfranchise Coloured voters in the Cape in 1955. To demonstrate outrage against what the women called the rape of the South African constitution, they wore black sashes when they picketed the government. Just before the African National Congress was banned in 1960, ANC activists who had led the struggle against women having to carry passes helped train Sash members to tutor people about what to do in case of raids and arrests.[30] At first called the Bail Fund Office, the Sash switched the name of its service center to the Advice Office and set up its first operation in 1958 in the Athlone location previously occupied by the ANC Women's League.[31] The Advice Offices provided legal council to women and men in the squatter communities.

Crossroads was raided the first time in May 1975. The attack ended with thirty-four arrests, surprising the women because, according to Mrs. B, they "had been told that this area was for Africans." She went on to say, "We could not take these notices seriously, because we had been told by some other inspectors to come here. When these notices expired the inspectors arrived, and on arresting the people they were not taken to the police station but ordered to take out and tie together their belongings. And they would proceed with demolition. This happened to three women. And after that we came together and decided to take up the issue with bantu affairs [the Bantu Administration Board] in the Observatory. We were a group of fifty-eight women and made our plea to Mr. [Fanie] Botha [the local commissioner charged with matters concerning blacks], Mr. McLachlan and Mr. Petersen. And they refused to grant us our request saying that we were given sufficient notice. They gave us about another month to stay. Then we approached the Black Sash. We had already made previous contact with the Black Sash. From then on we were arrested, would appear in court, be arrested again, several times, until 1976."[32]

A representative of the Black Sash Advice Office remarked on the newfound militancy of the women from Crossroads: "[T]he one thing we noticed was that these women were very independent. . . . When we told them that they were illegally in the area, they told us that in spite of that, they were determined to stay. There was no question that they would obey the law. Now that was the first time that we had heard of that. Until 1975, when you did everything you could to get permission for a woman to stay, and you failed, she went. But the women of Crossroads were the first women to sit in our office and say . . . 'We are not going.' "[33]

The Black Sash realized that the women from Crossroads had moved into another realm: They were not asking for rights under an unjust law; they were asking for justice. Sash official Noel Robb recalled: "We had to have a special meeting because up to then we'd only defended those who were legally here and helped them to get their rights. Now we were being asked to defend people with no rights, and this was quite a policy decision [for us]."[34] By asserting their rights as human beings rather than submitting to the laws that buttressed apartheid, the women of Crossroads embarked on a campaign that would help discredit the South African government.

Though many of the women at Crossroads initially knew little about politics, becoming activists solely to keep roofs over their families' heads, they quickly picked up political sophistication. Regina Ntongana, who succeeded Jane Yanta as head of the Women's Committee in 1976, explained how the committee gained its power: "Between 1975 and 1977, we came to be strong as women. We used to have meetings every day, sharing our views and thoughts on each and every thing. . . . We decided we must have a few [women] in front to lead so that we must be definitely sure who is going to work. So we elected thirteen women; I was one of them. At first the men didn't like it. They said we did things too fast . . . it wasn't easy for the men because they were working during the day . . . the women was going all over the place to find out what was going on. . . . So we knew more than the men. . . . Some of them were really jealous . . . they sometimes stopped us to have meetings."[35]

Many women formed networks around their efforts to accumulate necessities. From the city dump near Crossroads, women and children foraged in the refuse for wood, plastic, and string. To serve the needs of people in squatter settlements, there were about one hundred small businesses and trading shops. One of them in Modderdam, destroyed by the government in late 1977, was run by Mrs. Bella Phindi when anthropologist Andrew Silk interviewed her. She had started with some vegetables and built up her stock to include various food items. She had begun with a table outside her house and then added shelves to her living room, which became a shop. Shops, outdoor stands, schools, clinics, and child-care centers acted as gathering points where people informally met and reflected upon their lives and those of their neighbors.[36]

Despite the women's efforts, the shortage of social services put some necessities out of their reach. According to the medical officer of the Divisional Council reporting in July 1978: "In a period of six months, the number of births was 465, a growth rate of 1,000 per annum. There are 20 water taps, for the whole population, wastage of water remains a problem, there is always a certain amount of litter, night soil in 3,000 pails have to be removed twice weekly."[37] For waste removals and water spigots, local people had to pay 10 rand a month.

How bad conditions were depended on one's perspective. As Mrs. Ntongana explained, "I like staying here at Crossroads very much. I like it because now we pay rent, water has been installed, and they are servicing the toilets. I have a certain measure of security, and I'm not thinking of moving anywhere."[38] Despite the fact that they paid rent, women had no tenant rights when police came to raid their houses. Sometimes they seemed to have few rights of any sort. Describing the burning of Modderdam settlement in August 1977, one observer said that a group of women watching the spectacle began to sing. "In the middle of the hymn, the police moved forward a few feet. 'We don't like it when they sing, because we don't know what they are singing,' a policeman later told a reporter."[39]

The singing shows that despite hardships, women in the squatter communities had frequently been able to create what one person called "strong spirit" and a "good feeling."[40] A woman whom Andrew Silk talked to in another shanty town explained how the women came to know one another: "Here we often have a greater chance to make friends than in the country. Up there, most of the people you visit are relatives whom you have known your whole life. This can be quite boring. Here people make friends with those who happen to live next to them. Occasionally you might know some of the people from the village or from another squatter camp, but usually you make friends with people you have never seen before. We have some of the fights you might find elsewhere. Yet we find usually that there is good cooperation, for we all know each other's condition, and we all need the same things. When one of us is sick or has to bring children to hospital, usually we help out and take over her chores. When we get together to do the washing or cooking or just to talk, we usually discuss buying food or the chances of getting a job outside, or personal problems with our children or our husbands.

"What brings us together the most, though, is our desire to stay here. . . . Life would be harder if all of the new people were just scattered around. What matters to us is not so much the condition of our houses, but the help you get from people around you. You might think that people would only make friends with those who are most like them. . . . But here we find it is not so. There are some young village girls who have got to know the older ones from the town quite well. They teach them about this Cape Town."[41]

The women, many of whom had traveled with their children from shanty town to shanty town until they reached Crossroads, created loose associations through which they could advance themselves and their children. To serve the approximately nine thousand children who lived at Crossroads and played in the sand on which the squatter community was built, in 1976, the women created a school, Noxolo (Teach). Eighteen months later, they attached a community center. By 1978, Noxolo had four grades and four teachers for 352 students. Each child paid one rand, tuition that various church groups supplemented. On May 27, 1978, they opened the Sizamile lower primary school at Crossroads.[42] Describing how the schools were built, Mrs. Ntongana explained that "each child had to bring zincs, nails and poles, and we put the building together. It was just a shelter in the beginning. During the day Mrs [Jane] Yanta, she was our leader then, used to be busy helping the women who were teaching there. We didn't know when or how we would get money to pay them, but it was a start. At that time everyone was proud to help because people could see we were in need and that we must do something to get something."[43]

But constructing the school under adverse circumstances was the least of the women's problems; they also had to defend it against the government. Mrs. Ntongana reported with great sadness, "[The Administrative Board] came and demolished our school. Some of the teachers, they didn't have qualifications to teach, so they [the board] chased them away. Some were locked up. When the parents came back from work the school was flat. We didn't know what to do, but we didn't give in. We started to build another school. They demolished again. The third one they demolished with a bulldozer. It would be up two days then they would break it down. We didn't give up. As women we organized all over to get help. So the organizations like the churches and Black Sash did help. And in the end we did win. Eventually we got permission to build. That's how we got our . . . school. We called it 'Sizamile'—it means 'we are trying.' "[44] Except for one person, the entire staff of the school were women.[45]

Sizamile, too, was doomed. Many of the women refused to relinquish the school, continuing to teach when authorities came to demolish it. But at 1:30 A.M. on the morning of

June 5, 1978, six hundred riot police invaded the school. In the attack, a baby and two other people were reportedly killed. As the local women stood their ground, three hundred were arrested.[46]

On June 7, 1978, over two hundred women from Crossroads sneaked out the back of the camp, eluding police surrounding Crossroads, and marched on the Bantu Affairs Administration Board in Goodwood. Ma recalls that "the men [their husbands] were so scared." But the women were determined to confront authorities. Too numerous to fit inside the board's offices, the women motioned the officials to meet them outside. When the officials refused to come out to speak to the assembled crowd, they reluctantly agreed to allow seven delegates to represent them. Speaking only in Xhosa and therefore forcing the authorities to summon a translator, they demanded explanations about the destruction of the school and about the harassment they had suffered: being arrested as they went for water, being prevented from working, and having husbands arrested on the way to work. As Mrs. Ntongana recalled, "We were the only people demanding." The officials, ignoring the women's protestations that many of them had been born and lived their whole lives in Cape Town, promised to help the women with their luggage and transportation, but insisted that the women had to "return" to the "homelands."[47]

Recently recalling the old battles, Ma chuckled about how the women taunted the authorities. They knew the translator summoned from Langa, one of the oldest hostels in the area. And, of course, he knew that the women spoke English and could understand everything the officials said. The bureaucrats claimed that they had repeatedly sent notice that most of the women were illegally in the Cape and therefore that they had no rights to housing or schools. The women told the translator that they received papers, but not understanding them, they used them for toilet paper. Anyway, Ma recalls their saying, they were there to discuss the officials' illegal action, not where the women lived.[48]

Accused by authorities of being men's pawns in a power play, the women defended themselves by saying, "When your life is bitter, *you* do something." Mrs. Ntongana recalled saying, "You do not have to be told that you have nowhere else to go, no land to cultivate, no work, and no money in a 'homeland.' "[49] In an effort to intimidate the women, officials told them that they must not demonstrate, should not talk to reporters, and in the future should write letters and make appointments.

The seven women from Crossroads who had allowed themselves to be named spokeswomen for the group, including Regina Ntongana, Alexandria Luke, and Mary Gwabeni, were ordered to appear for questioning on June 17, 1978, and police acknowledged that they expected to arrest the women. Prepared for any eventuality, the women explained to a reporter that they had nothing to lose, and thought only of maintaining their homes in Crossroads. As Mrs. Ntongana recalled, "We were wearing the pain of not having houses."[50]

The Women's Committee solidified the organization by electing a permanent secretary and treasurer as well as a chairwoman for Wednesday afternoon weekly meetings at Noxolo School. Mrs. Ntongana, who at the time had a job in a restaurant in town, was persuaded to give it up to devote herself to the committee full-time.[51] Subcommittees on rents and "clean up" dealt with official attempts to expel those in arrears and the charge by authorities that Crossroads was derelict.

Leaving nothing to chance, the group made sure that the local press recognized its activities.[52] The trump card women used in 1978 was publicity. The women of Crossroads refused to be silenced about what was going on. They mounted a media campaign, believing "that a continuing blaze of publicity was the best protection against demolition and other harassment."[53]

The women weren't alone. They forged connections with liberal allies such as the Black Sash; the Quakers, who ran literacy classes at Noxolo school; the Institute of Race

Relations; the Urban Problems Research Unit; the Provincial Ecumenical Council; and the Anglican Church. Recognizing the need to unite the entire community, the women entered a Joint Committee with the two men's groups. Keeping up to date with the changing strategy of authorities, the Joint Committee organized frequent community-wide meetings. Since the women, whether working at home without wages or employed in clandestine trade, occupied Crossroads day and night and had established an organizational network throughout the camp, by 1978 women ran the Joint Committee.[54]

Despite increasing police attacks, in 1978 the women decided to show their determination to remain in their homes at Crossroads. One of their more ingenious tactics was to paint their houses. Regina Ntongana, who knows that people need to see progress no matter how trivial if they are to stay together, recalls that they "organized monies from the women and bought paint. The women divided Crossroads into sections and we decided we must paint the houses different colors to show that we meant to stay." When they finished, the houses were arrayed in orange, purple, pink, and green.[55] According to one observer who was unaware of house painting as a political strategy of the women, "many houses of Crossroads were painted in bright colors with trim done carefully in another color."[56]

Throughout 1978, women met in a church. With the advice of the Provincial Ecumenical Council and other religious groups, they used the media to advertise their situation. Gathering resources from their sponsors, the women printed bumper stickers and postcards, organized photo exhibits and slide shows, mobilized a petition campaign that gathered thirty-five thousand signatures, and launched a Day of Prayer and Solidarity throughout the world. They briefed sympathetic journalists about events at the settlement. They ran tours for visiting dignitaries and organized a solidarity week at the University of Cape Town.[57]

Despite their efforts, the government mounted the September 14, 1978, attack. Resisting in a number of ways, the women launched a play that November called *Imfuduso*, or Exodus, describing their lives at Crossroads. Performing both male and female parts, the women, according to Josette Cole, tried to demonstrate their belief "that the struggle to remain in the Western Cape was, essentially, a women's struggle."[58] Mrs. Ntongana remembers the play with delight. Having studied the mannerisms of government officials she calls Boers through their many encounters, she relished acting their parts; some women played police; others played squatters. In an effort to alert people throughout the country about what was happening at Crossroads, the women took the play on tour to the major cities of South Africa. By widening their audience, they sought to control public opinion about what the government was doing to them.

When asked why no men were invited to participate in the presentation, Mrs. Ntongana argued that "we had no men in the play because we felt it was really us—the women—who were really feeling the pain. We were the only ones who did fight for Crossroads. A man is not so strong. If the government would come, the men would run away. But a woman, she won't give in so easily. . . . What made us to be so strong is that we had really suffered. Some did have qualifications [passes], some did have but lost them. Others didn't have. We felt that we must stick together as women, no matter what's what."[59] Deeply religious, Ma was increasingly drawn to women in church organizations. With the help of a liberal group of women in the Dutch Reformed Church, to which she belonged, and to Kairos, a Dutch Christian feminist organization, the Crossroads women made a video of the play and showed it on Dutch television when the women from South Africa traveled there to publicize what was happening to them.[60]

For over a decade, from 1975 on, the women of Crossroads led by the Women's Committee grew in political experience and strategic skill. With ample media coverage, they publicized their plight, including the government's use of front-loaders as tanks to bulldoze their homes. Portraying themselves as victims in order to get media attention, many of the women were anything but: they were as astute as the government about getting their images across.

Their main adversary was the misnamed minister of co-operation and plural relations, Dr. Piet J. Koornhof, who came to power in November 1978. Presenting himself as a reformer, he tried to convince local citizens that he took all their interests to heart. Greeted as a "father" by a male leader, Koornhof embraced the paternalist metaphor saying, "A good father will always be careful not to arouse expectations which cannot be fulfilled, but he must also bear the best interests of his children at heart." By early 1979, he had made a deal with some of the citizens of Crossroads. Clearly attempting to revamp the government's image abroad, Koornhof tried to turn press attention from visions of police attacking innocent women as they fled from burning shanties, holding toddlers by the hand and bearing infants on their backs, to one more favorable to the government.[61]

Koornhof came up with a miraculous solution by proposing to construct permanent housing at New Crossroads near Nyanga, the settlement contiguous to Crossroads. At first, he implied that everyone presently living in the old community would move to better housing and would remain together. The problem, clear from the beginning, was that the new area was far too small to accommodate all the people who were already at Crossroads, let alone the refugees from nearby settlements who were sure to come.

Koornhof, who now claims, as do many former government officials, to have been an opponent of apartheid all the time, also led Crossroads people to believe that they would not be arrested even if they lacked documentation so long as they worked as craftspeople or held some other legal employment serving the community. Thus, Mrs. Rosie Makwethu could not understand when she was detained, tried, and "found guilty of being in the Peninsula illegally."[62] The solution Koornhof offered in April 1979 substituted eighteen-month permits for passes, which meant that women and others without passes could be deported at the end of stipulated time periods. The offer applied only to residents of Crossroads whom the government considered to be legally in the Cape, thereby splitting workers with documents from other migrant Africans and leaving out most of the women. It provided a photo opportunity for the South African government without really solving anything.[63]

Recognizing that clear laws about who would be allowed to remain in the Cape and who would be arrested would prevent chaos, the government finally authorized six-month residence permits in July 1979. Supposedly these would protect Crossroads' people against raids and arrests until January 31, 1980.[64] From the first, Koornhof began to backtrack, giving assurances only that some Crossroads people would move to the new development.

Despite the protests of some women and organized youth, the proposal was generally accepted by local people who hoped that permanent dwellings would enable them to lead a stable life. Irene Narwele, known as "Mawushe," now a member of the community work unit of the Surplus People Project, was one of Mrs. Ntongana's neighbors in Crossroads. Hoping to better her life and those of her children, Mawushe decided to take up the government's offer and move, while Mrs. Ntongana at the time viewed all those who accepted the compromise as sellouts. Ntongana, who has a keen sense of political strategy, thought the government had found a way of co-opting the community by tantalizing some people with the possibility of real houses. Ma also feared the loss of the power the Women's Committee had exercised.

Before the settlement, according to Josette Cole, "It had been members of the Women's Committee who to a large extent controlled access to information, outside contacts, and any resources coming into the community."[65] But increasingly, after May 1979, power was centralized, the powers of the Joint Committee circumscribed, and the Women's Committee increasingly excluded from caucus meetings dominated by Johnson Ngxobongwana, known informally as the mayor of Crossroads. By August, an Executive Committee chaired by Ngxobongwana and excluding the women had been elected. Making up the committee were fifteen men with responsibilities for different issues. Now the old committees had to report to these men. Meanwhile the repression of those who lacked the proper passes, the majority of whom were women, intensified throughout the Cape.

When, in 1980, the first phase of the housing development known as New Crossroads was ready, about five thousand people agreed to leave their shanties made of corrugated iron to move to the larger, brick houses, where the rents were more than four times as high.[66] Claiming that fewer than twenty-four thousand resided at Crossroads, the authorities discounted local government reports of six months earlier that put the number at least double that.[67] Only people listed under the surveys of old Crossroads done in 1976 and 1980 were allowed to move to New Crossroads, and this frequently excluded family members who were more recent immigrants. Like policies governing immigration elsewhere, excluding people according to the time they entered an area proved fruitless. What was unclear in the original agreement was that subleasers, people who rented space to build tents in the small back yards of more substantial shanties, and those who were not registered in the census because they had been at work or had been gone when the survey was taken, were ineligible to move—or to stay.

In January 1980, many residents discovered that instead of year-long passes, they had received temporary permits good only for three months. People who rented rooms were disqualified for resettlement, and many moved to an adjoining squatter settlement known as KTC. Male workers could move back into the dormitories reminiscent of concentration camp lagers, where the bed was a shelf with a space underneath where a few pots and pans and other belongings could fit. Women would be deported to the Ciskei or Transkei.[68]

While the government appeared to be upgrading the housing for those in Crossroads, they were, in effect, attempting to exile large numbers of women to the homelands. By October 1980, the community was divided into New and Old Crossroads. Those who did move to the larger houses in New Crossroads were marginally better off than they had been in the squatter community. The new settlement offered a bucket for excrement, two beds, a dresser, a table, and a primus stove, all of which had to be shared by as many as twenty people. One such house served as home to nine women, four men, and eleven children.[69] Yet, it seemed palatial compared to old Crossroads. While the construction improved, dangers still lurked in the new community. Around 9 A.M. on August 11, 1980, the loudspeakers used by the Crossroads Committee called out: "If a member of your family left for work this morning via the Nyanga Bus Terminus, you should check if he is lying dead."[70]

Toward the end of 1980, the old Women's Committee of Crossroads began working again in the new settlement and succeeded in placing teachers in the new schools and in getting certain design changes. But, as one exasperated Women's Committee member argued, many of the women had become "Mrs. My-house," and the former solidarity began to melt away. So desperate were some women for the promised housing that they were willing to take the benefits Koornhof offered at their neighbor's expense. Many of those who qualified for New Crossroads eagerly moved there, abandoning former allies who the government claimed did not belong in Cape Town. Trying to recreate the solidarity, a small group of women launched a more formal organization, Nomzamo, to deal with issues that the male Executive Board was ignoring, such as residence permits. But Nomzamo lasted only six months before it too disappeared, demonstrating the difficulty that the women, now divided between New and old Crossroads, had in maintaining their organizational power.[71]

Meanwhile rents were rising, nowhere more so than in Cape Town.[72] In New Crossroads, rents had increased by 6 rand a year beginning in 1982 and rose to 29 rand plus water costs within a year. By refusing to pay rent to the community councilors who collected it for providing water, waste, and garbage removal, the local people attacked the only representatives of the South African state with whom they regularly came in contact. Rent strikes spread throughout South Africa beginning in September 1984, launching what one commentator called "a significant non-violent indication of black anger."[73]

As with other social movements, rent strikes raised broader social and economic claims: that the aged be permitted to remain in their homes rent free; that the state of emergency be lifted and political prisoners released; and that the army be removed from the squatters' communities.[74] Having begun with housing, women escalated their demands to ask for entitlement due them as human beings. Issues concerning housing and conditions in the townships erupted into a major social movement in South Africa between 1984 and 1986.

Antagonism also increased between men and women. When the streets in New Crossroads were laid out according to a grid pattern and named for men, a local woman complained, "It was the women who created Crossroads. When the pot was cooked, the men came to dish it up. They do not know from where the fire came and therefore cannot rekindle it."[75]

Trying to overcome antagonism between the sexes, the women tried to create community solidarity. On January 21, 1985, 169 local women, including Regina Ntongana, meeting in a local field to discuss participating in a rent strike, were arrested. Along with Johnson Ngxobongwana of the Executive Committee that ruled both old and New Crossroads, they were charged with participating in an "illegal gathering." In order to get the women released, the committee sought the bail money of 50 rand each, some of which later disappeared.[76]

Ngxobongwana, who vanished into police hands following his detention in January 1985, returned to Crossroads, where his own political trajectory converged with the disem-

powerment of the women as a political force. Ngoxbong-
wana's activities became increasingly suspicious. Seemingly a
mixture of beatings and promises from Security Forces persuaded Ngxobongwana to change sides and utilize for his
own benefit the power he had been building internally; from
July 1985 on, Ngxobongwana seemed to have police com-
pliance for everything he did. Yet resistance increased in all
the squatter camps, and by October, greater Cape Town was
once again under martial law, and activists were rounded
up.[77]

In exchange for protection and mediation of disputes in
a settlement where people dared not go to the police, Johnson Ngxobongwana and his supporters became a mafia, and
gained enormous power and wealth. Rival factions emerged,
and Ngxobongwana and his group began to wear pieces of
white cloth on their heads and legs, leading people to call
them, without irony, the "white ones" or *witdoeke* in
Afrikaans. Using terror tactics to reduce the power of rival
gangs, the *witdoeke* even kidnapped Regina Ntongana and
her husband, who increasingly disagreed with the direction
the Executive Committee was taking.[78]

Whenever the police arrested people, Ngxobongwana
and his rivals collected bail funds, portions of which they
pocketed before the trials actually took place. Local people
were coerced into paying these fees, which were more protection money than anything else. The daughters of a family who in March 1986 refused to contribute to one such
fund faced death by axes wielded by Ngxobongwana's faction. Women and some of the "comrades" or youth gangs
gathered for a meeting; following that, the house of one of
the actual attackers mysteriously burned down. Later, two
men on Ngxobongwana's side were found dead as the result
of ax wounds. Retaliation against the "white ones" supported by the police led to further violence in New Crossroads. Then Ngxobongwana disappeared again for several
months.[79]

The faction fights escalated and frequently amounted to
banditry supported by vendetta inside the squatter camps.

With the youth gangs generally supported by the women on one side and Ngxobongwana and his troops on the other, few could avoid the crossfire. One child, "Saliswa [Qasana] was living with her father when their house burned down during a faction fight and, in January 1986, she was caught in a street battle and her ankles were so severely bruised by a stick that she had to be hospitalized."[80] After that, she developed asthma, which was made worse by the stress and irritation of the tear gas that frequently spread over the settlement. Having lived at Crossroads since its founding, "tied on [her] mother's back . . . as [she] ran from the police across the dunes of Crossroads," the child had even been imprisoned with her mother.[81] Instead of improving, her life got worse and worse.

Despite the ruined lives, the government had not achieved its goals. Recognizing the failure of passes to impose their authority over all Coloured and black people, and facing increased opposition from industry which needed a more fluid labor supply, the South African government substituted a policy of "orderly urbanization." Carrying passes became unnecessary, but to remain in the cities one still had to show proof of an "approved" accommodation, a nearly impossible task since the government had never built houses for black people in the Cape.[82] With the help of Ngxobongwana and black vigilantes within Crossroads, the South African government did drive off many women and other undocumented residents of squatter communities throughout the late winter of 1985 and the spring of 1986, forcing them to flee to other camps or, in defeat, to retreat to the Bantustans.

When Winnie Nkosi, chairwoman of the Crossroads' branch of the United Women's Organization, was kidnapped along with two other women, the police did nothing. Accused of supporting the "comrades" in fighting "the fathers," as Ngxobongwana and his henchmen had begun to call themselves, the women were being reeled in.[83] Whatever the equally violent activities of the "comrades," the women fixed their attention on Ngxobongwana and his crew.

The violence came to a head in May and June 1986 in Crossroads and nearby townships. Between May 17 and June 12, the *witdoeke* invaded the settlements of KTC, Nyanga, and Portland Cement around Crossroads, burned down shanties, robbed between forty thousand and seventy thousand squatters of their homes, and injured approximately four thousand residents.[84] With the aid of the South African security forces who banned the press, Ngxobongwana and his henchmen carried on the forced removals the government was unable to accomplish. Thousands lost their homes, in which some had lived for decades.[85] In the aftermath, twenty-five hundred people or more were taken to Khayelitsha, government land about twenty miles from Crossroads, on which people were asked to start over from scratch, living in tents on unimproved sand dunes.

Many women remained undaunted. Guarded by the youthful "comrades," 150 women from Crossroads and its collateral settlements marched on Parliament in Cape Town and vowed never to move.[86] Mrs. Nolulamile Manqaba's ten-month-old son, who had been sleeping in a tent at the Full Gospel Church, died when the *witdoeke* and the police set the tent on fire. She and other witnesses charged that the police had not just stood by but had aided the vigilantes. And an editorial in the *Cape Times* argued that the violence at Crossroads and its neighboring camps was not simply faction fighting. They questioned whether the events could be seen as "a sophisticated counter-insurgency operation in which conservative vigilantes are mobilized by a 'dirty tricks' squad to act against the 'comrades' and at the same time drive Crossroads refugees from their place of refuge to Khayelitsha? Is this just a more than usually ruthless and callous type of forced removal, as some seem inclined to believe?" As usual in these demonstrations, authorities, hoping to avoid the gaze of the press, invited a small delegation of women to go to the government offices to make written statements.[87]

Human interest stories followed one another, as the media tried to intervene in what seemed to be a war against

African mothers. One of the women who lost her home was a widow named Emile Mkehle, who at thirty-five worked as a domestic to support her five children, ranging in age between three and ten. She shared a home with eighteen members of her family, wherever they could find people to shelter them. About five days after the attack, a relief worker found them and provided them with food, their first meal in thirty-six hours. Although it was unclear what Mrs. Mkehle and her family would do, "She was adamant that her family would not move to Khayelitsha."[88] Another woman, who just wanted to be called Patience, lost her home in KTC after the initial attack in mid-May. Working as a cleaning woman to support her thirteen-month-old baby and her eight-year-old child as a single mother, she had lived with her sister's family in a shack that was burned down. She was part of the delegation that marched to Parliament to demand new shelters. Having caught cold from living in the open during the Cape's damp and cold winter, the child was now in the hospital. Her mother was certain that she would not go to Khayelitsha. "I cannot go to Khayelitsha to live in a tent—those tents are too wet."[89]

The *witdoeke* burned down what remained of the community center at Crossroads in August 1986. Following this act of vandalism, 160 women, claiming to be from all parts of Crossroads, demonstrated. Their march on the Nyanga Community Service office on August 19, 1986, was a protest against the barbed-wire fences that had been put up around their homes in Old Crossroads, to which they wished to return. Under press lights, carrying babies on their backs, the women milled around the offices that had previously served as headquarters of the Western Cape Development Board. After an hour, Mr. Nicky Schelhase came out to tell the women what they already knew: that the divisional commissioner of police was forbidding them to return to their homes. They were told that Schelhase would meet only with a small delegation of women the next day, if they agreed to choose representatives to speak with him.[90] Finally, the battle for Crossroads seemed to have come to an end.

As early as the late seventies, Mrs. Regina Ntongana had lamented about their persecution: "What is wrong with us? Why are they killing us? We blacks can also think. Our hair might be short outside, but our brains are long."[91] But even in August 1986, the women were not entirely defeated, and they learned from their experiences. In their efforts to occupy space from which they were barred, they asserted a sense of entitlement that overcame their diffidence about their abilities to make political decisions, intervene in governing processes, and even assume leadership positions in movements for political change.

The destruction of old Crossroads, which had functioned from 1975 until 1986, when many of the first inhabitants, including Mrs. Ntongana, were driven out, displayed the ends to which the government was willing to go to drive black people from Cape Town. The fact that ordinary women were able to create a sense of community identity and wring a sense of justice out of a social system that sought to bury them alive reveals certain new possibilities for democracy. In their struggles for urban housing, they helped establish new criteria for justice, standards that combined democracy with social need.

7

Surplus People and Grassroots Women's Leadership in the New South Africa

REGINA NTONGANA DOES NOT FIT a textbook definition of a leader. In fact, though her gift seems to be for belonging, she has reflected about what it means to lead. In her lilting, Xhosa-accented voice, she says the grassroots are like a bundle of clothing, all in different colors. What gives them shape is the wire over which they dry. The clothesline is the leader.[1]

Grassroots struggles at first seem inevitable, spontaneous, and un-self-conscious. They gain force from a sense of urgency that drives participants to disregard authority, often appealing to some higher moral law. But to propel themselves, grassroots movements have to gain incremental power best distributed democratically. As both a garment and a wire, Ntongana's authority comes from knowing every facet of a campaign, from helping to define a problem, to calculating the effect of certain kinds of demonstrations, to knowing what demands can be won in the short run and which must be organized over a long time. The immediate gains are important to her, as they are to the women with whom she gets involved. She has a talent for bringing out the creativity in others.

Like Dollie Burwell, who speaks about service, Ma would certainly say that she enjoys helping people. Ntongana is impatient with leaders who claim to know what people want without asking them, saying, "You can't build nothing if you are not interested in people from the grassroots." Ma enjoys engaging people and watching them decide things for themselves.

Ntongana's views about politics are intrinsically tied up with her experiences working with women. Seemingly isolated and incapable of overcoming either the government or local men, women of Crossroads frequently drew on women from outside the community. Such individual women and women's groups helped them learn to use the media to win public support for their cause. From the beginning of their struggle in 1975, the Crossroads' women had sought for and received support from the Black Sash through its Advice Office. Respectful of the difficulty homeless women had feeding, nurturing, and educating their children and their strong drive to enable their families and community to survive, the Black Sash, though focusing its attention on political rights, attempted to help the women it served in the squatter communities.[2] Mostly upper-middle-class white women, including the wife of the deputy director of the *Cape Times*, Sashers had access to the press, whom they alerted about the situation of Crossroads' women.[3]

Trying the new, hoping for the best, and attempting to forget the past is the ethos of survival in the new South Africa. Yet there are things even Regina Ntongana cannot forget, and some of them lie with Crossroads itself and with the origins of the Surplus People Project as a service organization serving the Western Cape. Founded by Ntongana, Josette Cole, and Lala Stein in 1986 as part of the National Land Committee, the organization took its place alongside other community groups fighting for squatters' rights. The odd name of the organization comes from the South African government's unconscious appropriation of the Marxist concept of "surplus value." According to Marx, the difference between the value workers create on their shift and the lesser time they would have to work to replenish themselves, to repay the depreciation on the tools and factories, and pay for the raw materials creates "surplus value," which results in profits for the owners. The white South African government coined the phrase "surplus people" for black women and children. Since the regime did not need most women and children to work for wages, they were "surplus people." The government tried to expel Mrs. Ntongana and millions of other women from urban areas all over South Africa and to send them to the wastelands called Bantustans or, euphemistically, Homelands. The resistance at Crossroads became emblematic of all those people throughout South Africa who would not be moved—and those who supported them.

If the watchword for Dollie Burwell is "social justice," the term synonymous with democracy in South Africa in the nineties is "social citizenship." "Social citizenship" entails economic and social rights conceived as human rights, among which one of the most important is decent housing. Mrs. Ntongana and her co-worker at the Surplus Peoples Project, Irene "Mawushe" Narwele, understand democracy in these social terms because of their experiences as squatters and as members of the women's committee at Crossroads. In order to preserve their homes, gain water, and get the sewage and other garbage collected, they needed to have a say. They organized to protect and preserve the shacks that they had built, and to improve their families' lives. For these women and others who have waged similar campaigns, participatory democracy, by which they and not authorities or professional bureaucrats decide how to achieve social and economic goals, is necessary for "social citizenship."

Josette Cole thinks so, too. Cole is a white South African who at thirteen emigrated to Toronto, Canada, with her family. She returned to South Africa in her twenties, six months before the student uprising in Soweto in 1976 that ended with the government massacre of five hundred black schoolchildren. She decided to fight for an end to apartheid or leave South Africa for good, and volunteered as a field representative for the Provincial Council of Churches. Slightly built, soft-spoken, but forceful and determined, she quickly became involved with the women at Crossroads and with women elsewhere in Cape Town who actively resisted the government's relocation policies. She had been a feminist and a Christian socialist in her student days in Toronto and now began attending the regular Friday morning meetings of the Cape Flats Committe for Interum Accommodation, organized in 1978 by various church groups supporting Crossroads.[4] Respectful, even awed by the clarity of women like Regina Ntongana, Cole became a participant observer: as she worked to abolish apartheid, she also committed herself to expressing the voices of the women who were refusing to obey influx-control laws.

Another regular participant in the Friday meetings supporting the people at Crossroads was Laurine Platzky. Platzky grew up as the daughter of a politically active widow, toddled to demonstrations against apartheid, and became the first woman elected president of the Student Representative Council of the University of Cape Town in 1972. She grew up protesting against apartheid, and she realized immediately that forced removals of squatter communities had become a linchpin of that detested system.

Josette Cole, Regina Ntongana, and Laurine Platzky met and found themselves to be kindred spirits. The two younger white women were driven to fight against apartheid as Mrs. Ntongana already had. Platzky mobilized students to publicize the way the government was persecuting women and robbing them of their South African citizenship by declaring them citizens of the Bantustans and maintaining that these wastelands under puppet governments were separate nations. In *We Will Not Move*, which Platzky helped get published under the auspices of the National Union of South African Students in 1978,[5] the voices of Mrs. Ntongana and the other women who proclaimed their rights to protect the homes they had built with their own hands could be heard in all their richness and passion. Beginning in 1980 Platzky, along with Cherryl Walker, now one of the foremost historians of women in South Africa, sociologist Jacqueline Cock, anthropologist Sheila Meintjes, and about fifty other volunteers nationwide carried out research on the effects of apartheid's land settlement policies on people of color all over the country. In 1983, the consortium began publishing volumes dealing with the regional impact of the governments' land policies, and in 1985 the group published *Surplus People*.[6] The Surplus People Project, a separate local organization that works on housing and land issues only in the Western Cape, followed in 1986. Until 1995, Josette Cole served as coordinator and general strategist and Regina Ntongana as a member of the Community Work Unit of the regional organization.

An autodidact, Regina Ntongana, who went to school for only three years, speaks three languages: Xhosa, English, and Afrikaans. She is a grassroots leader of the kind who can build a shack; can carry water long distances for washing, cooking, and drinking; and can confront authorities, challenging their assessments of her rights. Along with tens of thousands of others, she participated in a movement that challenged existing authority, undermined business profits, and contributed to the government's cancellation of the hated influx-control laws that forced black Africans to carry passes in their own country. Ma transfers the skills she developed as a member of the community at Crossroads into the work she does at the Surplus People Project. Ma is happiest when she is helping women do as she and Mawushe did—assess the situation, take a stand, work out concrete plans for securing support from local authorities, and see women empowered to take control. Yet she recognizes the skills of people such as her good friend Josette Cole.

Josette Cole is a dedicated strategist, determined to help create the kind of grassroots democracy and social justice that have eluded people in South Africa. While, in Mrs. Ntongana's words, Cole "gives herself over to the people," she also tries to analyze the possibilities that can result from efforts to help women regain rights over housing and land. Cole's article and book on Crossroads, finished just before the final battle for Crossroads and its collateral settlements at KTC, Nyanga, and Portland Cement, are essential reading for anyone concerned with the development of consciousness among poor women yearning for better housing and a responsive government.[7]

As a participant observer who periodically goes back to university to hone her skills in urban planning and economic history, Cole is one of the main chroniclers of the evolution of the Crossroads struggle as a political movement. Her reflections about the place of women in the community's struggle and her skill at hearing the voices of the women involved contribute to her ability to write about social history from within.

Among the services Josette Cole's writing has performed has been to introduce Regina Ntongana to readers who would otherwise not know her. In detailing the lives of individual women such as Ntongana, written in their own words, Cole shows how intrinsic the government's treatment of women was to the maintenance of apartheid. Even more significant, her works underscore how the exclusion of women marked an aspect of the decline of democracy in the self-government of local communities such as Crossroads. The confidence Cole gained from being a participant enables her to recognize and analyze feminist issues that other critics overlook. Boswell to Mrs. Ntongana's Dr. Johnson, Cole remains close friends with Ntongana.

Mrs. Ntongana and Mawushe now live in New Crossroads, which, though merely a mile a way from their former homes in old Crossroads, occupies another world. After the climactic days of Crossroads, Ma was in danger of being killed. For a while, she and her husband hid out with Laurine Platzky. Finally, Ma and her husband moved to New Crossroads, a development of modest brick two-room houses.

As field workers for the Surplus People Project, Mawushe and Ma provide training to women who have seized the initiative in their own struggles to achieve self-determination and decent housing. Though not all feminists, the staff of the Surplus People Project share a fundamental belief in women's intrinsic importance to creating democracy. Building informal democratic institutions to expand women's self-governing networks concerned with maintaining a high quality of everyday life is one of the issues to which the organization is committed. But at no time have the founders and staff of the Surplus People Project tried to supersede local organizations.

The Surplus People Project holds staff meetings on gender sensitivity. Mikki van Zyl, the "gender facilitator," ran these training sessions in 1993 in an effort to get male and female staff members to recognize the importance of gender equality to all the work the organization does: helping create democracy in South Africa. At one session, Mikki encouraged people to imagine a woman and her life—and to try to write down the time she spends on preparing food, working for wages, watching television, caring for kids, and relaxing. Then the group of two men and six women from the staff of about twenty tried to figure out how the woman they had imagined—frequently herself in the women's case—got through the day, with all the competing demands placed on her.

Mrs. Ntongana and Mawushe exuberantly entered into the role playing, the next task in the gender sensitivity training, as the middle-class participants squirmed. Mikki was not surprised, saying that poor and working people generally enjoy the play-acting more than other folks. The women were united, however, in nervous laughter mixed with jokes they tried to mute to avoid insulting the two men present.[8]

At the Surplus People Project office, Ma and Mawushe spend a lot of time on the phones, speaking in Xhosa, which animates them and gives a passion to their voices that even someone ignorant of the language can appreciate. Women's committees from different localities hear about the organization and call to find out how to get a lawyer, how to file papers giving themselves control over houses they have built, how to get a creche or child-care center started. Sometimes a delegation of women comes to the office.

Athlone, where the office is located, looks like East Los Angeles. Both urban areas are ethnic neighborhoods within white cities, neighborhoods that express the lives of racial minorities with Moslem Indians and mixed-race "Coloureds" predominating in Athlone and Mexican-Americans in East Los Angeles. Athlone combines residential neighborhoods with low-slung buildings and five-story tenements etched against high mountains, while East Los Angeles consists of run-down, two-story garden apartments and small individual houses, with flowers and tomato plants growing in the front yards. Both neighborhoods center on vital commercial areas in which the smell of spicy food cooking on open fires adds to the sharpness of the bright colors arrayed in the nearby stores. Few white tourists venture to either place, although the vitality of the local people and the variety of the food and markets are what tourists often think they crave.

Both areas seem inaccessible without cars; Cape Town resembles Los Angeles in its urban sprawl and bad public transportation. Unlike East Los Angeles, however, downtown Athlone lies along a commuter railroad track, making it possible for people from Cape Town's squatter communities and townships to come shopping or to pass through on the way to jobs in the white sections of town on the other side of the mountains. The Cape Town trains, largely used by black people, are cavernous, slow, and dirty, designed as they are to accommodate large numbers of standing bodies crushed in at rush hour as people try to get in from the townships and squatter settlements to jobs they feel lucky to have in the city. The other means of public transportation are minibuses, called taxis or "combis," that squeeze in up to sixteen Indian, Coloured, and black people in jump seats and on each other's laps. Combis run along main streets, picking up people and dropping them off along the way.

Mawushe and Ma, like grassroots versions of horse-and-buggy doctors, practice democracy by paying house calls. They usually travel to outlying communities on the metropolitan trains and combis. Advising local women is the part of their jobs they seem to like best, though it also is the most demanding. They deeply believe, as Ma says, that "even in our own townships—we are the people. We are the ANC. We are the government."9

One of the communities where she and Mawushe work is Malmesbury, about sixty miles north of Cape Town, in the midst of the beautiful, hilly orchards of the Western Cape. The history of the Western Cape lies in these hills, where Africans had farmed before their land was taken from them and they were turned into farm laborers and then migrants. At the nearby factories, male farm and cannery workers lived in barracks called hostels from which women and children were excluded. The women and children associated with the men followed them to the gates of Malmesbury beginning in the early eighties, much as Mrs. Ntongana and Mawushe had gone to Crossroads. Literally millions of South African blacks, having been pushed off the land they farmed, have migrated as homeless people to enormous squatter settlements on golf courses, in parks, on sand dunes, and around factories. Mawushe views property with an eye to building shacks. When Mawushe was invited along with other community activists to tea at the home of Bishop Desmond Tutu, who, as Anglican archbishop of Cape Town, lived in a palatial home owned by the church, Mawushe wickedly told him that several hundred families could comfortably live there; he was taken aback until she laughed her deep and hearty laugh.[10]

With no place else to go, single women looking for work and the women and children related to the men in the hostels camped outside the locked gates of the Malmesbury cannery, living in the surrounding reeds and mud, in rain and sun, just beyond the signs that prohibited them from entering the fenced compound. The men sneaked food, water, and mattresses out to their families. The women periodically tried to come into the compound, and they were repeatedly arrested.

The women, though drawn from different places, generally spoke Xhosa. More than five hundred women, sharing subhuman conditions living out of doors, gradually welded themselves into a community in the eighties and nineties. Even though influx-control laws that prohibited black women from living in the Cape ended in 1986, the company and the municipality still refused to allow the women to join their husbands within the compound: the company remained a law unto itself, and the city government regarded black women squatters as outsiders, undeserving of the rights of local citizens. Putting themselves in danger rather than have the men lose their jobs, the women tried to create homes for themselves and their children in shacks they built outside the gates.

In a particularly dramatic demonstration in 1987, the men carried mattresses into the surrounding field while women distracted the guards. When the police came in and tried to drive the women out, they fought back. One woman went into labor and delivered her baby in the ensuing melee. In one of those historical moments that has already become mythologized, the women tore down the gates and began to erect shacks within the company compound. As with all squatter settlements, the more than five hundred fifty households established inside as well as outside the old gates lacked sewage and water. From the women's perspective, the municipality should have provided water spigots, outdoor toilets, and electrical hookups on cement slabs on which they could construct their dwellings. The municipality preferred simply to drive them away.

Finally, in September 1989, the women learned that the town, claiming the women presented a health hazard, planned to evict them by December. Rather than submit, the women raised some money and sent a delegation to Athlone to speak to the Surplus People Project. The group helped the squatters organize meetings so that everyone in the settlement could have their say. As in Crossroads, the women took the initiative. In addition to sites with water hookups and electrical lines, the women wanted stands at the bus stop where they could sell prepared food to earn money. The Surplus People Project called in lawyers, who negotiated with the local authorities in Malmesbury, and the municipality tentatively agreed to permit the women to stay within the gates. But when negotiations bogged down, the police again raided the community.

The women remained, however, and painted over the signs forbidding them to be there, laid out their village, and named the streets, giving the shacks street numbers. Although established inside the compound, the women still lacked basic amenities. The hostels had only a few toilets, which were not even sufficient for the men who originally lived there. Women had to carry water great distances for cleaning and cooking. Once the women established their rights to be on the land, they wanted the same social services any other citizen got. They organized a demonstration, and with the support of local community groups, they marched to the civic center of Malmesbury and demanded that the town include them in its benefits.

During the period when the women fought to remain at the Malmesbury compound, they marched to the town clerk's office and demanded services. A committee negotiated with the municipal authorities for more than a year and finally, in December 1992, won an agreement that the town would supply 550 sites with water taps, toilets, and underground electrical connections. The women also demanded a creche or child-care facility, a clinic, and a small sewing factory to provide jobs.

Looking at the hamlet from the barnlike community center the women and men constructed, what stands out are the yellow huts seemingly woven together by the clothes lines covered with garments of all colors and sizes. Mrs. Ntongana seems to regard a woman named Maggie as the local leader. Maggie, who dresses Northern-style, in a plain skirt and blouse, apparently started the fad for canary yellow houses when she went down to the road and took a can of paint that a road crew painting lines down the highway had left overnight. Sheets of corrugated iron make up the walls of the shack, covered inside with newspapers to keep out the wind. On the walls hang ANC posters and calendars. Inside her tiny living room, Maggie has a set of pots scoured so finely that they resemble Dutch pewter in seventeenth-century paintings: you can see your face reflected on the surfaces. Filling the tiny space is a couch, a chair, a portable stereo cassette player, and speakers running from the one wire that serves as power source for the entire community. The kitchen, really a tiny alcove with a hot plate—there is no running water and no refrigerator—has a small table. The bedroom, filled by a chest of drawers and a double bed with a cotton bedspread, shows the work of an assiduous housekeeper.

Even the land around the shacks shows the handiwork of the women of Malmesbury. Mawushe admires their achievements: "These women, they are growing vegetables . . . But women themselves have had to make that soil better. They throw those tins [tin cans] in, and then they cover [them] with soil. And now they sow different kinds of fresh vegetables like carrots, beet roots, and onions. And now they showed me that production. It's rocky soil. Now they get big potatoes from that iron, that zinc, [those] rusty tins. People must be clever enough. They must be making more soil so that it will be filled with iron. We don't have money to buy these fertilizers, so they just come up with ideas."

Ma, Mawushe, and Mikki van Zyl traveled to the settlement for a meeting to discuss making a video and designing T-shirts commemorating the storming of the gates. As the women drew up to the compound in Mikki's beat-up gray car, they saw the settlement women gathered in front of the meeting hall, sitting on wooden folding chairs, enjoying the winter sun against whose rays they had protected their skin with dabs of white zinc ointment. The community center consists of a wooden shed with three rows of benches and about a dozen wooden folding chairs, and four plastic seats. In July 1993 the walls were covered with instructions about how to vote in the national elections, which were still nine months away.

On the stage with two women from the community, Mawushe acted as coordinator, speaking in Xhosa. She began with hymns, sung in rounds. Then about fifty women, some with babies wrapped up in bundles, sang in their seats and danced in the aisles. The clacking of their tongues, which makes Xhosa sound like it comes with castanets, was accentuated by snapping fingers. The energy pulsated through the room, undisturbed by the occasional infant crying.

Then the business began. When attention turned to the T-shirt design, one woman, dressed traditionally in a bandanna and long wrap-around skirt, but wearing two rhinestone earrings of red and blue, lifted her shirt and sweater to show a T-shirt that said "Freedom to Trespass." On the back was another statement: "The Land Belongs to the People." The women laughed contentedly. One mother nuzzled her six-month old infant dressed in a red velvet shirt. Another woman shouted, "From Apartheid to Freedom," and several women pinched each other's arms demonstrating their agreement about the T-shirt slogan.

Then Mikki van Zyl got up to discuss the video itself. Mikki, a white woman in her thirties, comes out of the feminist movement and South Africa's counterculture of the late eighties. She stands about six inches taller than Mawushe and about a foot taller than Mrs. Ntongana and most of the other women. Of Afrikaner descent, she speaks English and Afrikaans, but not Xhosa, so Mawushe had to translate for her. Mikki invited the women to make stick figure drawings of how they thought they had looked living outside the compound. She asked the women to imagine their new homes. A group of women agreed to play parts in the video and were excited about their debut as actresses.

The purpose of the video was to cement the women's solidarity, to enhance the community's historical memories of what they had already accomplished, and to enable them to consolidate their power so that they would remain a cohesive group for the elections the following April.

The elections, of course, only re-introduced questions about social citizenship and the degree to which, along with the right to vote, democracy entails social and economic rights such as child-care facilities, health-care clinics, and access to land on which to live and grow food.

Reminiscent of the video *Exodus* that Ma and her friends had made about their struggles at Crossroads, *The Women*

Who Didn't Turn Back (*Abafazi: Amangajikiyo*) finished in March 1994, a month before the election, was both an historical reconstruction and a program for action. As the workbook that accompanies the bilingual video says, "Of the people elected onto the committee representing the community, the number of women has steadily diminished."[11] Mawushe and others at the Surplus People Project are worried that now that the men no longer need the women to protect them against reprisals, the women are being shut out of decision-making. Mawushe says, "Women themselves must be part of what is happening in that negotiating." What is apparent is that certain issues remain prominent only when women are on the committees governing the settlement. For example, the women have elected a committee to look into the possibility of a child-care center. Although there is an ANC in Malmesbury and the women hold the party in great esteem, they don't expect the ANC to involve itself in everything important to them. Making the video was a way to re-ignite the women's faith in themselves and the issues with which they were concerned.[12]

To prepare the script, the women divided into workshops. In addition to deciding what key events they would depict and drawing them, the women discussed their hopes for the future and drew pictures of their imaginary lifestyle. Wearing turquoise T-shirts as costumes, the women acted out skits from the history of their movement. From the women's individual drawings, an artist from the Surplus People Project prepared a composite of the women's aspirations as they spoke of them in their workshops. One woman wanted a house where she would "plant a tree for shade on a sunny day, and a lawn with green grass, and flowers on a footpath from the doorway to the gate." She drew her neighbor's house with clothes on the lines. One woman wanted a house with a bed, a cat, an electric lamp, a kitchen table, and cups on the table. Another wanted chickens and pigs, and, "if God is on my side, to have a car."

What figured in the drawings were also a creche, a school, a hospital, a playground, and even a soccer field with parking facilities. One woman depicted her neighbor "taking soup to our children at school." The drawings showed two schools, a primary school and a high school in which the main language would be Xhosa. The other public facilities for which the women yearned were a hospital with gurneys and beds for the patients, and, most poignant of all, "an old age home with trees and chairs for the old people to sit in the sun . . . and Xhosa nurses to care for them."

Mixed in with the aspirations for public services and improved living conditions was the wish for a place for initiation ceremonies and a hut for the initiates. One woman drew a white flag to "show respect because the boy is now a man." The commitments to past rituals combined with aspirations to gain modern improvements such as hospitals and creches is indicative of the hopes for social citizenship—or social justice—in the New South Africa.

On the opposite periphery of Cape Town, the women who live in Nordhoek suffer similar problems and hopes. Malmesbury's people are part of the massive rural migration that resulted from the reduction of black land rights, but Nordhoek arose from gentrification and urban renewal in Cape Town and the resort area of Vish Hoek. While few people speak of forced removals in South Africa and urban renewal projects in the United States in the same breath, blatant similarities exist. What the two processes share is the willingness to redraw urban maps as if they represented patterns on paper instead of people's neighborhoods.

Focusing on spectacular views and access to the sea—as well as consolidating racial settlements—governments in both South Africa and the United States have supported developers and forced people from their homes in sections viewed as run-down and unworthy of repair. Projects to improve harbor areas such as the Harbor View development at Greenpoint in Cape Town meant destroying instead of improving a poor neighborhood in 1987 in order to introduce a series of malls with shops, restaurants, and bars. Such shopping centers, catering to tourists and affluent whites, proliferated in both South Africa and the United States in the eighties and nineties, as the South Sea Seaport in New York City and the Baltimore and Boston harbor developments attest. In order to clear the way in what were once stable working-class sections with run-down areas on their outskirts, poorer citizens were forced to move. Governments, which promoted such projects to develop commercial land, took no responsibility for where those displaced went. In some cases in the United States, gentrification of previously modest sections of cities forced rents so high that even people who had lived in the same neighborhoods all their lives could no longer afford to stay. If they did remain, they lived on the streets, contributing to what beginning in the eighties was viewed as the homeless problem.

In South Africa, specific attempts to separate the races led to the dissolution in the early seventies of neighborhoods such as District 6, where people of all colors had lived together, creating a rich, bohemian, artistic culture. People whom the police moved from downtown neighborhoods such as Greenpoint wound up in some of the same places as those who had been pushed off agricultural land in the countryside: in squatters' settlements, lacking shops, health care, and public transportation. As Regina Ntongana sees it, "If you miss the morning combi, you walk. If people get sick at night, you walk." Like most rapidly growing megalopoli, Cape Town spread out to include formerly outlying towns, making provision of improved public transportation into a major social demand.

Leaving Athlone at the relatively untraveled hour of 11 A.M., you meander through South Africa's recent urban history. The train from Athlone ends at Vish Hoek, a part of the greater Cape Town area on the Indian Ocean. Most poor people were forcibly removed from homes at Vish Hoek to make way for the development of a tourist industry there. From Vish Hoek you take a taxi or combi more than five miles up a hill, passing luxurious vacation homes, to get to the sandy bluff off the main road where Nordhoek is located and where those displaced from Greenpoint and Vish Hoek ended up as squatters. One of the many contradictions of South Africa is the sheer beauty of the impractical places poor people have to live. But while rich white people in Los Angeles and South Africa live on mountaintops and in canyons, they shield themselves from the elements with air conditioning, heating, and relatively solid homes, where electricity and clean, running water abound. They own the land under their houses; not so for the people in Nordhoek.

When we visited in the July winter of 1993, the people in Nordhoek were suffering the indignities of wind and floods. Left on high sand dunes, buffeted by the wind, flooded out in the winter, and scorched in the summer, the people in Nordhoek lacked solid dwellings, water, sewage, or schools. Mrs. Ntongana worked with them in their efforts to come together to create a community where they could sustain their lives. What the women wanted during the last days of apartheid were corrugated iron plates they called "zincs" to construct sturdy temporary housing.

The government had sent rolls of black plastic (from which garbage bags were generally made) for people to use to build tents to shelter themselves from the howling wind in Nordhoek. One woman, crouching as she washed clothes in a metal pan, told Ma the news about the scant building materials the government had provided and sent her in to talk to her mother-in-law, Winnie. Gathering in the relatively sturdy house of Winnie, a woman in her forties or fifties who had become the group leader of the settlement, women recounted meetings they had had with authorities and then the indignity of the arrival of the black, garbage-bag material Winnie and the other women referred to as "plastics." The wind was howling outside and everything was coated in sand. The women told how the wind had blown the roof off of a shanty they were using as a child-care center, and women ran to save the children. One woman got the kids into a metal container local people sometimes used for meetings just as a tree fell on top of the shack where the children had been. Another shack had recently gone up in flames when the wind blew over the gas burner local people use to cook their food. Nevertheless, the women talked about future meetings, as Mrs. Ntongana discussed what they must do next. At the end of the meeting, walking away disgusted once again by the government's lack of attention to poor black people, Ma muttered, "They want them to eat sand."[13]

Returning a year later with Ma was like acting a part in a propaganda film. In July 1994 following the South African elections in April, sounds of hammering mixed with South African rock 'n' roll coming from portable tape boxes that seemed to be everywhere. As Mrs. Ntongana walked through the unpaved streets, she stopped to talk in Xhosa to a man who was rolling something resembling clay in his hands. When they switched to English, Mrs. Ntongana introduced the man, who was the local ANC leader. Asked if he was a potter, he said no, he was softening putty for his new windows. He pointed back to his shack, to which he had added a precarious second story—complete with a large space for a picture window.

Walking around the neighborhood, Mrs. Ntongana stopped to talk to everyone, as if she were a visiting dignitary or a beloved aunt who had come home for a reunion. People were hammering on their own houses, painting them pastel colors, making cinder-block additions; everywhere, they were adding windows. Apart from the solidity of the settlement that July winter in contrast with the bleakness of the place the year before, the windows indicated a degree of confidence that few in crime-ridden South African squatter communities would have considered a year earlier.

After admiring changes, Ma visited the just completed clinic, which provides free prenatal and child care as well as other general medical services, then checked on how the community center and its dining room were progressing. Both structures were built with aid from abroad—from Sweden and Canada—since the South African government lacked the resources to carry out building development on a large scale during the first years of its rule.

After surveying the changes—which seemed like a Golden Book on enterprise and activity—Mrs. Ntongana found Winnie, who continues to convene a lot of the committees that govern the settlement. Sitting in Winnie's house, with its old but comfortable couch and chairs squeezed into a small space, Mrs. Ntongana conferred with Winnie and other women about local conditions—the lack of sewage or water in the houses of the shanties of the new immigrants at the edge of the neighborhood; the floods that had inundated various sections.

Some people tensed when a young woman in uniform came to the door. Addressing Winnie in a patronizing way, she spoke as if to a child or someone who was mentally incompetent, "Winnie, that meeting, are we going to have it this evening?" "Yes, we can have it," Winnie replied. "Are you sure?" the uniformed woman went on, as if she hadn't heard the reply. "So it's all right for this evening, 6 o'clock? Are you sure? O.K., at the creche tonight 6 o'clock?"

When the officer was gone, Mrs. Ntongana, Winnie, and the other women who had come and gone carrying babies returned to speaking in Xhosa. Ma later explained that the recent immigrants in the newer section of Nordhoek had been flooded out again in the heavy, cold rains. "The police came with clothes and food and everything. . . . They were spending nights here with the people, trying to pull them out."[14]

"When the floods wiped out some of the shacks a few weeks before, the police helped," Ma explained. That overcame some of the local people's hostility toward the authorities. The meeting scheduled for that night was to try to establish more formal connections between local community leaders and the police. Despite Ma's own unhappy relations with police and soldiers of the old South African government, she was willing to wipe the slate clean. Maintaining an optimistic view about the possibilities of constructing new democratic organizations and institutions is what the New South Africa is all about.

Nothing has been more gratifying to Ntongana than her return to work in Crossroads. Although her home in New Crossroads is scarcely a mile from her old home, she had not returned to the settlement, which new arrivals had begun re-filling after its initial destruction in 1986. Ma ordinarily would no more have crossed into that territory than a gang member in Chicago would have penetrated into some other gang's turf. So it was an odd Sunday in June of 1994 when she went for a walk in her old neighborhood.

"While I was walking along the street, I was thinking they are so dirty," she recalls. Then she ran into some women she knew. "The women, they were crazy when they saw me, and they asked me to have a chat with them. And I can see women are falling apart now. The street was so dirty. The toilets were blocked. Everything was just broke." The women claimed that they wanted Ma to help them organize themselves, but she said, "It wasn't clear that people had a good attendance." Two days later she returned for a meeting, this time with Mawushe, who also lives in New Crossroads. The women talked about creating a creche, but they planned to begin with a demonstration about cleaning up the refuse in the neighborhood. As Ma explained it, "They want to stand up, and they want to raise their voices."[15]

Being a strategist of grassroots movements, Ma counseled the women of Crossroads to elect delegates and have them come to the Surplus People Project office. Like the women of Malmesbury, those from Crossroads were having problems making their voices heard during the transition following the April 1994 elections. Having won the right to vote, the black women still had economic and social issues to resolve. In an effort to improve squatters' control over their living space, the ANC government had provided for people to buy their own homes. But the prices were often too high and the terms of the arrangements too difficult to master. What's more, many of the women and men were illiterate, so rumors about what was going on took the place of facts about legislation. Ma called the situation "unhealthy." She knows the problem from the inside: "People now must buy the houses. . . . They've got an ANC [chapter] organizing it, but it doesn't take their issues up. So that's why the people are worried. But the group wants to stand up for their own issues. They are the people suffering. They are oppressed. There are no leaders. Now it depends on the people."

When she speaks of "the people," Ma usually means women. Fierce commitment to democracy has been a hallmark of the women's movements she has known in South Africa, and Ma can't separate women's control over their own living situations from democracy. After sticking together through Crossroads, Ma and her husband had split up, and he died a few years ago. She has a son to whom she is devoted and a daughter devoted to her. But she is one of those heterosexual women in South Africa and elsewhere who presume a consensus among women about the inadequacy of men. When I asked Ma if she was a feminist, since she works primarily with women and has suffered some of the worst indignities male leaders can inflict, she stopped for a moment. Then she looked up at me and said, deliberately: "I am a Christian, and therefore I believe God has a reason for everything." Then she hesitated, waited a few beats, and added: "He must have had some reason for creating men."[16] This kind of essentialist view that presumes that all men share single social and psychological characteristics prevents women from making the same demands on men they make on women. But it also views men as somehow less capable of changing, of growing, of participating in truly new democratic institutions.

Democracy takes on a lot of meanings for Mrs. Ntongana and others in South Africa. For black South Africans and their allies, the hopes for the first democratic elections of April 1994 entailed what became known as "social citizenship": housing, health care, schools, jobs, transportation, and security were intrinsic parts of what black South Africans hoped to achieve. There was bound to be disappointment during the transition, the end of which no one can predict.

Josette Cole has moved on. Back to school and actively engaged first with the constitutional reform process to include social and economic rights in the new Bill of Rights, Cole has also worked on the Research Development Program, which was to plan the economic and social development of South Africa into the next century. Cole moves between her pleasures as a participant observer and analyst and her abilities as an administrator. Unlike many who become central to institutions, Cole has very little ego invested in being a leader. For her, helping displaced people establish themselves in homes is only a piece of the broader struggle for social justice. She is not interested in being part of an ongoing organization if its needs conflict with moving further toward defining new economic and social rights.[17]

For Regina Ntongana, the process of consolidation, of building the New South Africa, as it is half ironically called, is another phase of struggle. While some people who are transforming squatter communities into permanent settlements are frustrated with the changing regulations and tired of struggling, Ma sees things differently. She didn't even mind the outbreak of strikes following the 1994 elections, as the union movement tried to assure that it wouldn't be overlooked in the process of forming new social relations. Ma spoke in favor of strikes: "To me, the strike is to speak with somebody who don't listen to you—to show, 'I want this' . . . to make it clear, 'I want this.' They want things to be clear, to be spelled out. . . . They want everything to be finalized, especially the Constitution and the new laws, and they want everything—especially to have their voices [heard]. I appreciate it. I like it very much."[18]

Conclusion:
Social Movements and Democratic Practices

IN A NOVEL CHRONICLING THE BREAKUP of a marriage, an es-
tranged husband asks his wife why, if she's so wonderful, he
feels so bad. After reading about these new women of courage
who are transforming hopes for democracy, many of you may
wonder with a sigh why you are so pessimistic, when they are
so hopeful. Are these women merely crazy optimists whose
commitments to the possibilities of governing lives through a
new system of justice fail to affect the rest of us?

What impact could local associations that are so idealis-
tic and nearly invisible have on "real" politics, where elected
officials run governments and negotiate with other governments at every level? If democracy refers merely to political
campaigns and voting rituals organized by professionals, and
conflicts get resolved only according to the dictates of power
and property ownership, can there be any hope of transforming society to assure its benefits for all? Lois Gibbs,
Luella Kenny, Dollie and Kim Burwell, Regina Ntongana,
and Josette Cole think so. They believe in justice and think
they can achieve it through the introduction of new ethical
values.

These women have had the experience of righting
wrongs, of securing justice by working with people face to
face, and they have created informal organizations and loose
networks to keep their gains and teach others how to win
their collective rights. Also, having coordinated their activi-

ties with people in other regions and countries, they know that their experiences of local control are compatible with solving national and international problems. The injunction of the Third World Conference on Women held in Nairobi in 1985 under United Nations auspices to "Think Globally and Organize Locally" has become a powerful slogan for ordinary women throughout the world. Without writing down what they are doing and without contacting professional politicians and experts for advice about how to achieve their aims, poor and working-class women have been extending their reach beyond local grievances to express broad democratic goals.

Whether or not we have participated in mass acts of civil disobedience or faced down officials who were trying to destroy our homes, we can learn a lot about democracy from these poor and working-class women. Most Americans consider democracy abstractly without knowing or even imagining what it means to fight for it on a daily basis. Yet preoccupations with their own brand of direct democracy—meaning equal access to decision-making processes that enable everyone, regardless of sex, race, class, or ethnicity, to negotiate to win their own aims—permeate all the stories you've just read.

Growing from the insurgency of civil rights and black liberation movements, to the student struggles that erupted in May of '68 in France and the United States, through the mobilizations of mothers of people who disappeared into the prisons and torture chambers of the military dictatorships of Latin America from the sixties through the eighties, to feminist demonstrations around reproductive rights in Europe and the Americas, women have become ever more visible in protest movements over the final four decades of the twentieth century, claiming collective rights for their communities. But because of their loose organizational forms and informal leadership styles, women's protest activities have been largely overlooked or underestimated, especially in regard to their political significance for democracy and ethical beliefs in human rights.

Conclusion

When Dollie Burwell turned to her family for permission to go to South Africa as a peace monitor during the dangerous 1994 elections, her younger daughter, Mia, responded forcefully. Much as she feared for her mother's life, she said that Dollie had no choice: she had to go to pay her dues to all those who had died for black civil rights in the American South.[1] That sense of shared history, of solidarity across local and national boundaries, and of the ethical need to contribute to others that guide the lives of Dollie and Kim Burwell, Regina Ntongana, Josette Cole, Luella Kenny, and Lois Gibbs is difficult to explain in theoretical terms.

Even sociologists and political scientists who analyze collective action generally focus on formal organizations and underrate the significance of the kinds of activities in which the women considered here engage. What has become known as the "collective action" school, created primarily by American sociologists and political theorists, including Aldon D. Morris, Sidney Tarrow, and Charles Tilly, studies what has historically galvanized people to take action in pursuit of collective interests.[2] Primarily concerned with the growing sophistication of the processes by which ordinary people confront those in power, shape their own goals, and—most important—form complex organizations to express their wishes, the collective action school looks at the conditions that contribute to mobilizing as they have developed over the past two centuries in Europe and the United States.

While recognizing the importance of informal ties such as friendship networks and connections among church members, collective action theorists frequently view loose associations merely as tendencies guiding potential insurgents toward one organization rather than another. Networks then become means to certain organizational ends rather than strong webs connecting politically vital local groups. According to this line of thinking, leaders and key events directed by highly visible organizations assume greater significance than do processes by which large numbers of people resist oppression and develop programs for transforming society.[3]

Those groups that remain connected by loose, personal affiliations and umbrella organizations, such as those formed by the Burwells, Ntonganas, Coles, Kennys, and Gibbses, have importance, according to most versions of collective action theory, only as they participate in more extensive and denser organizations. But a theory that undervalues loosely knit ties in contrast to hierarchical organizations underestimates the continuities in certain forms of women's organizing. Whether as a means of maintaining everyday life in the poor neighborhoods of East London that historian Ellen Ross has documented, or of helping to sustain a community denigrated by authorities as Dollie and Kim Burwell have done, both survival and protest frequently rest on loose networks with strong bonds.[4]

A useful variant of collective action theory that makes clearer what these women are doing comes in the work of sociologists Naomi Rosenthal and Michael Schwartz.[5] Emphasizing the distinctions among three different kinds of associations, they identify one type of national organization they call "federal movement organization." This type of group, including the Southern Christian Leadership Conference (SCLC) and the National Organization for Women (NOW), is governed by formal rules and regulations and directed by leaders whose influence differs markedly from that of ordinary members.

The second group, "local movement organizations," exercise a great deal of autonomous judgment and may or may not be branches of national organizations such as SCLC or NOW. Relations between leaders and members of local movement organizations tend to be easy, but because these are nevertheless membership groups, support can ebb and flow.

Most relevant for this study is what Rosenthal and Schwartz call "primary movement groups." Distinguished by informality, these groups usually depend on regular contacts between individual members in their buildings, church groups, supermarkets, or squatter settlements. Rosenthal and Schwartz claim that the cohesion of such associations can be found in the friendships, frequent associations, informal ties, and recognition of leadership that emerges in groups—all of which vitiate any distinctions people may make between public and private life.[6]

Democratic political ideas and practices can develop through everyday encounters as demonstrated by the Burwells, Coles, Ntonganas, Kennys, Gibbses and women who attempted to improve everyday life through social reform movements in the past.[7] For instance, women's nineteenth-century campaigns to change society through networks they formed with other women contributed to utopian socialism, anarchism, and early trade unions.[8] Women's historical attraction to decentralized religious and political movements and their involvement in contemporary environmental, peace, and communitarian struggles also derive greater clarity when they are examined in the context of certain women's attempts to fight for the survival of their communities.[9] Key places such as churches, parks, and markets sometimes provide nodal points where people's political demands and social needs converge.[10]

To the extent that the Gibbses, Kennys, Ntonganas, Burwells, Coles, and their allies expect to democratize everyday life, they take part in a tradition of mobilizing to substitute human need for all other values. What is new is that instead of disappearing after initial grievances have been aired, or instead of being absorbed into larger, more complicated, hierarchical organizations, the new democratic organizations of women have been able to sustain themselves as networks over long periods of time and over great geographical distances. The kinds of women discussed here have attracted very little attention among scholars concerned with Europe and the United States. But political theorists and sociologists such as Sonia Alvarez, María del Carmen Feijoo, Elizabeth Jelin, Jane Jaquette, and Teresa Valdés,[11] writing about Latin America, have dedicated a great deal of work to why certain women gravitate to struggles about human rights, proposing more equitable distribution of resources. While collective action theorists have dealt with crises such as the civil rights movement in the South, neither they nor most other theorists focus on why so many of the participants in contemporary environmental, peace, and community movements are women. Their omission is especially surprising because, as Denise Riley has argued so forcefully, the category of "women" has been imbedded in the category "society" to such a degree since the nineteenth century that the social has all but been feminized and divorced from politics and questions of citizenship until quite recently.[12]

One reason women's movements were so visible in Latin America between the sixties and the eighties is that social and political needs converged with great violence there. During those two decades, more than ninety thousand people disappeared into the prisons, torture chambers, and unmarked graves of some of the bloodiest military dictatorships in history. To find their lost relatives, some wives and mothers of those attacked formed loose associations based on their common plight. The longevity of these bonds has led to their solidification into organizations such as the Association of the Mothers of the Plaza de Mayo, but their impact does not derive from the complexity of their organizations or the specialized roles that leaders have developed. These movements, though initially focused on motherhood, soon became committed to human rights, and some to the emancipation of women as full citizens. Yet because contemporary collective action theorists have generally devoted their attention to mobilizations against governments that claim to be democratic, their theories seldom try to explain the participation of masses of women demonstrating against the human rights abuses in Latin America or South Africa.

Another group of scholars such as Marjorie Agosín, Marguerite Bouvard, Patricia Chuchryk, Jo Fisher, Marysa Navarro, Jennifer Shirmer, and Lynn Stephen, securing the testimony of participants, have tried to illuminate how the experiences of the women as mothers and house-wives brought them into confrontation with the author-ities and how their consciousness of themselves as fighters for human rights developed and transformed them.[13] They claim that the women, who began by seeking lost relatives, soon began making demands that their govern-ments be transformed.

Apart from questioning the participants themselves,[14] many of the theorists of Latin American women's move-ments base their assessments on critiques of work that po-litical scientist Maxine Molyneux and I have done. For more than two decades, I have been trying to explain why women who proclaim their identity as wives and mothers according to the terms their culture dictates sometimes get involved in social movements focused on high prices, food or housing shortages, pollution, or unpopular wars. To characterize the state of mind exhibited by these women, who accept the division of labor by sex in their culture and historical period and sometimes demand privileges associ-ated with fulfilling their responsibilities, I coined the term "female consciousness."[15]

Female consciousness drove some women to behave as consumers of social goods and promoted their rescue of their families and communities in times of crisis. I wrote about how governments that attacked mothers demonstrating for basic social needs sometimes found themselves facing chal-lenges to the legitimacy of the government itself. Having ex-amined the activities of working-class women in Petrograd (St. Petersburg), Russia, and Turin, Italy, in 1917; in Málaga, Spain, in 1918; and in Veracruz, Mexico, in 1922, I argued that failures of governments to enable poor women to pro-vide food and housing for their families led some of them to challenge authorities. As one Tsarist general remarked in 1917, "When they asked for bread, we gave bread, and that was the end of it. But when the flags are inscribed 'down with the autocracy,' it's no longer a question of bread."[16] In a crisis, social need could quickly promote political chal-lenges capable of overthrowing empires.

Working on similar problems, British political scientist Maxine Molyneux developed a theory of gender interests.[17] Looking at a broad range of activities, Molyneux argued that when women act collectively to assure the preservation of their families, class, ethnic groups, and communities, they are pursuing what she called their "practical gender interests." In other words, they make gendered responses to threats to their families and communities. Both terms, "female consciousness" and "practical gender interests," attempt to explain why during certain crises, women such as Lois Gibbs, Luella Kenny, Dollie Burwell, or Regina Ntongana sometimes assume authority to speak for entire communities. Both terms also attempt to explain the standards according to which such women justify what they are doing.

In fact, there are even broader implications of Molyneux's theory of practical gender interests and of my ideas about female consciousness, because neither category is as clear-cut as it first appears. For example, we both refer to processes in which women move back and forth between specific survival needs and general demands for human emancipation and justice. Since our theories were concerned with poor women's participation in collective action, neither Molyneux nor I ever argued that women occupied a private sphere or that men occupied a public one.[18] We were both trying to explain why crises sometimes brought seemingly apolitical women into confrontation with police and soldiers. When women acting as mothers thought authorities could stop endangering their children—in Love Canal, Crossroads, and Warren County—some women did what they thought they had to do to save their families and communities. I also argued that even when the women opposed injustices on other grounds, tactically they sometimes chose to represent themselves as maternal figures, because police and soldiers were more reluctant to confront mothers than to attack the same women claiming their rights as citizens.

Sometimes women put their feminist face forward and stressed specific gender needs. To explain this aspect of women's activities, Molyneux developed the concept of "strategic gender interests," by which she meant focus on women's subordination and efforts to alter sexual discrimination. These include campaigns against sexual harassment or spousal abuse, or for women's suffrage, female education, reproductive rights, child care, and other services that women of all classes, races and ethnicities might need. The issues that galvanize women in these movements—the desire to exercise their full rights as citizens—don't necessarily conflict, either in Molyneux's theory or in practice, with goals to achieve collective benefits for families and communities.[19] In fact, one of the successes of the eighties has been the ways women who are fighting to improve the conditions of their communities all over the world have also fought for their own dignity and freedom from physical abuse. Feminist ideas have been reinvented or incorporated in social movements of women worldwide, as was evident in the Fourth World Conference on Women in Beijing, China, in 1995.

What the school of Latin American women and social movements theorists, including Argentine sociologist Elizabeth Jelin, have been arguing is that campaigns such as Dollie and Kim Burwell, Lois Gibbs, Luella Kenny, Regina Ntongana, and Josette Cole carried on provide "a new means by which to relate the political and the social . . . , in which the every day social practices are included alongside and in direct connection with ideological and institutional politics."[20]

Yet, in the far-reaching debate about social movements that has engaged many of the leading international social scientists, these women's movements, their demands that political authorities meet ethical standards, and their calls for justice have received little attention. Because such groups seldom leave records, because leadership in larger organizations frequently passes to men, and because journalists and scholars tend to focus on national organizations, local and primary groups connected by networks often disappear from view. Those works that have dealt with women's efforts to transform conditions under which they and their families live have largely treated them as peripheral to the real con-flicts.

Yes, the prophetic tradition the women who are crazy for democracy represent is visionary in its efforts to substi-tute universal human rights based on ethical programs for the political and social systems that now prevail. Yes, these women lack proposals for specific alternative systems of gov-ernment and economics to replace the old ones. But what they do is invaluable to the success of democracy because they challenge those who seek to deny the fundamental moral precepts at its core. Rather than accept the separation of social need from politics, the Gibbses, Kennys, Nton-ganas, Burwells, and Coles place their hopes on democracy.

Democracy is certainly not possible in the new millen-nium if it applies only to politicians elected to office through the work of campaigners who then withdraw and expect their candidates to intuit their will. While direct democracy, according to which we each negotiate for ourselves and our communities, is impractical on a national or international stage, representative democracy does not work without the continued activism of many ordinary citizens. If activists' views cannot and should not always prevail over other inter-ests, their opinions certainly deserve an equal hearing with those of elected officials. Without citizens' commitments to put their own bodies on the line and their willingness to demonstrate in front of courthouses and congresses, there can be no democracy. In the United States and South Africa, politics frequently concerns providing for human needs, about which grassroots activists have extensive experience. Moreover, elected officials require the constant encourage-ment of people who know what is happening at the local level.

Of course, grassroots activists themselves can always stand for and be elected to office, as Dollie Burwell has been in Warren County and her friend Lydia Kompe has been in South Africa. But even they need to be in constant contact with the people who do the everyday tasks that make all so-cieties function, applying democratic principles to daily life.

Conclusion

The question is not about principled leaders; it is about how to factor in committed citizens like most of the women discussed here, who work maintaining and reorienting activities that sustain and improve the conditions for social life and democracy.

The activities of the Burwells, Gibbses, Kennys, Ntonganas, and Coles over the past few decades make it seem that democracy as a process by which people collectively decide their social priorities is impossible without ongoing mobilization of the kind they turn to as their principal tool of direct democracy. Whether one focuses on the social division of labor by sex, the egalitarian potential of which democracy is capable, or these new notions of human rights that emphasize social need, the existence of the revolution in which women of courage are engaging indicates new and promising directions for democracy.

Notes

1. Introduction: Women Prophets and the Struggle for Human Rights

1. For a related argument about how contemporary grassroots movements for justice have emerged among women of color in the United States, see Iris Marion Young, *Justice and the Politics of Difference* (Princeton: Princeton University Press, 1990). Nancy Fraser discusses how people can turn claims for needs into justifications for social rights in her "Talking about Needs: Interpretive Contests as Political Conflicts in Welfare-State Societies," Symposium on Feminism and Political Theory, *Ethics*, Vol. 99, no. 2 (January 1989): 291–313.

2. My thinking about how women defending their homes in Crossroads and other squatter communities contributed to new views of politics has been strongly influenced by Linzi Manicom, "Ruling Relations: Rethinking State and Gender in South African History," *Journal of African History*, 33 (1992): 441–465.

3. Martin Luther King Jr. reluctantly became the leader of the Montgomery Improvement Association after the boycott was under way. See Clayborne Carson, "The Boycott that Changed Dr. King's Life," *New York Times Magazine*, January 7, 1996, p. 38. The success of the boycott rested on the organizational abilities of the Montgomery Women's Political Council, made up of local African-American women, including Jo Ann Gibson Robinson. See Jo Ann Gibson Robinson, *The Montgomery Bus Boycott and the Women Who Started It: The Memoir of Jo Ann Gibson Robinson*, edited, with a foreword, by David J. Garrow (Knoxville, TN: University of Tennessee Press, 1987).

4. For an assessment of Ella Baker's abilities as a creator of SCLC, SNCC (the Student Nonviolent Coordinating Committee), and other grassroots

organizations, see Ellen Cantarow and Susan Guchee O'Maley, "Ella Baker: Organizing for Civil Rights," in *Moving the Mountain: Working Women for Social Change*, edited by Ellen Cantarow with Susan Guchee O'Maley and Sharon Hartmann Strom (Old Westbury and New York: Feminist Press and McGraw-Hill, 1980), pp. 52–93; Charles Payne, "Ella Baker and Models of Social Change," *Signs*, Vol. 14, no. 2 (1989): 885–899.

5.   Contemporary ideas about charisma draw on the theories of Max Weber, who argued that the quality entailed the properties of magic that were incompatible with the modern, scientifically rationalist world. He claimed that charisma constituted one of three forms of authority, along with legal and rational systems and traditional systems. For the original formulations of Weber's ideas about charisma, see Max Weber, *The Sociology of Religion*, translated by Ephraim Fischoff, introduction by Talcott Parsons (Boston: Beacon Press, 1963); and Max Weber, *Max Weber on Charisma and Institution Building; Selected Papers*, edited with an introduction by S. N. Eisenstadt (Chicago: University of Chicago Press, 1968).

Given the time when Weber wrote and his privileging of one form of technical, scientifically based rationality over all other systems of ordering priorities, it is not surprising that the theory entirely ignores gender and women. But the fact that so little attention has been paid in recent works is quite distressing.

For a sampling of how the concept of charisma has been used to discuss political authority, see S. N. Eisenstadt, *Power, Trust, and Meaning: Essays in Sociological Theory and Analysis* (Chicago: University of Chicago Press, 1995); Clifford Geertz, "Centers, Kings, and Charisma: Reflections on the Symbolics of Power," in *Culture and Its Creators: Essays in Honor of Edward Shils*, edited by Joseph Ben-David and Terry Nichols Clark (Chicago: University of Chicago, 1977), pp. 150–171; Douglas Madsen and Peter G. Snow, *The Charismatic Bond: Political Behavior in Time of Crisis* (Cambridge, MA: Harvard University Press, 1991); Edward A. Shils, *The Constitution of Society* (Chicago: University of Chicago Press, 1982).

6.   Weber, *The Sociology of Religion*, p. 47.

7.   The subject of political culture has become very important to social historians trying to explain how collective groups sometimes resist authority by insisting on new meanings for old practices. Many of us, building on the work of anthropologists, have studied how parades, festivals, and customary celebrations can become occasions to hold political leaders and governments accountable for repression as well as to celebrate unity. Without changing political institutions, people can sometimes change political relationships through cultural means by playing with the meanings of symbols and rituals.

In addition to my own *Red City, Blue Period: Social Movements in Picasso's Barcelona* (Berkeley: University of California Press, 1992), some of the works that consider cultural politics are the articles in *Culture, Power and History: A Reader in Contemporary Social Theory*, edited by Nicholas B. Dirks, Geoff Eley, and Sherry B. Ortner (Princeton: Princeton University Press, 1994); Lynn Hunt, *Politics, Culture and Class in the French Revolution* (Berkeley: University of California Press, 1984); David Kertzer, *Ritual, Politics, and Power* (New Haven: Yale University Press, 1988); Pamela Radcliff, *From Mobilization to Civil War: The Politics of Polarization in the Spanish City of Gijón 1900–1939* (New York: Cambridge University Press, forthcoming); and Kathleen Wilson, *The Sense of the People: Politics, Culture, and Imperialism in England, 1715–1785* (Cambridge and New York: Cambridge University Press, 1995).

8.   For a truly brilliant historical investigation of the connection between women preachers and social transformation in the lives of working people, see Deborah M. Valenze, *Prophetic Sons and Daughters: Female Preaching and Popular Religion in Industrial England* (Princeton: Princeton University Press, 1985).

9.   For an insightful consideration of why charismatic leadership works so well in egalitarian movements, see Richard J. Ellis, "Explaining the Occurrence of Charismatic Leadership," *Journal of Theoretical Politics*, Vol. 3, no. 3 (1991): 305–319; 311.

10.   Temma Kaplan, "Female Consciousness and Collective Action: The Case of Barcelona, 1910–1918, in *Rethinking the Political: Gender, Resistance, and the State*," edited by Barbara Laslett, Johanna Brenner, and Yesim Arat (Chicago: University of Chicago Press, 1995), pp. 145–166. The article originally appeared in 1982.

11.   Excellent accounts of these and intermediate conferences carried on as part of the decade of women can be found in Charlotte Bunch, *Passionate Politics: Feminist Theory in Action* (New York: St. Martin's Press, 1987), pp. 283–305; and Judith Zinsser, "The Third Week in July," *Women's Studies International Forum*, Vol. 6, no. 5 (1983): 547–557; and "Nairobi Confab Ends on High Note," *New Directions for Women*, September/October 1985: 1, 12, 14.

12.   The foregoing description is based on my personal observations at the NGO Forum of the Fourth World Conference on Women in Beijing from August 30 to September 10, 1995, and from newspaper accounts in the *China Daily* (Beijing): August 26–September 9, 1995; the *International Herald Tribune* (Paris): August 26–September 9, 1995; and *New York Times*, August 25–September 17, 1995.

13.   For newspaper coverage of the bank and its significance, see Barbara Crossette, "The Second Sex in the Third World: A New Order," *New York Times*, September 10, 1995: Section 4, 1, 3; and Patrick E. Tyler, "Star at Conference on Women: Banker Who Lends to the Poor," *New York Times*, September 14, 1995: A6.

14.   The women's human rights community, made up of grassroots activists working in conjunction with feminist health care providers and lawyers, has blossomed in the late eighties and nineties. For a historical account, see Elisabeth Friedman, "Women's Human Rights: The Emergence of a Movement," in *Women's Rights, Human Rights: International Feminist Perspectives*, edited by Julie Peters and Andrea Wolper (New York and London: Routledge, 1995), pp. 18–35. Charlotte Bunch, one of the architects of the strategy of working through the United Nations to secure women's freedom from violence, describes the process in "Transforming Human Rights from a Feminist Perspective," *Women's Rights, Human Rights*, pp. 11–17. Another activist in the movement, Roxanna Carrillo, writes about it in "Violence Against Women: An Obstacle to Development," in *Gender Violence: A Development and Human Rights Issue* (NJ: Center for Women's Global Leadership, 1991), pp. 19–41.

15.   The debates about public and private realms into which male and female society were allegedly divided began as an heuristic devise in Louise Lamphere and Michelle Zimbalast Rosaldo's *Women, Culture, and Society* (Stanford, CA: Stanford University Press, 1974) and was modified considerably in Michelle Zimbalast Rosaldo's "The Use and Abuse of Anthropology: Reflections on Feminism, and Cross-Cultural Understanding," *Signs*, Vol. 5, no. 3 (spring 1980): 389–417, but that false dichotomy, taken from liberal contract theory, permeated feminist theory for far too long. For a recent critique of this typology, see Carole Pateman, "Feminist Critiques of the Public Private Dichotomy," in *The Disorder of Women: Democracy, Feminism and Political Theory* (Stanford, CA: Stanford University Press, 1989), pp. 118–140.

16.   Denise Riley, *"Am I That Name?" Feminism and the Category of "Women" in History* (Minneapolis: University of Minnesota Press, 1990); Iris Marion Young, "Gender as Seriality: Thinking about Women as a Social Collective," in *Rethinking the Political*, pp. 99–124.

17.   The idea of rights has come under attack from legal scholars who constitute the Critical Legal Studies school. They argue that since the law upholds the interests of the wealthy and powerful against the poor and weak, of individuals against communities, political rights, such as voting, cannot help achieve justice without massive income and property redistribution and transformation of all social relations in an egalitarian way. In fact, according to critical legal scholars, the illusion of rights may make people quiescent about injustice, lulling them into thinking that they have power to achieve social goods when in fact they do not. For an interesting analysis of some of the issues Critical Legal Studies raise, see Elizabeth M. Schneider, "The Dialectic of Rights and Politics: Perspectives from the Women's Movement," *New York University Law Review* 61 (1986): 589–662.

   Critical Legal Studies' judgments about rights do not apply to the rights language the grassroots women activists discussed here employ:

these women speak in public, not in the courts, about a form of justice related to human need, which is how they define rights.

2. Suburban Blight and Situation Comedy

1. Most of the foregoing remarks about Luella Kenny's feelings come from phone and personal interviews I conducted with her in Grand Island, New York, on August 14, 1994; October 28 and 29, 1994; June 28, 1995; and November 22, 1995.

2. Personal interview with Barbara Quimby, Grand Island, New York, October 29, 1994.

3. The figures on dumping come from the *New York Times*, which claimed the chemical company dumped metal barrels in the water or along the banks of the canal. Then Hooker sold the land to the school board. See Donald G. McNeil Jr., "Upstate Waste Site May Endanger Lives," *New York Times*, August 2, 1978, pp. A1, B9.

4. Love Canal is one of the best-studied instances of toxic-waste damage in the world, and numerous books and articles have been written about it. For a sampling of work, see Adeline Gordon Levine, *Love Canal: Science, Politics, and People* (Lexington, MA: Lexington Books, D. C. Heath and Company, 1982); and Michael H. Brown, *Laying Waste: The Poisoning of America by Toxic Chemicals* (New York: Pantheon, 1979), p. 5.

5. Brown, *Laying Waste*, pp. 52–53.

6. Brown, *Laying Waste*, p. 46.

7. Brown, *Laying Waste*, pp. 6–7.

8. Levine, *Love Canal*, pp. 30–31.

9. Interview with Debbie Cerrillo, October 30, 1994, Grand Island, New York.

10. Lois Marie Gibbs, *Love Canal: My Story*, as told to Murray Levine (Albany, NY: State University of New York Press, 1982), p. 10.

11. Levine, *Love Canal*, p. 33.

12. Gibbs, *Love Canal*, pp. 6, 81; Levine, *Love Canal*, pp. 93, 106. Even supposed male allies sometimes denigrate women as "hysterical housewives." For one activist's response, see Cora Tucker, "Women Make It Happen," *Empowering Ourselves: Women and Toxic Organizing*, edited by Robbin Lee Zeff, Marcia Love, and Karen Stilts (Arlington, VA: Citizens Clearinghouse for Hazardous Waste, Inc., 1989), p. 4.

13. Brown, *Laying Waste*, p. 46, 48; Gibbs, *Love Canal*, pp. 6, 10, 20–21, 141, endnote 3; for a list of the chemicals found in Love Canal and the human damage they could cause, see Levine, *Love Canal*, p. 41.

14. Donald G. McNeil Jr., "Health Chief Calls Waste Site a 'Peril,' " *New York Times*, August 3, 1978, p. A1.

15. Brown, *Laying Waste*, p. 27; Levine, *Love Canal*, pp. 34–35.

16. McNeil Jr., " 'Peril,' " *New York Times*, August 3, 1978, p. A1.

17. Levine, *Love Canal*, p. 36.

18. McNeil Jr., " 'Peril,' " *New York Times*, August 3, 1978, p. A1.

19. Gibbs, *Love Canal*, p. 92.

20. Levine, *Love Canal*, p. 37.

21. Levine, *Love Canal*, p. 37.

22. Levine, *Love Canal*, pp. 42–44.

23. Brown, *Laying Waste*, p. 31.

24. Levine, *Love Canal*, p. 42.

25. Levine, *Love Canal*, p. 55.

26. Brown, *Laying Waste*, p. 44.

27. Personal interview with Luella Kenny, Grand Island, New York, October 28, 1994; Brown, *Laying Waste*, pp. 44–45.

28. Luella Kenny, October 28, 1994.

29. "Luella Kenny," in *Empowering Ourselves*, pp. 11–12.

30. Levine, *Love Canal*, p. 46.

31. Levine, *Love Canal*, p. 68.

32. Gibbs, *Love Canal*, p. 81.

33. Cited in Levine, *Love Canal*, p. 93.

34. Brown, *Laying Waste*, p. 53.

35. Brown, *Laying Waste*, p. 54.

36. Gibbs, *Love Canal*, pp. 10–16, 23–25, 82, 94–95.

37. Cited in Levine, *Love Canal*, p. 100.

38. Figures provided by Dr. Haughie of the Department of Health in a letter dated March 15, 1979, and cited in Levine, *Love Canal*, p. 106.

39. Phone interview with Debbie Cerrillo, August 27, 1994; Gibbs, *Love Canal*, p. 94.

40. Levine, *Love Canal*, pp. 201–202.

41. Gibbs, *Love Canal*, pp. 96–97; personal interview with Lois Gibbs, July 10, 1995, Falls Church, Virginia.

42. Gibbs, *Love Canal*, p. 99; Levine, *Love Canal*, p. 107.

43. Phone interview with Debbie Cerrillo, August 8, 1994.

44. Luella Kenny, October 28, 1994.

45. Lois Gibbs, July 10, 1995, reminiscing about Marie Pozniac, who died in November 1993.

46. Gibbs, *Love Canal*, p. 125.

47. Luella Kenny, October 28, 1994.

48. Gibbs, *Love Canal*, p. 134.

49. Luella Kenny, October 28, 1994.

50. Levine, *Love Canal*, pp. 143–44. Barbara Quimby recalls that almost all notification from the government came Friday afternoons or evenings. From interview, October 29, 1994.

51. Personal interview with Patricia Brown, October 29, 1994, Love Canal, New York. I am very grateful to Brown for taking me around Love Canal and sharing her recollections with me.

52. Gibbs, *Love Canal*, pp. 142–145; Levine, *Love Canal*, pp. 148–149.

53. For a particularly vivid account of the hostage taking, see Harriet G. Rosenberg, "Housewives and Hostages at Love Canal: A Narrative of Resistance," paper presented at the American Anthropological Association Annual Meetings, Chicago, Illinois, November 20–24, 1991, p. 1; for a detailed firsthand account of the demonstration, see Gibbs, *Love Canal*, pp. 145–155.

54. Barbara Quimby, October 29, 1994.

55. Levine, *Love Canal*, p. 149.

56. Rosenberg, "Housewives and Hostages," pp. 8, 11; Gibbs, *Love Canal*, pp. 145–155; 159.

57. Barbara Quimby, October 29, 1994.

58. Gibbs, *Love Canal*, p. 156.

59. Gibbs, *Love Canal*, p. 157.

60. Gibbs, *Love Canal*, p. 157.

61. Brown, *Laying Waste*, p. 48.

62. Levine, *Love Canal*, note 3, pp. 171–172, 190.

63. Gibbs, *Love Canal*, p. 164; Levine, *Love Canal*, p. 207.

64. Gibbs, *Love Canal*, pp. 165–166.

65. Gibbs, *Love Canal*, p. 76.

66. Barbara Quimby, October 29, 1994.

67. Bob Hall, "Lessons from the Grassroots," in *Environmental Politics: Lessons from the Grassroots*, edited by Bob Hall (Durham: The Institute for Southern Studies, 1988), pp. 1–12, 6.

68. Gibbs, *Love Canal*, p. 92.

69. Debbie Cerrillo, October 30, 1994.

70.   Personal interview with Adeline Levine and Murray Levine, Buffalo, New York, October 28, 1994.

71.   Gibbs, *Love Canal,* pp. 6, 10, 141, endnote 3; Rosenberg, "Housewives and Hostages," pp. 7, 12.

72.   Barbara Quimby, October 29, 1994.

73.   Luella Kenny, October 29, 1994.

74.   Barbara Quimby, October 29, 1994.

75.   Harriet Rosenberg, "From Trash to Treasure: Housewife Activists and the Environmental Justice Movement," in *Articulating Hidden Resistance: Exploring the Influence of Eric Wolf* (Berkeley: University of California Press, 1995), pp. 190–204.

76.   Cora Tucker, "Women Make It Happen," in *Empowering Ourselves,* p. 4.

3.   *"When it rains, I get mad and scared": Women and Environmental Racism*

1.   Phone conversation with Dollie Burwell, Afton, North Carolina, November 19, 1992.

2.   Personal interview with Vernice Miller, New York, February 24, 1993.

3.   Dollie Burwell, speaking at the Redefining Motherhood Conference, Dartmouth College, May 15, 1993.

4.   Personal interview with Dollie Burwell, Warrenton, North Carolina, January 25, 1993.

5.   Dollie Burwell, January 25, 1993.

6.   *News and Observer* (Raleigh), September 1, 1978; "PCB Suspect Plotted Cover-Up, State Claims," *News and Observer,* March 6, 1979; and "PCB Dumping Described in Court," *News and Observer,* May 24, 1979, found in the file on PCB spills in the Clipping Collection of Wilson Library, the University of North Carolina, Chapel Hill, subsequently referred to as PCB Spills; *New York Times,* January 19, 1979, p. A12; *New York Times,* June 5, 1979, p. A19; *The Christian Science Monitor,* June 24, 1981, Vol. 73, p. 2. The sequence of events is summarized in Nicholas Freudenberg, *Not in Our Backyards! Community Action for Health and the Environment,* foreword by Lois Marie Gibbs. (New York: Monthly Review Press, 1984), pp. 182–184; and additional evidence is provided in Robert D. Bullard, *Dumping in Dixie: Race, Class, and Environmental Quality* (Boulder, CO: Westview Press, 1990), pp. 35–39.

7.   The evidence comes from Freudenberg, *Not in Our Backyards!* pp. 182–183. The story is detailed in "PCB Dumping Described in Court," *News and Observer*, May 24, 1979: PCB Spills. In *Dumping in Dixie*, Robert D. Bullard explains the spill from a slightly different perspective. According to him, the oil tainted with PCB was bought for resale from the Raleigh company, but EPA standards changed in 1978 and the oil could no longer be resold. Having agreed to dispose of the oil, the Ward company simply drained it from the truck along the roadside. See pp. 35–36.

8.   Quoted by Alan A. Block and Frank R. Scarpitti, *Poisoning for Profit: The Mafia and Toxic Waste in America* (New York: Morrow, 1985), p. 62, cited in Harriet G. Rosenberg, "From Trash to Treasure: Housewife Activists and the Environmental Justice Movement," in *Articulating Hidden Resistance: Exploring the Influence of Eric Wolf* (Berkeley: University of California, 1995), p. 194.

9.   Ginny Carroll, "Three Enter Guilty Pleas in PCB Trial," *News and Observer*, May 6, 1979: PCB Spills. For damages and costs that the state of North Carolina tried to recover, see *News and Observer*, September 1, 1978: PCB Spills. William Sanjour, the chief of the Environmental Protection Agency and an expert on hazardous wastes, challenged the use of dumps for PCB-contaminated material. For an explanation of his views see Bullard, *Dumping in Dixie*, p. 38. In fact, the only safe ways to dispose of material with PCB are burial in sealed areas, chemical neutralization, and incineration. The state and the EPA argued that it was too costly in time and money to use the new mobile incineration system to dispose of the PCB. See "On-Site PCB Disposal Called Too Expensive," *Durham Morning Herald*, Regional Edition, August 6, 1982, p. 1B.

10.   "PCB Dumping Described in Court," *News and Observer*, May 24, 1979: PCB Spills.

11.   Sharon Begley, "Toxic Waste Still Pollutes Roadways," *Newsweek*, October 27, 1980.

12.   "Mother's milk found to have PCB similar to toxic spills," *News and Observer*, September 25, 1982: PCB Spills.

13.   Joyce Brown, "U.S. Advises Against In-Place Treatment of PCB-Tainted Soil," *News and Observer*, June 5, 1979: PCB Spills; Dollie Burwell's presentation at the Redefining Motherhood Conference, Dartmouth College, May 15, 1993; Freudenberg, *Not in Our Backyards!* p. 183; *The Christian Science Monitor*, June 24, 1981, p. 2.

14.   Bullard, in *Dumping in Dixie*, p. 36, elaborating on findings published in the Commission for Racial Justice, *Toxic Wastes and Race in the United States: A National Report on the Racial and Socioeconomic Characteristics of Communities with Hazardous Waste Sites* (New York: United Church of Christ Commission for Racial Justice, 1987), p. xi. This study, done after the dumping and the demonstrations, seems to be the most ac-

curate. The newspapers, focusing on Warren County, generally claimed it was 59.5 percent African-American. See, for example, F. Alan Boyce, "PCB Protest—Environmental Issue Being Clouded?" *News and Observer* (Raleigh), September 19, 1982. But Jenny Labalme says in *A Road to Walk: A Struggle for Environmental Justice* (Durham: The Regulator Press, 1987), p. 4, that Warren County was 64 percent black and that Shocco Township, where the site was established, was 75 percent African-American. Of 100 North Carolina counties, according to Labalme, Warren ranked 97th in per-capita income. Whatever the correct figures, it is clear that Afton, the unincorporated township of Shocco, and Warren County were among the poorest places in a poor state.

15. Ken Geiser and Gerry Waneck, "PCBs and Warren County," *Science for the People* 15 (July/August 1983), pp. 13–17, 17, cited in Bullard, *Dumping in Dixie*, pp. 36–37; *New York Times*, August 11, 1982, p. 15(N), D17(L); John Hackman, "The Hazard that Won't Go Away," originally in the *Charlotte Observer*, *The Warren Record*, Vol. 85, no. 41, October 20, 1982, pp. 1B, 12B. He quotes Tom McCord, president of the Chem-Security Company of Belvue, Washington, who had the contract to build North Carolina's first privately owned hazardous-waste landfill in Anson City, southeast of Wadesboro. Admitting that a landfill was the cheapest, not the best, way to dispose of toxic material, he claimed that saving money would have a ripple effect on the poor community surrounding the site.

16. Dollie Burwell, January 25, 1993

17. Quoted by Vernice Miller, November 7, 1992, lecture at Eugene Lang College of the New School for Social Research; Charles Lee, "The Integrity of Justice: Evidence of Environmental Racism," *Sojourners* 25 (1991).

18. Personal interview with Ken Ferruccio, Afton, North Carolina, October 1, 1994.

19. Freudenberg, *Not in Our Backyards!* pp. 183–184; Dollie Burwell confirms that she made the contacts. Interview, January 25, 1993.

20. Eleanor Lee, "Landfill Vandalism in Warren is Probed," *Durham Morning Herald*, Regional Edition, August 24, 1982, p. 1B.

21. "Guards Posted at Landfill," *Durham Morning Herald*, Regional Edition, August 26, 1982, p. 1B; "News Conference Held: Liner Is Repaired at PCB Dump Site," *The Warren Record*, Vol. 85, no. 34, September 1, 1982, pp. 1, 14. Elissa McCrary, "Trucks Roll Daily to PCB Landfill," *Durham Morning Herald*, Regional Edition, September 22, 1982, p. 1B; Eleanor Lee, "Two Warren Men Explore PCB Detoxification," *Durham Morning Herald*, Regional Edition, August 21, 1982, p. 1B; "News Conference Held: Liner is Repaired at PCB Dump Site," *The Warren Record*, Vol. 85, no. 34, September 1, 1982, pp. 1, 14, 1.

22. "Warren County Residents Vow to Fight PCB Landfill," *The Fayetteville Observer*, September 13, 1982, p. 1B.

23.   Freudenberg, *Not in Our Backyards!* p. 183; "People of Color and the Struggle for Environmental Justice," *Program Guide: The First National People of Color Environmental Leadership Summit,* October 24–27, 1991, p. 4.

24.   Dollie Burwell, January 25, 1993.

25.   Bullard, *Dumping in Dixie,* p. 36.

26.   Dollie Burwell, January 25, 1993.

27.   Dollie Burwell, January 25, 1993; "Afton Residents Hear Work on PCB Landfill" (*New York Times* Service) *Durham Morning Herald,* Regional Edition, August 12, 1982, p. 1B. Jenny Labalme, a student at Duke who covered the demonstrations as a history student and journalist, wrote and did the photographs for *A Road to Walk* and "Dumping on Warren County," in *Environmental Politics: Lessons from the Grassroots,* edited by Bob Hall (Durham: Institute for Southern Studies, 1988), pp. 23–30. I am grateful to her for her work and for the phone conversations we had in February 1993 about the 1982 demonstrations.

28.   "155 Arrested During Warren PCB Protest," *Durham Morning Herald,* Regional Edition, September 21, 1982, p. 1B; F. Alan Boyce, "Warren PCB Protest: Landfill Used for 2nd Day," *Durham Morning Herald,* Regional Edition, September 17, 1982, p. 1B.

29.   Dollie Burwell, "Reminiscences from Warren County, North Carolina," in *Proceedings: The First National People of Color Environmental Leadership Summit,* edited by Charles Lee. The Washington Court on Capitol Hill, Washington, D.C., October 24–27, 1991 (New York: The United Church of Christ Commission for Racial Justice, 1992), p. 125. The film clip of Kim in the demonstration appeared on *CBS Nightly News,* September 15, 1982, available from the TV News Archive, Vanderbilt University, Nashville, Tennessee.

30.   "PCB Dump Action Nets 114 Arrests," *The Fayetteville Observer,* September 28, 1982, p. 1A; "Protest Over PCB Continuing Here," *The Warren Record,* Vol. 85, no. 38, September 29, 1982, p. 14; personal interview with Dollie Burwell, November 1, 1995.

31.   "Clark Blasts Continuing PCB Protest," *Durham Morning Herald,* Regional Edition, September 29, 1982, p. B1.

32.   Dollie Burwell, January 25, 1993; see also F. Alan Boyce, "39 People Arrested in 3rd Day of Protests Over PCB Landfill," *Durham Morning Herald,* Regional Edition, September 18, 1993, p. B1.

33.   Most of this account comes from interviews with Dollie Burwell on January 25, 1993, and November 1, 1995; for newspaper coverage of the arrest of Walter Fauntroy, see "PCB Dump Action Nets 114 Arrests," *The Fayetteville Observer,* September 28, 1993, pp. 1A; 2A; 2A; "Delegate Arrested During PCB Protest," *Durham Morning Herald,* Regional Edition, September 28, 1982, p. B1.

34. *Toxic Wastes and Race*, p. xiii.

35. *Toxic Wastes and Race*, Table 2, p. 19.

36. Vernice D. Miller, facilitator: "Regional Group Workshop: Northeast, Puerto Rico and Eastern Canada (R1)," *Program Guide: The First National People of Color Environmental Leadership Summit*, pp. 17–18; p. 17.

37. "Four Arrested at PCB Protest," *Durham Morning Herald*, Regional Edition, October 2, 1982, p. 1B.

38. "No Arrests Made Tuesday as PCB Storage Nears End," *The Warren Record*, Vol. 85, no. 39, October 6, 1982, pp. 1, 4.

39. Quoted in "Protest Over PCB Continuing Here," *The Warren Record*, Vol. 85, no. 38, September 29, 1982, pp. 1, 14.

40. "No More Waste Landfills Seen in Warren County," *The Fayetteville Observer*, Wednesday, September 29, 1982: PCB Spills.

41. Harriet G. Rosenberg, "Housewives and Hostages at Love Canal: A Narrative of Resistance," paper presented at the American Anthropological Association Annual Meetings, Chicago, Illinois, November 20–24, 1991, p. 13; *New York Times*, September 16, 1982, p. 11(N), p. A18(L); Dake Russakoff, *The Washington Post*, October 11, 1982, p. A1.

42. Dollie Burwell, January 25, 1993.

43. Personal interview with Dollie Burwell, Warrenton, North Carolina, September 29, 1994.

44. Dollie Burwell, January 25, 1993.

45. "Clayton favored in 1st District: Election of black woman would be a first for state," *The Herald Sun* (Durham, North Carolina), October 30, 1992, p. C4.

46. Cora Tucker, "Women Make it Happen," in *Empowering Ourselves: Women and Toxics Organizing*, edited by Robbin Lee Zeff, Marsha Love, and Karen Stults (Arlington, VA: Citizens Clearinghouse for Toxic Waste, Inc., 1989), p. 5.

47. Personal interview with Kenneth Ferruccio, Afton, North Carolina, 1994.

48. Benjamin F. Chavis Jr.'s introduction to Dollie Burwell, *Proceedings: The First National People of Color Environmental Leadership Summit*, p. 125.

4. *Homemaker Citizens and New Democratic Organizations*

1. B. Drummond Ayres Jr., "Law to Ease Voter Registration Has Added 5 Million to the Rolls," *New York Times*, September 3, 1995, A1.

2.   Mary G. Dietz, "Context is All: Feminism and Theories of Citizenship," *Daedalus*, Vol. 116 (Fall 1987), pp. 1–24; 14.

3.   Personal interview with Lois Gibbs, Falls Church, Virginia, July 10, 1995.

4.   Lois Gibbs, July 10, 1995.

5.   Personal interview with Dollie Burwell, Afton, North Carolina, September 30, 1994.

6.   Lois Marie Gibbs, "Some Thoughts on Women Who Move From Being Local Grassroots Leaders to Full-time Organizers," in *Empowering Ourselves: Women and Toxics Organizing*, edited by Robbin Lee Zeff, Marsha Love, and Karen Stults (Arlington, VA: Citizens Clearinghouse for Hazardous Waste, Inc., 1989), pp. 37–41; 37.

7.   Interview with Dollie Burwell by Melynn Glusman, April 19, 1995, part of the Project on Women's Activism and Grassroots Leadership at the University of North Carolina at Chapel Hill. Tape 41994-KB.

8.   Dollie Burwell, Mellon Seminar, Duke University, Durham, North Carolina, November 1, 1995.

9.   Phone interview with Adeline and Murray Levine, June 17, 1995; Lois Gibbs, July 10, 1995.

10.   Personal interview with Debbie Cerrillo, Grand Island, New York, October 30, 1994.

11.   Lois Gibbs, July 10, 1995.

12.   The Leaders of the Love Canal Homeowners Association, *Love Canal: A Chronology of Events that Shaped a Movement* (Falls Church, VA: Citizens Clearinghouse for Hazardous Waste, Inc., 1984), nn.

13.   Adeline Gordon Levine, *Love Canal: Science, Politics, and People* (Lexington, MA: D. C. Heath and Co., 1982), pp. 199–201; 204.

14.   Gibbs, "Some Thoughts," *Empowering Ourselves*, p. 40.

15.   Gibbs, "Some Thoughts," *Empowering Ourselves*, pp. 37–41; 38–39. See also the straightforward advice on organizing in *Leadership Handbook on Hazardous Waste* (Arlington, VA: Citizens Clearinghouse for Hazardous Waste, 1983).

16.   *Leadership Handbook*, pp. 9–10; 26.

17.   Adeline and Murray Levine, June 17, 1995.

18.   Gibbs, "Some Thoughts," *Empowering Ourselves*, p. 37.

19.   *Love Canal: A Chronology*, 1978, nn.

20.   Lois Gibbs, July 10, 1995.

21.   Debbie Cerrillo, October 30, 1994.

22.   Debbie Cerrillo, October 30, 1994.

23. Phone interview with Luella Kenny, June 17, 1995.

24. Personal Interview with Dollie Burwell, Afton, North Carolina, September 29, 1994.

25. Personal interview with the Reverend Leon White, Durham, North Carolina, September 30, 1994.

26. Lois Gibbs, July 10, 1995.

27. Gibbs, "Some Thoughts," *Empowering Ourselves*, pp. 37–38.

28. Cora Tucker, "Women Make it Happen," in *Empowering Ourselves*, pp. 4–6; 4.

29. Lois Gibbs, July 10, 1995.

30. Lois Gibbs, July 10, 1995. Gibbs was not alone in having her marriage disrupted by her increasing engagement in a social movement. One of the Madres of the Plaza de Mayo in Argentina, who became active in the struggle against the military rulers who had abducted and murdered her son, said once that her husband had suffered more than she. When I asked what she meant, she said, "My husband has lost his wife as well as his son," by which she meant that she no longer was a full-time wife and mother once she became a human rights advocate. Although the issue of women activists' changing identities has not received the attention it deserves, students of grassroots movements in South America have written more extensively than most about the issue. One example can be found in Lynn Stephen, "Women's Rights are Human Rights: The Merging of Feminine and Feminist Interests Among El Salvador's Mothers of the Disappeared (CO-MADRES)," *American Ethnologist*, Vol. 22, no. 4 (1995), 1–22; 10–11.

31. Lois Gibbs, July 10, 1995.

32. Dollie Burwell, September 30, 1994.

33. "Personal Growth," in *Empowering Ourselves*, pp. 31–32.

34. Lois Gibbs, July 10, 1995.

35. Dollie Burwell, September 29, 1994.

36. Personal interview with Dollie Burwell, Warren County, North Carolina, February 11, 1995.

5. Generation X, Southern Style

1. Personal interview with Kim Burwell, Afton, North Carolina, October 1, 1994.

2. *Leadership Initiative Project Proposal Narrative: Building, Expanding, Deepening and Consolidating Youth Organizing in Eastern North Carolina*, A Plan for a Two-Year Program of Leadership Development, Organizing, and Networking, (1993). Contact Person: Angela Brown, director.

3. Interview with Kim Burwell by Melynn Glusman, April 19, 1995, in Warren County, North Carolina, part of the Project on Women's Activism and Grassroots Leadership at the University of North Carolina at Chapel Hill. Tape 41995-KB.

4. For a survey of black youth movements, including the Youth Task Force, see Corliss Hill and Tara Roberts, "Children of the Dream," *Essence*, 25th Anniversary Issue (May 1995), pp. 240–244.

5. The degree to which young people in the NAACP and CORE as well as SNCC (the Student Non-Violent Coordinating Committee) carried on some of the most dangerous work of the civil rights movement is apparent in Anne Moody's *Coming of Age in Mississippi* (New York: Dell, 1968).

6. Kim Burwell, October 1, 1994.

7. Quoted from "The Youth Task Force Organizing Project Proposal Narrative (for 1995–96)." Available from Angela Brown, Youth Task Force, Atlanta, Georgia.

8. Flier "A National Call to Struggle. Countdown 2000: Setting the Black Youth Agenda. Don't Punk Out! March 3–5. A National Student and Youth Shut-in during the 30th Anniversary Commemoration of Bloody Sunday & Selma to Montgomery March." Contacts listed are Kimberly Burwell, Leadership Initiative Project, and Minnie White, Young People's Institute.

9. The following discussion comes from a taped argument between Dollie and Kim Burwell on October 1, 1994.

10. Dollie and Kim Burwell, February 11, 1995.

11. The only time Dollie absolutely forbade Kim to join her was during the demonstration in Forsyth County, Georgia, in 1987. When a white man decided to commemorate Martin Luther King Jr.'s birthday that year in a town from which blacks had been barred since 1912 (after three black men were lynched for allegedly raping a white woman), the organizer received a death threat and withdrew. The march went on until stopped at Cummings, Georgia, where Klan members threw rocks and bottles on January 17, 1987. Mobilizing the troops, Jesse Jackson, Dick Gregory, Coretta Scott King, and Hosea Williams called on affiliates of the Southern Christian Leadership Conference to come to the Martin Luther King Center in Atlanta and then go in buses to Forsyth County on January 24, 1987, for a "March Against Fear and Intimidation." Twelve thousand to twenty thousand people marched, Dollie among them, in one of the biggest civil rights demonstrations since the sixties. A crowd of whites, including David Duke, chanted "Nigger Go Home." Fifty-five white hecklers were arrested. Having expected trouble, Dollie had refused to let Kim join her. Scared by Dollie's adamancy, Kim stayed glued to the television. *New York Times Index* 1987, p. 175; Melynn Glus-

man interview with Kim Burwell, April 19, 1995; Dollie and Kim Burwell, November 1, 1995.

12. Kim Burwell, October 1, 1994.

13. Kim Burwell, Mellon Seminar, Duke University, Durham, North Carolina, November 1, 1995.

14. Kim Burwell, October 1, 1994.

15. Kim Burwell, October 1, 1994.

16. Kim Burwell, October 1, 1994.

17. Personal interview with Dollie Burwell, Warren, North Carolina, January 25, 1993; Kim Burwell, October 1, 1994.

18. Kim Burwell, October 1, 1994.

19. Kim Burwell, April 19, 1995, interview with Melynn Glusman; Kim Burwell, November 1, 1995.

20. Kim Burwell, October 1, 1994; phone interview with Angela Brown, Atlanta, Georgia, November 20, 1995; phone interview with Oliematta (Olie) Taal, Atlanta, Georgia, January 27, 1996; "The Youth Task Force Organizing Project Proposal Narrative for 1995–96," p. 2.

21. Oliematta (Olie) Taal, January 27, 1996.

22. Flier, "A National Call to Struggle."

23. Kim Burwell, November 1, 1995.

24. Kim and Dollie Burwell, November 1, 1995.

25. Kim Burwell at the Mellon Seminar on Women and Grassroots Leadership, Duke University, Durham, North Carolina, November 1, 1995.

26. Kim Burwell, November 1, 1995.

27. Dollie and Kim Burwell, November 1, 1995.

28. Kim Burwell, October 1, 1994.

29. Dollie Burwell, January 25, 1993.

30. Kim Burwell, October 1, 1994.

6. *"We sleep on our own graves": Women at Crossroads*

1. Personal interview, Regina Ntongana, Surplus People Project offices, Athlone, Cape Town, South Africa, July 16, 1993.

2. Gay W. Seidman's " 'No Freedom without the Women': Mobilization and Gender in South Africa, 1970–1992," in *Rethinking the Political: Gender, Resistance, and the State*, edited by Barbara Laslett, Johanna Bren-

ner, and Yesim Arat (Chicago: University of Chicago Press, 1995), pp. 210–239.

3.   Linzi Manicom, "Ruling Relations: Rethinking State and Gender in South African History," *Journal of African History*, 33 (1992): 441–465; 447. In this lucid and thoughtful article, Manicom claims that apartheid, though concerned with regulating labor and making sure that a desperate and hungry supply was always willing to work no matter what the wages or working conditions, also used gender as a means by which to enhance the power of the government and its control over every aspect of life.

4.   For a comprehensive survey of influx control legislation and its effect on housing for blacks, see Laurine Platzky and Cherryl Walker for the Surplus People Project, *The Surplus People: Forced Removals in South Africa* (Johannesburg: Ravan Press, 1985), especially pp. 25–30. See also, "Pass Law Misery," *Cape Herald*, February 9, 1984, p. 4. For a far-reaching analysis of the development of apartheid as a social system, see Deborah Posel, *The Making of Apartheid 1948–1961: Conflict and Compromise*, Oxford Studies in African Affairs (Cape Town and Oxford: Oxford University Press, 1991).

5.   Lauretta Ngcobo, *and they didn't die* (New York: George Brazzilier, 1991), pp. 204–205.

6.   "Pass Law Misery," *Cape Herald*, February 9, 1984, p. 4. For a review of the legislation see Platzky and Walker, *Surplus People*, pp. 141–142.

7.   Because of the need at the time to protect the identity of activists, Josette Cole simply used initials to refer to people such as Mrs. Regina Ntongana, the chairwoman of the Women's Committee in Crossroads. For the quotation, see Cole, " 'When Your Life is Bitter You Do Something,' Women and Squatting in the Western Cape: Tracing the Origins of Crossroads and the Role of Women in Its Struggle," in *South African Research Papers*, edited by Dave Kaplan, Department of Economic History (University of Cape Town P. B. Rondebosch 7700, Cape Town: University of Cape Town, South Africa, June 1986), p. 16.

8.   Ngcobo, *and they didn't die*, pp. 42–43.

9.   Jane Barnstable, "Helping Them to Help Each Other," *The Cape Times*, July 10, 1979, p. 6.

10. For estimates about arrests for violating pass laws, see Platzky and Walker, *Surplus People*, pp. 9, 33. The description of the life of women without passes is from Poppie Nongena [pseud.], quoted in Elsa Joubert, *The Long Journey of Poppie Nongena* (Johannesburg: Jonathan Ball Publishers, 1980), p. 255. In her book, *Imperial Leather: Race, Gender and Sexuality in the Colonial Contest* (New York and London: Routledge, 1995), pp. 299–328, Anne McClintock claims that *The Long Journey* is a fictionalized version of a real life, and is a "hybrid," neither a novel nor an oral history. She rightly questions why white South Africans who supported apartheid

would treat the book as a human interest story, and wonders what interests the two women coming from such different positions of power had in speaking to each other. I'm using the narrative here merely to highlight more ample newspaper, survey, and personal accounts and thus add another type of evidence to a broader picture of the political effects of apartheid on the everyday life of ordinary women of color.

11.   Since many of the people at Crossroads were there without passes, it is impossible to get an accurate count of the population at any time. For the figure of 105,000 see Marianne Thamm and Glynnis Underhill, "Focus: Crossroads 'War Zone,' " *Cape Times*, May 21, 1986, available in the Surplus People Project Resource Collection: Press Clips, Crossroads, Box 1 (Pre-1992), File Crossroads, 1985/86/87.

12.   The significance of Crossroads to the struggle for democracy and justice in South Africa became apparent to me when I read Josette Cole, *Crossroads: The Politics of Reform and Repression 1976–1986* (Johannesburg: Ravan Press, 1987), and her earlier monograph, " 'When Your Life is Bitter, You Do Something.' " Cole, a volunteer for the Western Province Council of Churches, supported the people at Crossroads who were resisting expulsions and then became the chronicler of their efforts.

13.   Mrs. N (really Mrs. Regina Ntongana) quoted in *We Will Not Move: The Struggle for Crossroads* (Cape Town: The National Union of South African Students, 1978), p. 21.

14.   Pamela Reynolds, *Childhood in Crossroads: Cognition and Society in South Africa* (Cape Town, Johannesburg, and Grand Rapids, MI: David Philip Publisher and William B. Eerdmans Publishing, 1989), pp. 208–209.

15.   "Women's Movement Statement Following the Raid," *We Will Not Move*, p. 69.

16.   Reynolds, *Childhood in Crossroads*, pp. 16, 97; Andrew Silk, *A Shanty Town in South Africa: The Story of Modderdam* (Johannesburg: Ravan Press, 1981), p. 83.

17.   Mrs. N. quoted in *We Will Not Move*, p. 19.

18.   From a statement by Mrs. Sheena Duncan, national president of Black Sash, "Eight million blacks 'have lost citizenship,' " *Argus*, February 11, 1983, reproduced in *South African Pressclips*, February 13, 1983, p. 49.

19.   "Land and People: Profile of South Africa," C2 of *Land in South Africa* (Johannesburg: Human Awareness Programme, February 1989).

20.   "Three hundred believed arrested: Three reported dead in raid," *Cape Times*, September 15, 1978, pp. 1, 6; 1. Jonathan Wacks film: *Crossroads / South Africa: The Struggle Continues*, video at the Schomburg Collection, New York Public Library, done about this time, shows the

growing cohesion of the women and their assumption of leadership positions in the community.

21.   Cole draws on an article by K. Showers, "A note on women, conflict and migrant labour," p. 57, for her own assessment. Cole, "When Your Life is Bitter You Do Something," p. 54.

22.   Nazeem Howa, "Meet Aunty Dora Jassen, the Woman Everyone Calls 'Mayoress Vrygrond,' " *Cape Herald*, February 16, 1984, p. 2.

23.   Mrs. Ntongana, quoted as "N," "When Your Life is Bitter, You Do Something," pp. 16–17.

24.   Reynolds, *Childhood in Crossroads*, p. 15.

25.   Reynolds, *Childhood in Crossroads*, p. 16.

26.   Mrs. B. in *We Will Not Move*, pp. 23–24.

27.   As quoted from one of the earlier settlers in Cole, *Crossroads*, p.11.

28.   Reynolds, *Childhood in Crossroads*, p. 20.

29.   Cole, *Crossroads*, p. 13.

30.   One of the heroic stories in South African history is the long resistance of women to carrying passes. For especially moving histories see Cherryl Walker, *Women and Resistance in South Africa* (New York: Monthly Review Press, 1982; 1991); and Julia Wells, "Why Women Rebel: A Comparative Study of South African Women's Resistance in Bloemfontein (1913) and Johannesburg (1958)," *Journal of South African Studies*, 10, 1 (1984): 55–70.

31.   Kathryn Spink, *Black Sash: The Beginning of a Bridge in South Africa* (London: Methuen, 1991), pp. 24, 33, 64.

32.   Mrs. B. in *We Will Not Move*, pp. 24–25.

33.   N. Robb of the Advice office is quoted in an interview with Josette Cole (Cape Town, 1984) in Cole, *Crossroads*, pp. 13–14.

34.   Cited in Cole, "When Your Life is Bitter You Do Something," p. 42.

35.   Quoted in Cole, *Crossroads*, p. 20. More than a decade later, Mrs. Ntongana still recalled the growing animosity of the men. Regina Ntongana, July 16, 1993.

36.   Reynolds, *Childhood*, pp. 56, 97; Silk, *A Shanty Town in South Africa*, pp. 43–44. Sociologists Naomi Rosenthal and Michael Schwartz call such associations primary movement groups. See their article "Spontaneity and Democracy in Social Movements," *International Social Movement Research*, Vol. 2, pp. 33–59.

37.   The report is cited in a revealing lecture delivered by Brigadier V. D. Ubsthvizen to an audience at the University of Cape Town. Although the lecture defends the government's position and attempts to show that

because of overcrowding and crime, Crossroads is a health hazard, still the statistics appear to be accurate though the solution—namely, forcibly evicting the population—does not follow. See the lecture titled "The State on Crossroads Speech by Brig. V. D. Westhuizen to Audience at UCT," in *We Will Not Move*, pp. 82–89; 85. For an outline of his charges, blaming the people at Crossroads for everything from unemployment to the housing shortage and the crime wave, see "Report Compiled by Brig. V. D. Westhuizen," *We Will Not Move*, pp. 90–91.

38.   Mrs. N. quoted in *We Will Not Move*, p. 21.

39.   Silk, *A Shanty Town*, p. 144, quoting the police from an article in the *Cape Times*, August 13, 1977.

40.   Quoted in Silk, *A Shanty Town*, p. 31.

41.   Quoted in Silk, *A Shanty Town*, pp. 31–32.

42.   Reynolds, *Childhood at Crossroads*, p. 56. Cole disagrees about the special role women played and attributes the building of the Sizamile and Noxolo schools to local residents of both sexes. Cole, *Crossroads*, p. 18. For a discussion of the schools, see Mr. T., "Three Interviews: The Early History of Crossroads"; "Chronology of Events at Crossroads"; "The Squatter Camp at Crossroads—A Response to Apartheid," SANA (Southern African News Agency) Bulletin 1978/4; *We Will Not Move*, pp. 17; 27–28; 58–59; 59.

43.   Quoted in Cole, "When Your Life is Bitter You Do Something," p. 17.

44.   Quoted in Cole, "When Your Life is Bitter You Do Something," p. 17. Mrs. Ntongana has merged Sizamile and Noxolo in her recollection.

45.   Reynolds, *Childhood in Crossroads*, p. 51. Mrs. Ntongana happily recalls her brief stint as a teacher. Personal interview with Regina Ntongana, Nordhoek, Cape Town, South Africa, July 19, 1993.

46.   Jonathan Wacks's film: *Crossroads / South Africa: The Struggle Continues*, video at the Schomburg Collection, New York Public Library. The *Cape Times* says that the rumored death of the baby could not be verified.

47.   Mrs. Ntongana is the best source for the meeting and how the women viewed it. It is her reflection that appears in " 'We Are Not Moving': An Account of the Women of Crossroads Delegation to BAAB-Following Police Pass Raids on the Camp," *We Will Not Move*, p. 68. She told the same story nearly twenty years later in a personal interview, Athlone, Cape Town, July 22, 1994.

48.   Regina Ntongana, July 22, 1994.

49.   "We Are Not Moving," *We Will Not Move*, p. 68.

50.   "The Raids and Some Community Responses: The Women," and "We Are Not Moving," *We Will Not Move*, pp. 67; 68. Regina Ntongana, July 16, 1993.

51.   Cole, "When Your Life is Bitter You Do Something," p. 18.

52.   Cole, *Crossroads,* p. 22.

53.   Quote from K. Kiewet and K. Weichel, *Inside Crossroads* (Cape Town, 1981), p. 51, cited in Cole, *Crossroads,* p. 22. The team of volunteer researchers known as the Surplus People Project worried because in order to save Crossroads, they had appealed to the population at large through the media, bumper stickers, and public exhibitions, rather than promote more community participation. See *Forced Removals in South Africa. The SPP Reports,* Vol. 3 (Capetown and Pietermaritzburg: The Surplus People Project, 1983), p. 51.

54.   Cole, *Crossroads,* pp. 22–23.

55.   Mrs. Regina Ntongana quoted in Cole, "When Your Life is Bitter You Do Something," p. 19. See also Keri Swift, "The Raids and Some Community Responses: The Women," *We Will Not Move,* p. 67.

56.   Reynolds, *Childhood in Crossroads,* p. 96.

57.   Cole, *Crossroads,* pp. 23–24.

58.   Quoted in Cole, *Crossroads,* p. 62.

59.   Mrs. Ntongana quoted in Cole, "When Your Life is Bitter You Do Something," p. 23.

60.   Regina Ntongana, July 23, 1993.

61.   "Minister goes to squatter township," *Cape Times,* November 22, 1978, p. 1. An earlier editorial titled "Looking for Scapegoats," printed in *Cape Times,* September 20, 1978, p. 8, counters the government's charges that the churches were provoking Crossroads' residents to resist. The newspaper claimed that people have only to remember "the photographs which have been published in the newspapers" to realize what was happening.

62.   Leon Beller. "Crossroads Arrests Despite Koornhof," *Cape Times,* July 4, 1979, p. 11.

63.   Cole, *Crossroads,* pp. 31–35, 37.

64.   Staff reporter, "First 6-month permits issued," *Cape Times,* July 24, 1979, p. 15.

65.   Cole, *Crossroads,* p. 45.

66.   Barry Streek, "F—Julle! That's what a commissioner told Crossroads squatters," *Golden City Pass,* reproduced in *South African Pressclips,* July 18, 1982, p. 30, says that the basic rent at New Crossroads was 29.50 rand plus water costs, up three or four times the 7 to 10 rand that had been paid at Old Crossroads.

67.   Cole, *Crossroads,* p. 52, places the number at about fifty thousand. Newspaper estimates go even higher.

68.   Reynolds, *Childhood in Crossroads,* p. 210; Joseph Lelyveld, "Pretoria Firm," *New York Times,* August 9, 1981, p. A29.

69. Reynolds, *Childhood in Crossroads*, p. 210.

70. Quoted in Reynolds, *Childhood in Crossroads*, p. 41.

71. Cole, *Crossroads*, pp. 67–69.

72. "Price of Residential Land Skyrockets in Cape Town's Indian Areas," *Cape Herald*, December 29, 1983, p. 4.

73. Quotation from "Eviction Dilemma," *Financial Mail*, July 25, 1986, reproduced in *South African Pressclips*, week ending July 27, 1986, no. 29, pp. 18–19.

74. "Eviction Dilemma," *Financial Mail*, July 25, 1986, reproduced in *South African Pressclips*, week ending July 27, 1986, no. 29, pp. 18–19; 19.

75. Quoted in Reynolds, *Childhood in Crossroads*, p. 97.

76. "169 Crossroads Women in Court," *Cape Times*, January 25, 1985, p. 1; " 'Where is our bail money?,' ask angry residents," *Grassroots*, May 1986, p. 8. See also Cole, *Crossroads*, pp. 104–105, 118.

77. Cole, *Crossroads*, pp. 114–115.

78. Laurine Platzky, July 28, 1993; Cole, *Crossroads*, pp. 88–89, 100.

79. Cole, "Crossroads: A special kind of removal," *Cape Times*, May 23, 1986, p. 8; Cole, *Crossroads*, p. 123. Other journalists concur with Josette Cole that the police were supporting the witdoeke in their destruction of Crossroads and its satellites. *Grassroots* and even the *Cape Times* seemed certain that the police were supporting Johnson Ngxobongwana. For instance, an article in the May 19, 1986, *Cape Times* said, "Reporters saw Casspirs (armored cars) standing by without apparently intervening—an accusation which was emphatically denied by the police last night," in Yazeed Fakier and Tony Weaver, "3 die in battles between squatter rivals: Thousands homeless," *Cape Times*, May 19, 1986, p. 1. A statement signed by groups ranging from Catholic Justice and Peace to Black Sash to the United Democratic Front to Jews for Justice alleged "collusion between the security forces and the Witdoeke vigilantes." See "Cape Town must bear witness to forced removal," *Cape Times*, June 3, 1986, p. 8.

80. Reynolds, *Childhood in Crossroads*, p. 203.

81. Reynolds, *Childhood in Crossroads*, p. 217.

82. Allister Sparks, "Pass laws may be scrapped, but still there is no freedom," *Cape Times*, May 1, 1986, p. 8; Barry Streek, "Powers to control squatting condemned," *Cape Times*, June 4, 1986, p. 2.

83. Cole, *Crossroads*, pp. 119–120.

84. The numbers dislodged vary from thirty thousand to seventy thousand, according to accounts, although the later ones, written in retrospect, give higher estimates. See "Crossroads killers still run free," *Grassroots*, Vol. 8, no. 3 (June 1987), p. 6, which says that fifty died and forty thousand lost their homes during the attack on Crossroads and its

collateral communities of KTC, Portland Cement, Nyanga, and Nyanga Bush. In "Houses for sale in Crossroads," *Cape Times,* July 4, 1987, the municipal reporter estimates that up to seventy thousand people lost their homes in the attack a year earlier. For numbers of people hurt, see Chris Erasmus, "4,000 squatters hurt 'in gunfire,' " *Cape Times,* June 23, 1987. Consult Cole, *Crossroads,* p. 132, 142.

85.   Reynolds, *Childhood in Crossroads,* p. 203; Cole, *Crossroads,* p. 135, says three thousand makeshift dwellings were destroyed in the fighting. The exclusion of the press is reported in Marianne Thamm and Glynnis Underhill, "Crossroads 'war zone,' " *Cape Times,* May 21, 1986, in SPP Press Clips, Crossroads Box 1, Pre-1992, File Crossroads, 1985/86/87.

86.   "Govt, squatters heading for showdown," *Cape Times,* May 23, 1986, p. 1; Chris Bateman and Renke Moodie, "Crossroads: Shawco call to government," *Cape Times,* June 4, 1986, p. 2; Andrew Donaldson, "Women plead at Parliament," *Cape Times,* June 10, 1986, p. 2.

87.   Donaldson, "Women Plead at Parliament," *Cape Times,* June 10, 1986, p. 2. "Beyond belief," editorial in *Cape Times,* June 10, 1986, p. 6. The questions and the charges were repeated in "A national scandal," *Cape Times,* June 11, 1986, p. 10.

88.   Chris Bateman, "Haven for widow, family," *Cape Times,* June 13, 1986, p. 7.

89.   Chris Erasmus, "We have lost all—even hope," *Cape Times,* June 24, 1986, p. 11.

90.   "Squatters Want Camp Wire Cordon Removed," *Star,* August 20, 1986, reproduced in *South African Pressxlips,* August 24, 1986, no. 33, p. 15.

91.   Quoted in *We Will Not Move,* p. 70.

7.   Surplus People and Grassroots Women's Leadership in the New South Africa

1.   Personal Interview with Regina Ntongana, Surplus People Project offices, Athlone, Cape Town, South Africa, July 16, 1993.

2.   Personal discussion with Sheena Duncan, founder and past president of Black Sash, Johannesburg, July 28, 1993; personal conversation with Sue Sparks, member of Black Sash, Johannesburg, South Africa, July 30, 1993; personal conversation with Mary Burton, past president of Black Sash, Cape Town, July 21, 1994.

3.   Personal interview with Laurine Platzky, July 18, 1993, Gardens, Cape Town, South Africa.

4.   Personal interviews with Josette Cole, Cape Town, South Africa, July 19 and 24, 1993.

5. *We Will Not Move: The Struggle for Crossroads* (Cape Town: National Union of South African Students, 1978).

6. Laurine Platzky and Cheryl Walker for the Surplus People Project, *The Surplus People: Forced Removals in South Africa* (Johannesburg: Ravan Press, 1985).

7. See her early monograph, " 'When Your Life is Bitter, You Do Something,' Women and Squatting in the Western Cape: Tracing the origins of Crossroads and the role of women in its struggle," *South African Research Papers*, edited by Dave Kaplan (Cape Town: Department of Economic History, the University of Cape Town, June 1986). Also see Cole's *Crossroads: The Politics of Reform and Repression 1976–1986* (Johannesburg: Ravan Press, 1987).

8. Personal attendance at this session, SPP offices, Athlone, Cape Town, July 23, 1993.

9. Personal interview with Regina Ntongana, SPP offices, Athlone, South Africa, July 22, 1994.

10. Personal discussion with Irene "Mawushe" Narwele on the ride back from Malmesbury, July 20, 1993.

11. Workbook to be used with the video *Abafazi Abangajikiyo: The Women Who Didn't Turn Back* (Surplus People Project Gender Programme, 1994), p. 4.

12. Personal interview with Irene "Mawushe" Narwele, Athlone, Cape Town, South Africa, July 22, 1994.

13. Regina Ntongana, Nordhoek, Cape Town, July 23, 1993.

15. Regina Ntongana, Nordhoek, July 19, 1994.

15. Regina Ntongana, July 22, 1994.

16. Regina Ntongana, July 23, 1993.

17. Phone interview with Josette Cole, August 3, 1995.

18. Regina Ntongana, July 22, 1994.

8. Conclusion: Social Movements and Democratic Practices

1. Personal interview with Dollie Burwell, Durham, North Carolina, November 1, 1995.

2. Aldon D. Morris, "Black Southern Student Sit-In Movement: An Analysis of Internal Organization," *American Sociological Review* 46 (1981): 744–67; *The Origins of the Civil Rights Movement* (New York: The Free Press, 1984); Aldon Morris and Cedric Herring, "Theory and Research in

Social Movements: A Critical Review," in the *Annual Review of Political Science*, Vol. 2 (1987): 138–198. For the best cross-section of recent work done in social movement theory, see the book Morris edited with Carol McClurg Mueller, *Frontiers in Social Movement Theory* (New Haven: Yale University Press, 1992).

Sidney Tarrow, *Peasant Communism in Southern Italy* (New Haven: Yale University Press, 1967); *Struggling to Reform: Social Movements and Policy Change during Cycles of Protest* (Ithaca, NY: Cornell University Press, 1983); *Democracy and Disorder: Protest and Politics in Italy, 1965–1975* (New York: Oxford University Press, 1989); an article he produced with Bert Klandermans and Hanspeter Kriesi, "From Structure to Action: Comparing Movement Participation across Cultures," *International Social Movement Research*, Vol. 1 (1988): 41–83.

Charles Tilly, *The Vendee* (Cambridge, MA: Harvard University Press, 1964); "Collective Violence in European Perspective," in *Violence in America: Historical and Comparative Perspectives*, edited by Hugh Davis Graham and Ted Robert Gurr (New York: Praeger, 1969), pp. 4–45; "Food Supply and Public Order in Modern Europe," in *The Formation of National States in Western Europe*, edited by Charles Tilly (Princeton: Princeton University Press, 1975), pp. 380–455; *From Mobilization to Revolution* (Reading, MA: Addison-Wesley, 1978); *The Contentious French* (Cambridge, MA: Harvard University Press, 1986).

3. Personal communication from Naomi Rosenthal, March 26, 1996.

4. Ellen Ross, "Survival Networks: Women's Neighborhood Sharing in London before World War II," *History Workshop Journal* 15 (1983): 4–27.

5. Naomi Rosenthal and Michael Schwartz, "Spontaneity and Democracy in Social Movements," *International Social Movement Research*, Vol. 2 (1989): 33–59.

6. While Rosenthal and Schwartz ("Spontaneity and Democracy in Social Movements," p. 46) emphasize the organic democracy found in primary movement groups, they realize that such affinity groups can also attempt to achieve profoundly undemocratic goals—as certain white supremacy groups and right-to-life movements have done. Although the structure of primary movement group behavior is basically fluid and personal, allowing the group itself to work democratically, the achievements of the groups may be racist or sexist. Blame for what primary movement groups do must rest with the mass base as well as with individual leaders even more than in more highly differentiated movements.

7. For a cross-section of historical works on women's collective efforts to improve the quality of life and achieve social justice, see Nancy F. Cott, *The Bonds of Womanhood: "Women's Sphere" in New England, 1780–1835* (New Haven: Yale University Press, 1977); Paula Giddings, *When and*

Where I Enter: The Impact of Black Women on Race and Sex in America (New York: W. W. Morrow, 1984); Linda Gordon, *Pitied But Not Entitled: Single Mothers and the History of Welfare, 1890–1935* (New York: The Free Press, 1994); Jacquelyn Dowd Hall, *Revolt against Chivalry: Jessie Daniel Ames and the Women's Campaign against Lynching* (New York: Columbia University Press, 1993); Dolores Hayden, *The Grand Domestic Revolution: A History of Feminist Designs for American Homes, Neighborhoods, and Cities* (Cambridge, MA: MIT Press, 1981); Nancy A. Hewitt, *Women's Activism and Social Change: Rochester, New York, 1822–1870* (Ithaca: Cornell University Press, 1984); Robert G. Moeller, *Protecting Motherhood: Women and the Family in the Politics of Postwar West Germany* (Berkeley: University of California, 1993); Annelise Orleck, *Common Sense and a Little Fire: Women and Working-Class Politics in the United States, 1900–1965* (Chapel Hill: University of North Carolina Press, 1995); Ellen Ross, *Love and Toil: Motherhood in Outcast London, 1870–1918* (New York: Oxford University Press, 1993); and Kathryn Kish Sklar, *Florence Kelley and the Nation's Work* (New Haven: Yale University Press, 1995).

8.   Sheila Rowbotham, Joan W. Scott, Barbara Taylor, and Dorothy Thompson have examined the contributions that working-class and middle-class women, who hoped to transform their roles in family, work, and politics, made to utopian socialism and incipient labor unions. See Rowbotham, *Hidden from History: Rediscovering Women in History from the 17th Century to the Present* (New York: Vintage, 1976), pp. 39–46, and her *Women, Resistance & Revolution: A History of Women and Revolution in the Modern World* (New York: Vintage, 1974), pp. 36–58; Scott, "Men and Women in the Parisian Garment Trades: Discussions of Family and Work in the 1830s and 1840s," in *The Power of the Past: Essays for Eric Hobsbawm*, edited by Pat Thane, Geoffrey Crossic, and Roderick Floud (Cambridge, England: Cambridge University Press, 1984), pp. 67–93; Taylor, *Eve and the New Jerusalem: Socialism and Feminism in the Nineteenth Century* (New York: Pantheon, 1983); and Thompson, "Women and Nineteenth-Century Radical Politics: A Lost Dimension," in *The Rights and Wrongs of Women*, edited by Juliet Mitchell and Ann Oakley (Harmondsworth, England: Penguin Books, 1976), pp. 112–148.

I have argued elsewhere that sensitivity to gender, both on the job and in the home, enabled anarchist women to challenge authority in every aspect of their lives. See my *Anarchists of Andalusia, 1868–1903* (Princeton: Princeton University Press, 1977) and "Women and Spanish Anarchism," in *Becoming Visible: Women in European History*, first edition, edited by Renate Bridenthal and Claudia Koonz (Boston: Houghton Mifflin, 1977), pp. 400–421.

9.   Deborah M. Valenze offers brilliant historical analyses of how women participants in religious reform hoped to reorder social priorities

in "Cottage Religion and the Politics of Survival," in *Equal or Different: Women's Politics 1800–1914*, edited by Jane Rendall (Oxford: Basil Blackwell, 1987), pp. 31–56, and in *Prophetic Sons and Daughters: Female Preaching and Popular Religion in Industrial England* (Princeton: Princeton University Press, 1985).

For theorists and historians who have been concerned with women's activities in modern peace campaigns, see Barbara Epstein, *Political Protest & Cultural Revolution: Nonviolent Direct Action in the 1970s and 1980s* (Berkeley: The University of California, 1991); *Rocking the Ship of State: Toward a Feminist Peace Politics*, edited by Adrienne Harris and Ynestra King (Boulder, CO: Westview Press, 1989); Sarah Ruddick, *Maternal Thinking: Toward a Politics of Peace* (Boston: Beacon Press, 1989); Amy Swerdlow, *Women Strike for Peace: Traditional Motherhood and Radical Politics in the 1960s* (Chicago: University of Chicago Press, 1993).

For works on women and environmental struggles, see Irene Dankelman and Joan Davidson, *Women and the Environment in the Third World: Alliance for the Future* (London: Earthscan Publishers in association with IUCN, 1988); Celine Krauss, "Blue-Collar Women and Toxic-Waste Protests: The Process of Politicization," in *Toxic Struggles: The Theory and Practice of Environmental Justice*, edited by Richard Hofrichter (Philadelphia: New Society Publishers, 1993), pp. 106–117; Radha Kumar's *The History of Doing: An Illustrated Account of Movements for Women's Rights and Feminism in India, 1800–1990* (London and New York: Verso, 1993), pp. 182–190; Annabel Rodda, *Women and the Environment* (London and Atlantic Highlands, NJ: Zed, 1993); and Joni Seager, *Earth Follies: Coming to Feminist Terms with the Global Environmental Crisis* (New York: Routledge, 1993).

10.   Urban planner and feminist critic Dolores Hayden discusses how important certain landmarks are to community solidarity in *The Power of Place: Urban Landscapes as Public History* (Cambridge, MA: MIT Press, 1995).

11.   Sonia E. Alvarez, *Engendering Democracy in Brazil: Women's Movements in Transition Politics* (Princeton: Princeton University Press, 1990); María del Carmen Feijoo and Monica Gogna, "Women in the Transition to Democracy," in *Women and Social Change in Latin America*, edited by Elizabeth Jelin (London and New Jersey: Zed Books, 1990), pp. 79–134; Jane S. Jaquette, ed., *The Women's Movement in Latin America: Participation and Democracy*, second edition (Boulder, CO: Westview Press, 1994); Elizabeth Jelin, ed., *Women and Social Change in Latin America*; Teresa Valdés with Marisa C. Weinstein, *Organizaciones de Pobladoras y Construcción Democrática en Chile* (Santiago: FLASCO, 1989).

12.   Denise Riley, *"Am I That Name?" Feminism and the Category of "Women" in History* (Minneapolis: University of Minnesota Press, 1988). See especially p. 50, where she argues: "Insofar as the concerns of the so-

cial *are* familial standards—health, education, hygiene, fertility, demography, chastity and fecundity—and the heart of the family is inexorably the woman, then the woman is also solidly inside of that which has to some degree already been feminized. The 'social' does not merely admit women to it; something more constructive than a matter of entry or access is going on; it is as if 'women' became established as a new kind of sociological collectivity."

13.   Marjorie Agosín, *The Mothers of the Plaza de Mayo: The Story of Renée Epelbaum, 1976–1985*, translated by Janice Molloy (Trenton, NJ: The Red Sea Press, Inc., 1990); Marguerite Bouvard, *Revolutionizing Motherhood: The Mothers of the Plaza de Mayo* (Wilmington, DE: Scholarly Resource Books, 1994); Patricia Chuchryk, "Subversive Mothers: The Women's Opposition to the Military Regime in Chile," in *Women, the State and Development*, edited by Sue Ellen M. Charlton, Jana Everett, and Kathleen Staudt (Albany: State University of New York Press, 1989), pp. 130–151; Jo Fisher, *Mothers of the Disappeared* (London: Zed Books, 1989); Marysa Navarro, "The Personal is Political: The Madres de Plaza de Mayo," in *Power and Popular Protest: Latin American Social Movements*, edited by Susan Eckstein (Berkeley: University of California Press, 1989), pp. 241–258; Jennifer Schirmer, "Those Who Die for Life Cannot be Called Dead: Women and Human Rights Protest in Latin America," in *Surviving Beyond Fear: Women, Children and Human Rights in Latin America*, edited by Marjorie Agosín (Fredonia, NY: White Pine Press, 1993), pp. 31–57; and Schirmer, "The Seeking of Truth and the Gendering of Consciousness: The CO-MADRES of El Salvador and the CONAVIGUA Widows of Guatemala," in *'Viva': Women and Popular Protest in Latin America*, edited by Sarah A. Radcliffe and Sallie Westwood (London: Routledge, 1993), pp. 30–64. Lynn Stephen carried out conversations with the Salvadoran grassroots leader María Teresa Tula, published as *Hear My Testimony! María Teresa Tula, Human Rights Activist of El Salvador* (Boston: South End Press, 1994); see also Stephen's *Power from Below: Women's Grassroots Organizing in Latin America* (Austin: University of Texas Press, forthcoming).

14.   Increasingly, feminist scholars have challenged the veracity of oral history and testimonials, much as they have other sources. The argument is that the closeness of the relationship between the person speaking—who is usually a person with less formal education than the writer—and the terms of the relationship, which almost always includes unequal power relations between the two parties, preclude some of the caution scholars exercise with written texts. Particularly trenchant criticism and self-criticism can be found in Ruth Behar, *Translated Woman: Crossing the Border with Esperanza's Story* (Boston: Beacon Press, 1993); John Beverley, "The Margin at the Center of *Testimonio* (Testimonial Narrative)," in *De/Colonizing the Subject: The Politics of Gender in Women's Autobiography*, edited by Sidonie Smith and Julia Watson (Minneapolis: University of

Minnesota Press, 1992), pp. 91–114; Belinda Bozzoli, *Women of Pho-keng: Consciousness, Life Strategy, and Migrancy in South Africa, 1900–1983* (Portsmouth, NH: Heinemann, 1991); Marsha Darling, "The Disinherited as Source: Rural Black Women's Memories," *Michigan Quarterly Review* 26, no. 1 (Winter 1987): 48–63; Doris Sommer, " 'Not Just a Personal Story': Women's *Testimonios* and the Plural Self," in *Life/Lines: Theorizing Women's Autobiography*, edited by Bella Brodzki and Celeste Schenck (Ithaca: Cornell University Press, 1988), pp. 107–130; Judith Stacey, "Can There Be a Feminist Ethnography?" and Daphne Patai, "U.S. Academics and Third World Women: Is Ethical Research Possible?" in *Women's Words: The Feminist Practice of Oral History*, edited by Sherna Berger Gluck and Daphne Patai (New York and London: Routledge, 1991), pp. 111–119; 137–153; Marcia Wright, *Strategies of Slaves & Women: Life-Stories from East/Central Africa* (New York: Lilian Barber Press, Inc., and London: James Currey, 1993).

15.   Temma Kaplan, "Female Consciousness and Collective Action: The Case of Barcelona, 1910–1918," in *Rethinking the Political: Gender, Resistance, and the State*, edited by Barbara Laslett, Johanna Brenner, and Yesim Arat (Chicago: University of Chicago Press, 1995), pp. 145–166. The article originally appeared in 1982.

16.   Temma Kaplan, "Women and Communal Strikes in the Crisis of 1917–22," in *Becoming Visible: Women in European History*, second edition, edited by Renate Bridenthal, Claudia Koonz, and Susan Mosher Stuard (Boston: Houghton Mifflin, 1987), pp. 429–449, p. 436.

17.   Maxine Molyneux, "Mobilization Without Emancipation? Women's Interests, the State, and Revolution in Nicaragua," *Feminist Studies* 11, no. 2 (Summer 1985): 227–253, 230–235.

18.   Several critics have rebuked Molyneux and me for implying that women were preoccupied with private rather than public matters, when we were in fact arguing that the working-class women we were studying would not accept any distinction between needs and the political authority to fulfill them. Molyneux and I were concerned with consciousness and democratic priorities in movements for social change; we never accepted the idea of separate spheres.

In debate with those orthodox Marxists who believe that women simply act as undifferentiated members of a working class or revolutionary group and that certain issues, such as reproductive rights or resistance to domestic violence, could not be raised until some time in the future, we argued that women as well as men constituted "the people," the revolutionary group, or the working class. For one of Molyneux's critiques of ways socialist societies underestimated gender, see "Socialist Societies Old and New: Progress toward Women's Emancipation," *Monthly Review*, Vol. 34, no. 3 (July-August 1982): 56–100.

Among the critics who chastise us for binary thinking are Sallie Westwood and Sarah Radcliffe, "Gender, Racism, and the Politics of Identities in Latin America," in *'Viva': Women and Popular Protest in Latin America*, edited by Sallie Westwood and Sarah Radcliffe (London: Routledge, 1993), pp. 1–29; and Lynn Stephen, "Women's rights are human rights: the merging of feminine and feminist interests among El Salvador's mothers of the disappeared (CO-MADRES)," *American Ethnologist*, Vol. 22, no. 4 (1995): 1–20, 16–17.

19.   Although there are no logical reasons for disputes between women acting in social movements to protect their communities and those standing up for their own rights as women and as citizens, historically the groups have sometimes crossed swords over class and racial priorities. For a discussion of the rough battles that Latin American women of different classes and ethnicities waged first against one another and then together, see Nancy Saporta Sternbach, Marysa Navarro-Aranguren, Patricia Chuchryk, and Sonia E. Alvarez, "Feminisms in Latin America: From Bogotá to San Bernardo," in *Rethinking Politics*, pp. 240–281.

In the United States, white and black women argued in the seventies about whether sisterhood was more powerful than racial differences. The disputes were particularly acute around issues of reproductive rights. Black women, aware that many women of color were being sterilized right after childbirth in many city hospitals, wanted rights to abortions linked to opposition to sterilization abuse. The reproductive rights movement was launched to encompass broad needs. See Rosalind Petchesky, "Reproductive Freedom: Beyond Women's Right to Choose," *Signs*, Vol. 5, no. 4 (1980): 661–685; Adele Clarke and Alice Wolfson, "Class, Race, and Reproductive Rights," in *Women, Class, and the Feminist Imagination: A Socialist-Feminist Reader*, edited by Karen V. Hansen and Ilene J. Philipson (Philadelphia: Temple University Press, 1990), pp. 258–267.

20.   My translation of Elizabeth Jelin, "Los Movimientos Sociales en la Argentina contemporánea: una introducción a su estudio," in *Los Nuevos Movimientos Sociales/1* (Buenos Aires: Centro Editor de América Latina, 1985), p. 18.

Bibliography

Special Collections

Mayibuye Centre for History and Culture in South Africa, University of the Western Cape: Photographic Archive and Library

The Museum of Broadcasting, New York City

Schomburg Center for Research in Black Culture of the New York Public Library

The TV News Archive, Vanderbilt University, Nashville, Tennessee

South African Historical Archive, University of Witswatersrand, Newspaper and Poster Collection

Surplus People Project Resource Collection: Press Clips, Box 1(Pre-1992), File Crossroads, 1985/86/87

The Wilson Library, the University of North Carolina, Chapel Hill, Clipping Collection on PCB Spills

Interviews

The interviews were of various lengths, some amounting to whole days and weekends spent together, some more informal conversations, and some phone interviews.

Phone interview with Angela Brown, Atlanta, Georgia, November 20, 1995.

Personal interview with Patricia Brown, October 29, 1994, Love Canal, New York.

Personal conversation with Mary Burton, past president of Black Sash, Cape Town, July 21, 1994.

Whole days spent with Dollie Burwell, Warrenton, North Carolina, January 25, 1993; Afton and Warrenton, September 29, 30,

October 1, 2, 1994; Afton, February 11, 12, 1995; Durham, North Carolina, October 31, November 1, 1995.

Phone interviews with Dollie Burwell, November 19, 1992; June 7, 1993; June 5, 1995; January 1, 1996.

Interview with Dollie Burwell by Melynn Glusman, April 19, 1995, part of the Project on Women's Activism and Grassroots Leadership at the University of North Carolina at Chapel Hill. Tape 41994-KB.

Personal interviews with Kim Burwell, Afton, North Carolina, September 30 and October 1, 1994; February 11, 1995; whole day spent together, November 1, 1995.

Interview with Kim Burwell by Melynn Glusman, April 19, 1995, in Warren County, North Carolina, part of the Project on Women's Activism and Grassroots Leadership at the University of North Carolina at Chapel Hill. Tape 41995-KB.

Phone interview with Debbie Cerrillo, August 8, 1994; personal interview with Debbie Cerrillo, October 30, 1994, Grand Island, New York.

Personal interviews with Josette Cole, Cape Town, South Africa, July 16, 19, 24, 1993; July 22, 25, 1994.

Phone interview with Josette Cole, August 2, 1995.

Personal discussion with Sheena Duncan, founder and past president of Black Sash, Johannesburg, July 28, 1993.

Personal interview with Deborah Ferruccio, Afton, North Carolina, October 1, 1994.

Personal interview with Ken Ferruccio, Afton, North Carolina, October 1, 1994.

Personal interview with Lois Gibbs, Falls Church, Virginia, July 10, 1995.

Personal interviews with Luella Kenny, Grand Island, New York, October 28 and 29, 1994; phone interviews, August 15, 1994; June 28, 1995; November 22, 1995.

Phone interview with Jenny Labalme, Indianapolis, Indiana, February 20, 1993.

Personal interview with Adeline (Addie) Gordon Levine and Murray Levine, Buffalo, New York, October 28, 1994; phone interview with Adeline and Murray Levine, June 17, 1995.

Personal interview with Vernice Miller, Manhattan, February 24, 1993.

Whole days spent with Irene "Mawushe" Narwele, July 20, 1993; July 22, 1994.

Whole days spent with Regina Ntongana, Cape Town, South Africa, July 16, 19, 20, 23, 1993; July 19, 1994; July 22, 1994.

Personal interview with Laurine Platzky, Gardens, Cape Town, South Africa, July 18, 1993; phone interview January 28, 1996.

Personal interview with Barbara Quimby, Grand Island, New York, October 29, 1994.

Bibliography

Personal conversation with Sue Sparks, member of Black Sash, Johannes-
    burg, South Africa, July 30, 1993.
Phone interview with Oliematta (Olie) Taal, January 27, 1996.
Personal interview with the Reverend Leon White, Durham, North Car-
    olina, September 30, 1994.

Books and Articles

Abafazi Abangajikiyo: The Women Who Didn't Turn Back. Surplus People
    Project Gender Programme, 1994.
Ackelsberg, Martha A. "Communities, Resistance, and Women's Ac-
    tivism: Some Implications for a Democratic Polity." In *Women and
    the Politics of Empowerment.* Edited by Ann Bookman and Sandra
    Morgen. Philadelphia: Temple University Press, 1988.
Agosín, Marjorie. *The Mothers of the Plaza de Mayo: The Story of Renée
    Epelbaum, 1976–1985.* Translated by Janice Molloy. Trenton, NJ:
    The Red Sea Press, Inc., 1990.
Alvarez, Sonia E. *Engendering Democracy in Brazil: Women's Movements in
    Transition Politics.* Princeton: Princeton University Press, 1990.
Behar, Ruth. *Translated Woman: Crossing the Border with Esperanza's Story.*
    Boston: Beacon Press, 1993.
Beverley, John. "The Margin at the Center of *Testimonio* (Testimonial
    Narrative)." In *De/Colonizing the Subject: The Politics of Gender in
    Women's Autobiography.* Edited by Sidonie Smith and Julia Watson.
    Minneapolis: University of Minnesota Press, 1992.
Block, Alan A., and Frank R. Scarpitti. *Poisoning for Profit: The Mafia and
    Toxic Waste in America.* New York: Morrow, 1985.
Bookman, Ann, and Sandra Morgen, eds. *Women and the Politics of Em-
    powerment.* Philadelphia: Temple University Press, 1988.
Bouvard, Marguerite Guzman. *Revolutionizing Motherhood: The Mothers
    of the Plaza de Mayo.* Wilmington, DE: Scholarly Resource Books,
    1994.
Bozzoli, Belinda. *Women of Phokeng: Consciousness, Life, Strategy, and Mi-
    grancy in South Africa, 1900–1983.* Portsmouth, NH: Heinemann,
    1991.
Brecher, Jeremy, and Tim Costello, eds. *Building Bridges: The Emerging
    Grassroots Coalition of Labor and Community.* New York: Monthly
    Review, 1990.
Brown, Angela. *Leadership Initiative Project Proposal Narrative: Building,
    Expanding, Deepening and Consolidating Youth Organizing in Eastern
    North Carolina.* A Plan for a Two-Year Program of Leadership De-
    velopment, Organizing, and Networking. 1993.
Brown, Michael H. *Laying Waste: The Poisoning of America by Toxic
    Chemicals.* New York: Pantheon, 1979; 1980.

Bullard, Robert D. *Dumping in Dixie: Race, Class, and Environmental Quality.* Boulder: Westview Press, 1990.
———, ed. *Unequal Protection: Environmental Justice & Communities of Color.* San Francisco: Sierra Club Books, 1994.
Bunch, Charlotte. *Passionate Politics: Feminist Theory in Action.* New York: St. Martin's Press, 1987.
———. "Transforming Human Rights From a Feminist Perspective." In *Women's Rights, Human Rights: International Feminist Perspectives.* Edited by Julie Peters and Andrea Wolper. New York and London: Routledge, 1995.
Bunch, Charlotte, and Roxanna Carrillo. *Gender Violence: A Development and Human Rights Issue.* New Brunswick, NJ: Center for Women's Global Leadership, 1991.
Bunch, Charlotte, and Niamh Reilly. *Demanding Accountability: The Global Campaign and Vienna Tribunal for Women's Human Rights.* New Jersey and New York: Center for Women and Global Leadership and the United Nations Development Fund for Women (UNIFEM). 1994.
Cantarow, Ellen, and Susan Guchee O'Maley. "Ella Baker: Organizing for Civil Rights." In *Moving the Mountain: Working Women for Social Change.* Edited by Ellen Cantarow, Susan Guchee O'Maley, and Sharon Hartmann Strom. Old Westbury and New York: Feminist Press and McGraw-Hill, 1980.
Carrillo, Roxanna. "Violence Against Women: An Obstacle to Development." In *Gender Violence: A Development and Human Rights Issue.* New Jersey: Center for Women's Global Leadership, 1991.
Carson, Clayborne. "The Boycott that Changed Dr. King's Life." *New York Times Magazine,* January 7, 1996, p. 38.
Castells, Manuel. *The City and the Grassroots: A Cross-cultural Theory of Urban Social Movements.* Berkeley: The University of California, 1983.
Chuchryk, Patricia. "Subversive Mothers: The Women's Opposition to the Military Regime in Chile." In *Women, The State and Development.* Edited by Sue Ellen M. Charlton, Jana Everett, and Kathleen Staudt. Albany: State University of New York Press, 1989.
Clarke, Adele, and Alice Wolfson. "Class, Race, and Reproductive Rights." In *Women, Class, and the Feminist Imagination: A Socialist-Feminist Reader.* Edited by Karen V. Hansen and Ilene J. Philipson. Philadelphia: Temple University Press, 1990.
Cole, Josette. *Crossroads: The Politics of Reform and Repression 1976–1986.* Johannesburg: Ravan Press, 1987.
———. " 'When Your Life is Bitter You Do Something,' Women and Squatting in the Western Cape: Tracing the Origins of Crossroads and the Role of Women in its Struggle." In *South African Research Papers.* Edited by Dave Kaplan. Department of Economic History,

Bibliography

University of Cape Town P. B. Rondebosch 7700, Cape Town: University of Cape Town, South Africa, June 1986.

Cott, Nancy F. *The Bonds of Womanhood: "Women's Sphere" in New England, 1780–1835.* New Haven: Yale University Press, 1977.

Dankelman, Irene, and Joan Davidson. *Women and the Environment in the Third World: Alliance for the Future.* London: Earthscan Publishers in association with IUCN, 1988.

Darling, Marsha. "The Disinherited as Source: Rural Black Women's Memories." *Michigan Quarterly Review* 26, no. 1 (Winter 1987): 48–63.

Dietz, Mary G. "Context is All: Feminism and Theories of Citizenship." *Daedalus*, Vol. 116 (Fall 1987): 1–24.

Dirks, Nicholas B., Geoff Eley, and Sherry B. Ortner, ed. *Culture, Power and History: A Reader in Contemporary Social Theory.* Princeton: Princeton University Press, 1994.

Eisenstadt, S. N. *Power, Trust, and Meaning: Essays in Sociological Theory and Analysis.* Chicago: University of Chicago Press, 1995.

Ellis, Richard J. "Explaining the Occurrence of Charismatic Leadership." *Journal of Theoretical Politics*, Vol. 3, no. 3 (1991): 305–319.

Epstein, Barbara. *Political Protest & Cultural Revolution: Nonviolent Direct Action in the 1970s and 1980s.* Berkeley: The University of California, 1991.

Feijoo, María del Carmen, and Monica Gogna. "Women in the Transition to Democracy." *Women and Social Change in Latin America.* Edited by Elizabeth Jelin. London and New Jersey: Zed Books, 1990.

Fisher, Jo. *Mothers of the Disappeared.* London: Zed Books, 1989.

Forced Removals in South Africa. The SPP Reports. Vol. 3. Capetown and Pietermaritzburg: The Surplus People Project, 1983.

Fraser, Nancy. "Talking about Needs: Interpretive Contests as Political Conflicts in Welfare-State Societies." Symposium on Feminism and Political Theory. *Ethics*, Vol. 99, no. 2 (January 1989): 291–313.

Freudenberg, Nicholas. *Not in Our Backyards! Community Action for Health and the Environment.* Foreword by Lois Marie Gibbs. New York: Monthly Review Press, 1984.

Friedman, Elisabeth. "Women's Human Rights: The Emergence of a Movement." In *Women's Rights, Human Rights: International Feminist Perspectives.* Edited by Julie Peters and Andrea Wolper. New York and London: Routledge, 1995.

Geertz, Clifford. "Centers, Kings, and Charisma: Reflections on the Symbolics of Power." In *Culture and Its Creators: Essays in Honor of Edward Shils.* Edited by Joseph Ben-David and Terry Nichols Clark. Chicago: University of Chicago, 1977.

Gibbs, Lois Marie, and the staff of the Citizens Clearinghouse for Hazardous Waste. *Dying from Dioxin: A Citizen's Guide to Reclaiming*

Our Health and Rebuilding Democracy. Boston: South End Press, 1995.

Gibbs, Lois Marie. *Love Canal: My Story.* As told to Murray Levine. Albany: State University of New York Press, 1982.

———. "Some Thoughts on Women Who Move From Being Local Grassroots Leaders to Full-time Organizers." In *Empowering Ourselves: Women and Toxics Organizing.* Edited by Robbin Lee Zeff, Marsha Love, and Karen Stults. Arlington, VA: Citizens Clearinghouse for Hazardous Waste, Inc., 1989.

Giddings, Paula. *When and Where I Enter: The Impact of Black Women on Race and Sex in America.* New York: W. W. Morrow, 1984.

Gluck, Sherna Berger, and Daphne Patai, eds. *Women's Words: The Feminist Practice of Oral History.* New York and London: Routledge, 1991.

Gordon, Linda. *Pitied But Not Entitled: Single Mothers and the History of Welfare, 1890–1935.* New York: Free Press, 1994.

Gordon, Mary. *Good Boys and Dead Girls and Other Essays.* New York: Viking, 1991.

Hall, Bob, ed. *Environmental Politics: Lessons from the Grassroots.* Durham: The Institute for Southern Studies, 1988.

Hall, Jacquelyn Dowd. *Revolt against Chivalry: Jessie Daniel Ames and the Women's Campaign against Lynching.* New York: Columbia University Press, 1993.

Harris, Adrienne, and Ynestra King, ed. *Rocking the Ship of State: Toward a Feminist Peace Politics.* Boulder, CO: Westview Press, 1989.

Hayden, Dolores. *The Grand Domestic Revolution: A History of Feminist Designs for American Homes, Neighborhoods, and Cities.* Cambridge, MA: MIT Press, 1981.

———. *The Power of Place: Urban Landscapes as Public History.* Cambridge, MA: MIT Press, 1995.

Hewitt, Nancy A. *Women's Activism and Social Change: Rochester, New York, 1822–1870.* Ithaca: Cornell University Press, 1984.

Hill, Corliss, and Tara Roberts. "Children of the Dream." *Essence.* 25th Anniversary Issue, May 1995: 240–244.

Hirsch, Marianne, and Evelyn Fox Keller, eds. *Conflicts in Feminism.* New York and London: Routledge, 1990.

Hunt, Lynn. *Politics, Culture and Class in the French Revolution.* Berkeley: University of California Press, 1984.

Jaquette, Jane S., ed. *The Women's Movement in Latin America: Participation and Democracy.* Second edition. Boulder, CO: Westview Press, 1994.

Jelin, Elizabeth. "Los Movimientos Sociales en la Argentina contemporánea: una introducción a su estudio." In *Los Nuevos Movimientos Sociales/1.* Buenos Aires: Centro Editor de América Latina, 1985.

———. *Women and Social Change in Latin America.* London and New Jersey: Zed Books, 1990.

Bibliography

Joubert, Elsa, *The Long Journey of Poppie Nongena.* Johannesburg: Jonathan Ball Publishers, 1980.

Kaplan, Temma. *Anarchists of Andalusia, 1868–1903.* Princeton: Princeton University Press, 1977.

———. "Female Consciousness and Collective Action: The Case of Barcelona, 1910–1918." *SIGNS*, Vol. 7, no. 3 (Spring 1982): 545–566. Reprinted in *Rethinking the Political: Gender, Resistance, and the State.* Edited by Barbara Laslett, Johanna Brenner, and Yesim Arat.. Chicago: University of Chicago Press, 1995.

———. "Impediments to the New Communalism." In *Building Bridges: The Emerging Grassroots Coalition of Labor and Community.* Edited by Jeremy Brecher and Tim Costello. New York: Monthly Review, 1990.

———. *Red City, Blue Period: Social Movements in Picasso's Barcelona.* Berkeley: University of California Press, 1992.

———. "Women and Communal Strikes in the Crisis of 1917–22." In *Becoming Visible: Women in European History.* Second edition. Edited by Renate Bridenthal, Claudia Koonz, and Susan Mosher Stuard. Boston: Houghton Mifflin, 1987.

———. "Women and Spanish Anarchism." In *Becoming Visible: Women in European History.* First edition. Edited by Renate Bridenthal and Claudia Koonz. Boston: Houghton Mifflin, 1977.

Kertzer, David. *Ritual, Politics, and Power.* New Haven: Yale University Press, 1988.

Krauss, Celine. "Blue-Collar Women and Toxic-Waste Protests: The Process of Politicization." In *Toxic Struggles: The Theory and Practice of Environmental Justice.* Edited by Richard Hofrichter. Philadelphia: New Society Publishers, 1993.

Kumar, Radha, *The History of Doing: An Illustrated Account of Movements for Women's Rights and Feminism in India, 1800–1990.* London and New York: Verso, 1993.

Labalme, Jenny. *A Road to Walk: A Struggle for Environmental Justice.* Durham: The Regulator Press, 1987.

Lamphere, Louise, and Michelle Zimbalist Rosaldo, eds. *Women, Culture, and Society.* Stanford, CA: Stanford University Press, 1974.

"Land and People: Profile of South Africa." In *Land in South Africa.* Johannesburg: Human Awareness Programme, February 1989.

Leadership Handbook on Hazardous Waste. Arlington, VA: Citizens Clearinghouse for Hazardous Waste, 1983.

Lee, Charles. "The Integrity of Justice: Evidence of Environmental Racism." *Sojourners* 25 (1991).

Levine, Adeline Gordon. *Love Canal: Science, Politics, and People.* Lexington, MA: Lexington Books, D.C. Heath and Company, 1982.

Love Canal: A Chronology of Events that Shaped a Movement. By the leaders of the Love Canal Homeowners Association. Falls Church, VA: Citizens Clearinghouse for Hazardous Waste, Inc., 1984.

McClintock, Anne. *Imperial Leather: Race, Gender and Sexuality in the Colonial Contest.* New York and London: Routledge, 1995.

Madsen, Douglas, and Peter G. Snow. *The Charismatic Bond: Political Behavior in Time of Crisis.* Cambridge, MA: Harvard University Press, 1991.

Manicom, Linzi. "Ruling Relations: Rethinking State and Gender in South African History." *Journal of African History* 33 (1992): 441–465.

Miller, Vernice D. "Building on Our Past, Planning for Our Future: Communities of Color and the Quest for Environmental Justice." In *Toxic Struggles: The Theory and Practice of Environmental Justice.* Edited by Richard Hofrichter. Philadelphia: New Society Publishers, 1993.

Moeller, Robert. *Protecting Motherhood: Women and the Family in the Politics of Postwar West Germany.* Berkeley: University of California Press, 1993.

Molyneux, Maxine. "Mobilization Without Emancipation? Women's Interests, the State, and Revolution in Nicaragua." *Feminist Studies* 11, no. 2 (Summer 1985): 227–253.

———. "Socialist Societies Old and New: Progress toward Women's Emancipation." *Monthly Review,* Vol. 34, no. 3 (July-August 1982): 56–100.

Montgomery, David. *Citizen Worker: The Experience of Workers in the United States with Democracy and Free Markets during the Nineteenth Century.* New York and Cambridge, England: Cambridge University Press, 1993.

Moody, Anne. *Coming of Age in Mississippi.* New York: Dell, 1968.

Morris, Aldon D. "Black Southern Student Sit-In Movement: An Analysis of Internal Organization." *American Sociological Review* 46 (1981): 744–67.

———. *The Origins of the Civil Rights Movement.* New York: The Free Press, 1984.

——— and Cedric Herring. "Theory and Research in Social Movements: A Critical Review." In *Annual Review of Political Science,* Vol. 2 (1987).

——— and Carol McClurg Mueller. *Frontiers in Social Movement Theory.* New Haven: Yale University Press, 1992.

Myerson, Michael. *Nothing Could Be Finer.* New York: International Publishers, 1978.

"A National Call to Struggle. Countdown 2000: Setting the Black Youth Agenda. Don't Punk Out! March 3–5. A National Student and Youth Shut-in during the 30th Anniversary Commemoration of Bloody Sunday & Selma to Montgomery March." Contacts listed are Kimberly Burwell, Leadership Initiative Project, and Minnie White, Young People's Institute.

Bibliography

Navarro, Marysa. "The Personal is Political: The Madres de Plaza de Mayo." In *Power and Popular Protest: Latin American Social Movements*. Edited by Susan Eckstein. Berkeley: University of California Press, 1989.

Ngcobo, Lauretta. *and they didn't die*. New York: George Brazzilier, 1991.

Orleck, Annelise, *Common Sense and a Little Fire: Women and Working-Class Politics in the United States, 1900–1965*. Chapel Hill: The University of North Carolina Press, 1995.

Parsons, Talcott. Introduction to Max Weber, *The Sociology of Religion*. Translated by Ephraim Fischoff. Boston: Beacon Press, 1963.

Patai, Daphne. "U.S. Academics and Third World Women: Is Ethical Research Possible?" *Women's Words: The Feminist Practice of Oral History*. New York and London: Routledge, 1991.

Pateman, Carole. "Feminist Critiques of the Public Private Dichotomy." In *The Disorder of Women: Democracy, Feminism and Political Theory*. Stanford, CA: Stanford University Press, 1989.

Payne, Charles. "Ella Baker and Models of Social Change." *Signs*, Vol. 14, no. 2, (1989): 885–899.

Petchesky, Rosalind. "Reproductive Freedom: Beyond Women's Right to Choose." *Signs*, Vol. 5, no. 4 (1980): 661–685.

Platzky, Laurine, and Cherryl Walker for the Surplus People Project. *The Surplus People: Forced Removals in South Africa*. Johannesburg: Ravan Press, 1985.

Posel, Deborah. *The Making of Apartheid 1948–1961: Conflict and Compromise*. Oxford Studies in African Affairs. Cape Town and Oxford, England: Oxford University Press, 1991.

Proceedings, First National People of Color Environmental Leadership Summit. Edited by Charles Lee. The Washington Court on Capitol Hill Washington, D.C., October 24–27, 1991. New York: The United Church of Christ Commission for Racial Justice, December 1992.

Program Guide: The First National People of Color Environmental Leadership Summit. Sponsored by United Church of Christ Commission for Racial Justice, October 24–27, 1991.

Radcliff, Pamela. *From Mobilization to Civil War: The Politics of Polarization in the Spanish City of Gijón 1900–1939*. New York: Cambridge University Press, forthcoming.

Reynolds, Pamela. *Childhood in Crossroads: Cognition and Society in South Africa*. Cape Town, Johannesburg, and Grand Rapids, MI: David Philip Publisher and William B. Eerdmans Publishing, 1989.

Riley, Denise. *"Am I That Name?" Feminism and the Category of "Women" in History*. Minneapolis: University of Minnesota Press, 1988.

Robinson, Jo Ann Gibson. *The Montgomery Bus Boycott and the Women Who Started It: The Memoir of Jo Ann Gibson Robinson*. Edited, with a foreword, by David J. Garrow. Knoxville, TN: The University of Tennessee Press, 1987.

Rodda, Annabel. *Women and the Environment.* London and Atlantic Highlands, NJ: Zed, 1993.

Rosaldo, Michelle Zimbalast. "The Use and Abuse of Anthropology: Reflections on Feminism, and Cross-Cultural Understanding. *Signs,* Vol. 5, no. 3 (Spring 1980): 389–417.

———— and Louise Lamphere, eds. *Women, Culture, and Society.* Stanford, CA: Stanford University Press, 1974.

Rosenberg, Harriet G. "From Trash to Treasure: Housewife Activists and the Environmental Justice Movement." In *Articulating Hidden Resistance: Exploring the Influence of Eric Wolf.* Berkeley: University of California Press, 1995.

————. "Housewives and Hostages at Love Canal: A Narrative of Resistance." Paper presented at the American Anthropological Association Annual Meetings, Chicago, Illinois, November 20–24, 1991.

Ross, Ellen. *Love and Toil: Motherhood in Outcast London, 1870–1918.* New York: Oxford University Press, 1993.

Rowbotham, Sheila. *Hidden from History: Rediscovering Women in History from the 17th Century to the Present.* New York: Vintage, 1976.

————. *Women, Resistance & Revolution: A History of Women and Revolution in the Modern World.* New York: Vintage, 1974.

Ruddick, Sarah. *Maternal Thinking: Toward a Politics of Peace.* Boston: Beacon Press, 1989.

Schirmer, Jennifer. "Those Who Die for Life Cannot be Called Dead: Women and Human Rights Protest in Latin America." In *Surviving Beyond Fear: Women, Children and Human Rights in Latin America.* Edited by Marjorie Agosín. Fredonia, NY: White Pine Press, 1993.

————. "The Seeking of Truth and the Gendering of Consciousness: The CO-MADRES of El Salvador and the CONAVIGUA Widows of Guatemala." In *'Viva': Women and Popular Protest in Latin America.* Edited by Sarah A. Radcliffe and Sallie Westwood. London: Routledge, 1993.

Schneider, Elizabeth M. "The Dialectic of Rights and Politics: Perspectives from the Women's Movement." *New York University Law Review* 61 (1986): 589–662.

Scott, Joan W. *Gender and the Politics of History.* New York: Columbia University Press, 1988.

————. "Men and women in the Parisian Garment Trades: Discussions of Family and Work in the 1830s and 1840s." In *The Power of the Past: Essays for Eric Hobsbawm.* Edited by Pat Thane, Geoffrey Crossic, and Roderick Floud. Cambridge, England: Cambridge University Press, 1984.

Seager, Joni. *Earth Follies: Coming to Feminist Terms with the Global Environmental Crisis.* New York: Routledge, 1993.

Seidman, Gay W. "'No Freedom without the Women': Mobilization and Gender in South Africa, 1970–1992." In *Rethinking the Political:*

Bibliography

Gender, Resistance, and the State. Edited by Barbara Laslett, Johanna Brenner, and Yesim Arat. Chicago: University of Chicago Press, 1995.

Shils, Edward A. *The Constitution of Society.* Chicago: University of Chicago Press, 1982.

Silk, Andrew. *A Shanty Town in South Africa: The Story of Modderdam.* Johannesburg: Ravan Press, 1981.

Sklar, Kathryn Kish. *Florence Kelley and the Nation's Work.* New Haven: Yale University Press, 1995.

Sommer, Doris. " 'Not Just a Personal Story': Women's *Testimonios* and the Plural Self." In *Life/Lines: Theorizing Women's Autobiography.* Edited by Bella Brodzki and Celeste Schenck. Ithaca: Cornell University Press, 1988.

Spink, Kathryn. *Black Sash: The Beginning of a Bridge in South Africa.* London: Methuen, 1991.

Stacey, Judith. "Can There Be a Feminist Ethnography?" *Women's Words: The Feminist Practice of Oral History.* Edited by Sherna Berger Gluck and Daphne Patai. New York and London: Routledge, 1991.

Stephen, Lynn. *Hear My Testimony! María Teresa Tula, Human Rights Activist of El Salvador.* Boston: South End Press, 1994.

———. *Power from Below: Women's Grassroots Organizing in Latin America.* Austin: University of Texas Press, forthcoming.

———. "Women's Rights Are Human Rights: The Merging of Feminine and Feminist Interests among El Salvador's Mothers of the Disappeared (CO-MADRES)." *American Ethnologist,* Vol. 22, no.4 (1995): 1–20.

Sternbach, Nancy Saporta, Marysa Navarro-Aranguren, Patricia Chuchryk, and Sonia E. Alvarez. "Feminisms in Latin America: From Bogotá to San Bernardo." In *Rethinking the Political: Gender, Resistance, and the State.* Edited by Barbara Laslett, Johanna Brenner, and Yesim Arat. Chicago: University of Chicago Press, 1995.

Swerdlow, Amy. *Women Strike for Peace: Traditional Motherhood and Radical Politics in the 1960s.* Chicago: University of Chicago Press, 1993.

Tarrow, Sidney, *Democracy and Disorder: Protest and Politics in Italy, 1965–1975.* New York: Oxford University Press, 1989.

———. *Peasant Communism in Southern Italy.* New Haven: Yale University Press, 1967.

———. *Struggling to Reform: Social Movements and Policy Change during Cycles of Protest.* Ithaca, NY: Cornell University Press, 1983.

Tarrow, Sidney, Bert Klandermans, and Hanspeter Kriesi. "From Structure to Action: Comparing Movement Participation across Cultures." *International Social Movement Research,* Vol. 1 (1988): 41–83.

Taylor, Barbara. *Eve and the New Jerusalem: Socialism and Feminism in the Nineteenth Century.* New York: Pantheon, 1983.

Thompson, Dorothy. *The Chartists: Popular Politics in the Industrial Revolution.* Aldershott: M.T. Smith, 1984.

———. *Outsiders: Class, Gender and Nation.* London: Verso, 1993.

———. "Women and Nineteenth-Century Radical Politics: A Lost Dimension." In *The Rights and Wrongs of Women.* Edited by Juliet Mitchell and Ann Oakley. Harmondsworth, England: Penguin Books, 1976.

Tilly, Charles. "Collective Violence in European Perspective." In *Violence in America: Historical and Comparative Perspectives.* Edited by Hugh Davis Graham and Ted Robert Gurr. New York: Praeger, 1969.

———. *The Contentious French.* Cambridge, MA: Harvard University Press, 1986.

———. "Food Supply and Public Order in Modern Europe." In *The Formation of National States in Western Europe.* Edited by Charles Tilly. Princeton: Princeton University Press, 1975.

———. *From Mobilization to Revolution.* Reading, MA: Addison-Wesley, 1978.

———. *The Vendee.* Cambridge, MA: Harvard University Press, 1964.

Tilly, Charles, and Edward Shorter. *Strikes in France, 1830–1968.* New York: Cambridge University Press, 1974.

Toxic Wastes and Race in the United States: A National Report on the Racial and Socioeconomic Characteristics of Communities with Hazardous Waste Sites. Edited by Charles Lee. New York: United Church of Christ Commission for Racial Justice, 1987.

Tucker, Cora. "Women Make it Happen." In *Empowering Ourselves: Women and Toxics Organizing.* Edited by Robbin Lee Zeff, Marsha Love, and Karen Stults. Arlington, VA: Citizens Clearinghouse for Hazardous Waste, Inc., 1989.

Valdés, Teresa, and Marisa C. Weinstein. *Organizaciones de Pobladoras y Construcción Democrática en Chile.* Santiago: FLASCO, 1989.

Valenze, Deborah M. *Prophetic Sons and Daughters: Female Preaching and Popular Religion in Industrial England.* Princeton: Princeton University Press, 1985.

Wacks, Jonathan. *Crossroads / South Africa: The Struggle Continues.* Video at the Schomburg Collection, New York Public Library.

Walker, Cherryl. *Women and Resistance in South Africa.* New York: Monthly Review Press, 1982; 1991.

Weber, Max, *The Sociology of Religion.* Translated by Ephraim Fischoff. Boston: Beacon Press, 1963.

———. *Max Weber on Charisma and Institution Building; Selected Papers.* Edited and with an introduction by S.N. Eisenstadt. Chicago: University of Chicago Press, 1968.

Wells, Julia. "Why Women Rebel: A Comparative Study of South African Women's Resistance in Bloemfontein (1913) and Johannesburg (1958)." *Journal of South African Studies* 10, 1 (1984): 55–70.

Westwood, Sallie, and Sarah Radcliffe. "Gender, Racism, and the Politics of Identities in Latin America." In *'Viva': Women and Popular Protest in Latin America*. Edited by Sallie Westwood and Sarah Radcliffe. London: Routledge, 1993.

We Will Not Move: The Struggle for Crossroads. Cape Town: The National Union of South African Students, 1978.

Wilson, Kathleen. *The Sense of the People: Politics, Culture, and Imperialism in England, 1715–1785*. Cambridge and New York: Cambridge University Press, 1995.

Wright, Marcia. *Strategies of Slaves and Women: Life-stories from East/Central Africa*. New York: Lilian Barber Press, 1993.

Young, Iris Marion. *Justice and the Politics of Difference*. Princeton: Princeton University Press, 1990.

————. "Gender as Seriality: Thinking about Women as a Social Collective." In *Rethinking the Political: Gender, Resistance, and the State*. Edited by Barbara Laslett, Johanna Brenner, and Yesim Arat. Chicago: University of Chicago Press, 1995.

"The Youth Task Force Organizing Project Proposal Narrative (for 1995–96)." Available from Angela Brown, Youth Task Force, Atlanta, Georgia.

Zeff, Robbin Lee, Marsha Love, and Karen Stults. *Empowering Ourselves: Women and Toxic Organizing*. Arlington, VA: Citizens Clearinghouse for Hazardous Waste, Inc., 1989.

Zinsser, Judith M. "The Third Week in July." *Women's Studies International Forum*, Vol. 6, no. 5 (1983): 547–557.

————. "Nairobi Confab Ends on High Note." *New Directions for Women* (September/October 1985): 1, 12, 14.

Periodicals

Cape Herald (Cape Town), 1983–1984

Cape Times (Cape Town), 1977–1987

Charlotte Observer (Charlotte), September–October 1982

China Daily (Beijing), August 26-September 9, 1995

Christian Science Monitor (Boston), 1982, 1983

Chapel Hill Newspaper (Chapel Hill), 1979

Durham Morning Herald (Durham), August–October 1982

Everyone's Backyard (Arlington), 1993–1996

Fayetteville Observer (Fayetteville), August–October 1982

Grassroots: Non-Profit Community Newsletter (Cape Town), 1980–1987

Herald Sun (Durham), October 30, 1992

International Herald Tribune (Paris), August 26–September 9, 1995

New York Times (New York), 1978–1982; 1984–86; August 25–September 17, 1995

News and Observer (Raleigh), 1978–1979
South African Pressclips (Johannesburg), 1982–1983, 1986
Warren Record (Warrenton), February–October , 1982
Washington Post, 1982

Public Lectures

Dollie Burwell, speaking at the Redefining Motherhood Conference, Dartmouth College, May 15, 1993.

Dollie Burwell, Mellon Seminar on Women and Grassroots Leadership, Duke University, Durham, North Carolina, November 1, 1995.

Kim Burwell, Mellon Seminar on Women and Grassroots Leadership, Duke University, Durham, North Carolina, November 1, 1995.

Vernice Miller, November 7, 1992, lecture at Eugene Lang College of the New School for Social Research.

Index

Index

Index

Index